THE HAMMER OF THE SCOTS

Edward I and the
Scottish Wars of Independence

David Santiuste

Pen & Sword
MILITARY

First published in Great Britain in 2015 by
PEN AND SWORD MILITARY
an imprint of
Pen and Sword Books Ltd
47 Church Street
Barnsley
South Yorkshire S70 2AS

Copyright © David Santiuste, 2015

ISBN 978 1 78159 012 6

The right of David Santiuste to be identified
as the author of this work has been asserted by him in
accordance with the Copyright, Designs and Patents Act 1988.

Printed and bound in England
by CPI Group (UK) Ltd, Croydon, CR0 4YY

Typeset in Times by CHIC GRAPHICS

Pen & Sword Books Ltd incorporates the imprints of Pen & Sword
Archaeology, Atlas, Aviation, Battleground, Discovery, Family
History, History, Maritime, Military, Naval, Politics, Railways,
Select, Social History, Transport, True Crime, Claymore Press,
Frontline Books, Leo Cooper, Praetorian Press, Remember When,
Seaforth Publishing and Wharncliffe.

For a complete list of Pen and Sword titles please contact
Pen and Sword Books Limited
47 Church Street, Barnsley, South Yorkshire, S70 2AS, England
E-mail: enquiries@pen-and-sword.co.uk
Website: www.pen-and-sword.co.uk

Contents

Preface

This is a book about Edward I and Scotland, although I first encountered Edward during a visit to Wales. As a child with a precocious interest in history, I was awestruck by the castles of Wales, as well as by the beautiful landscape, and thus I began to learn something of Edward's impact on a country I came to love. My sympathies at that time were very much with Edward's Welsh rival Llywelyn ap Gruffydd (I knew little then of Llywelyn's own ruthless spirit), yet Edward nevertheless exerted a magnetic force. I later went on to study in Scotland – another country that still bears the scars of Edward's ambition – where I have remained for most of my adult life. This project has therefore provided an opportunity to write about my adopted home, whilst also exploring the life of one of the figures who first inspired my passion for medieval history. My view of Edward has become more complex over the years, but my interest in his story has endured.

Edward I is a fascinating character, and he is very much the central figure in the work I offer here. It must be stressed, however, that this book is not envisaged as a biography as such; certainly I have no ambitions to supplant the two existing biographies of Edward by Marc Morris and Michael Prestwich (both of which are excellent books). My own focus is specifically on Edward's role in the first phase of the Scottish Wars of Independence, as well as on the political events that led to the outbreak of war and later sustained it, although I have also sought to explain the wider impact of his campaigns in Scotland. The conflict and upheaval that resulted affected people at all levels of society, throughout the whole of the British Isles. In order to make sense of the decisions that Edward made, and of the challenges he faced, a number of other stories must also be told alongside Edward's own.

Edward's reign as king of England was a pivotal moment in British history. By the time he inherited his throne, in 1272, the English kings were also lords of Ireland. In 1282, following the fall of the House of Gwynedd, Edward destroyed the last vestiges of independent power in Wales. Scotland remained a separate kingdom, but Edward would come closer than any other English medieval king to establishing effective hegemony over the whole of Britain and Ireland. As we shall see, it would be simplistic to argue that Edward set out to *conquer* Scotland, at least at first, but he was determined to assert what he saw as his rightful *lordship* over England's northern neighbour. Having failed to realise this by political means, during the period from 1296 to 1307 he campaigned repeatedly in Scotland, seeking to force the Scots to acknowledge his rule.

If Edward had been able to achieve a lasting victory in Scotland – and it has been suggested there were real opportunities to accomplish this in 1296 and 1304 – then the later history of the British Isles would surely have been very different. That Edward was *not* ultimately successful, of course, owed much to the tenacious resistance of the Scots. Two of the Scottish leaders – Robert the Bruce, the later victor of Bannockburn, and William Wallace – have become legendary figures. The efforts of others, such as John Comyn and Andrew Murray, as well as countless nameless Scotsmen, must also be acknowledged. It should also be remembered, however, that Edward was rarely able to focus exclusively on Scotland, and the conflict must therefore be situated within the wider context of his life and times.

This book is primarily intended for motivated lay readers who would like to learn more about Edward I and his Scottish wars. As far as the first phase of the Wars of Independence is concerned (as opposed to the later campaigns of Robert the Bruce, which are now very well served), I felt there might be space for another book that could provide a bridge between popular histories and more specialist studies; my hope is that some readers will be encouraged to explore the subject further. Irrespective of whether my own work is successful or not, my recent experience as a tutor of adult learners, as well as a member of several historical societies, has convinced me there is a genuine need for historical writing of this type.

In addition to the two historians referred to above, I hope my debts to the work of various others (perhaps especially Geoffrey Barrow and Fiona Watson) will be adequately reflected in the notes and bibliography. It remains here to acknowledge some more personal obligations, expressing my gratitude to a number of people who have helped to make this book possible.

Thanks must go to all the team at Pen & Sword, but especially Rupert Harding. Dr Toby Capwell passed on some helpful advice (though any errors are my own). The project was partially funded by the K Blundell Trust, whose grants provide a wonderful source of assistance for younger writers.

I owe a great deal, as ever, to members of my family. My partner, Caroline, accompanied me on research trips, re-drew the family trees and has helped in innumerable other ways; above all I would like to thank Caroline for her continued support and understanding during the spring and summer of this year, as the text neared completion. I am also grateful to Caroline's parents, Robert and Florence: it was a pleasure to spend some time writing at their beautiful home. My father, Harry, has again provided vital support and encouragement.

Words cannot express how much I owe to my mother, Marion Santiuste *née* Kingsbury, who unfortunately did not live to see this project completed. I dedicate this book to her memory.

David Santiuste
Edinburgh, October 2014

A Note on Money

During the reign of Edward I – and, indeed, until 1971 – English currency was measured in pounds, shillings and pence (£ s d). Twelve (silver) pennies made a shilling, and twenty shillings made a pound. A mark was a unit of account, equating to 160 pennies, i.e. two-thirds of a pound. Attempts to provide modern equivalents for medieval prices can be unhelpful; not only do such figures quickly become outdated, but it should also be remembered that relative values fluctuate (due to a bewildering range of factors).

To provide some context for the figures given throughout the text, a skilled craftsman (such as a trained carpenter) might have expected to earn around four pence for a day's work; an unskilled labourer would have done well to earn half that sum, and might only have expected a penny. An annual income of £20 would have supported a very comfortable lifestyle; a man with an annual income of £5,000, such as an earl, would obviously have been considered extremely wealthy. It has been estimated that in 1284 Edward I's own income was around £27,000 (of which £8,000 came from customs duties), although this figure does not include any income from taxes on wealth or other extraordinary sources of revenue.

Maps

Map 1: The British Isles

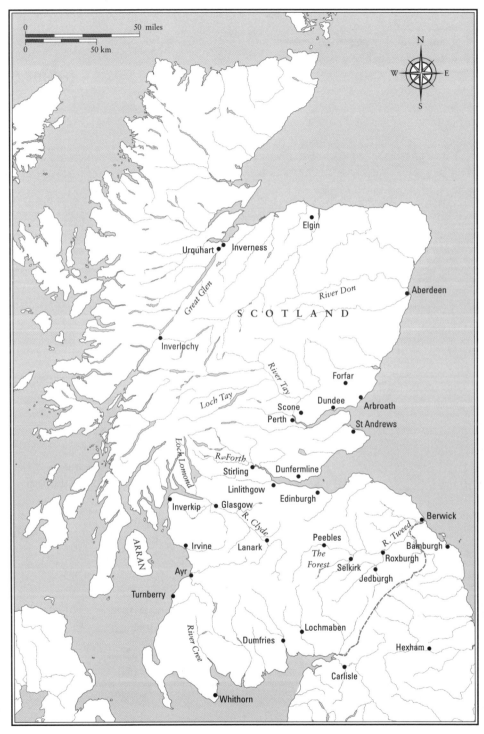

Map 2: Scotland

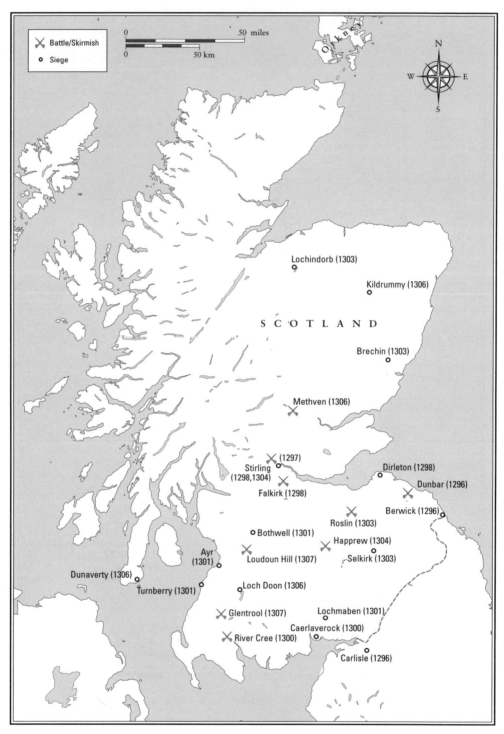

Map 3: Military Engagements

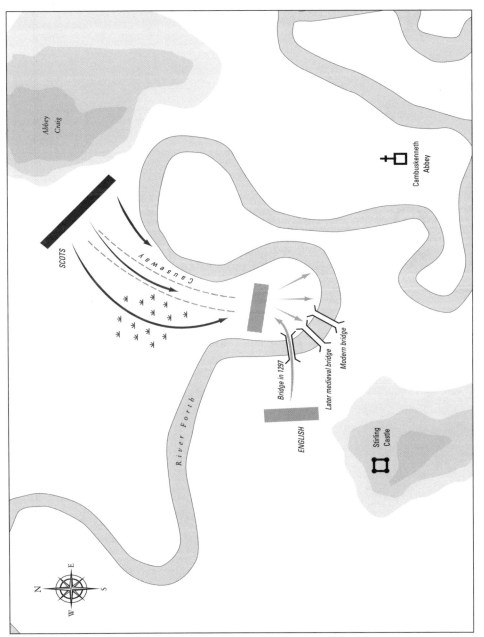

Map 4: The Battle of Stirling Bridge

Abbey
Craig

SCOTS

Causeway

River Forth

ENGLISH

Bridge in 1297

Later medieval bridge

Modern bridge

Cambuskenneth
Abbey

Stirling
Castle

N
E
W
S

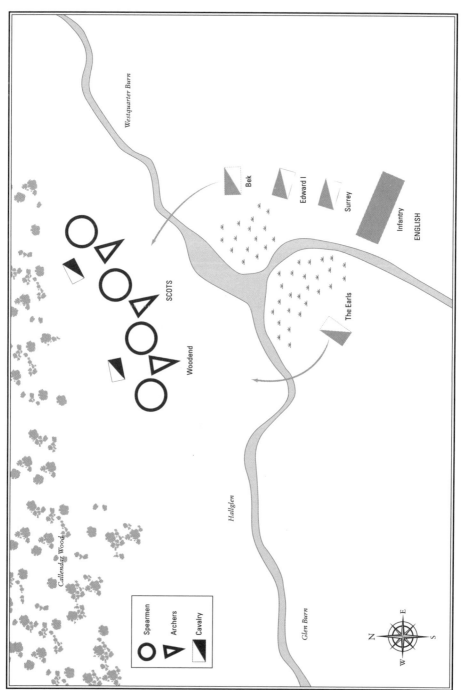

Map 5: *The Battle of Falkirk*

Genealogical Tables

Edward I and his family

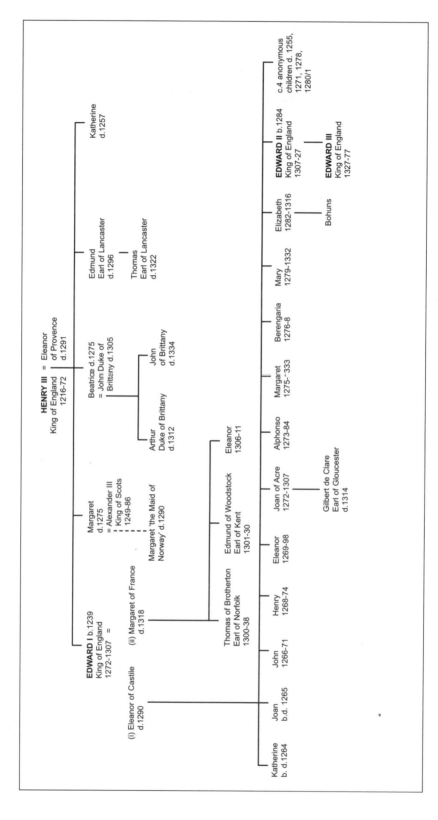

The Scottish Succession

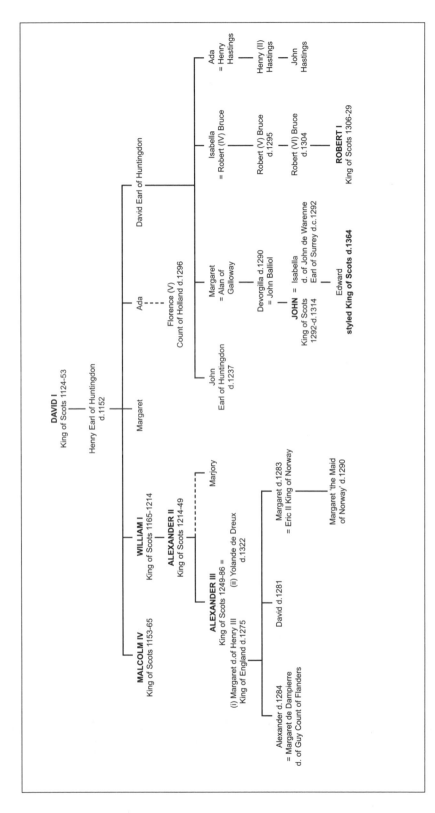

The Bruce and Comyn Families

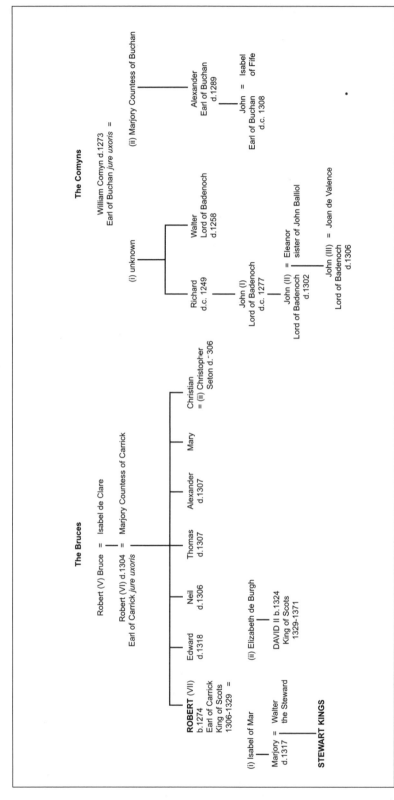

List of Plates

1. A possible likeness of Edward I, from the sedilia at Westminster Abbey. (© *The Dean and Chapter of Westminster*)
2. Stirling Castle. *(© William McKelvie/Dreamstime.com)*
3. The projected site of the Battle of Falkirk. (*Author*)
4. Caerlaverock Castle. (*Courtesy of Simon Ledingham*)
5. Reconstruction drawing of the siege of Bothwell, by David Simon. (© *Crown Copyright Historic Scotland reproduced courtesy of Historic Scotland*)
6. Detail from The Queen Mary Psalter, depicting contemporary arms and armour. (*Image courtesy of the British Library*)
7. A statue of William Wallace, by William Grant Stevenson. (© *Paul Geddes/Dreamstime.com*)
8. Dunfermline Abbey. (© *Philip Dickson/Dreamstime.com*)
9. A contemporary illustration of a Welsh archer. (*The National Archives: E 36/274*)
10. The Coronation Chair at Westminster Abbey and the Stone of Destiny. (© *The Dean and Chapter of Westminster*)
11. Lanercost Priory. (© *Patricia Hofmeester/Dreamstime.com*)
12. A statue of Robert Bruce, king of Scots, by Pilkington Jackson. (*Author*)

Chapter 1

Setting the Scene

The king of England sits straight-backed on his horse, surrounded by a mass of armed men. His snow-white hair is concealed by a helmet, upon which is mounted a gleaming circlet. He surveys his enemy's dispositions with a cold eye, exuding arrogance and disdain. King Edward gives the word, and the royal army advances towards the Scottish host. When the troops in the van seem about to close with the enemy, however, they suddenly come to a halt. The king's attendants look on aghast as the soldiers cheerfully greet the Scots, and then abruptly change sides.

'Irish', spits the king, with a brief shake of his head, but he remains unperturbed. He gives the impression, like a chess grand-master, that he has anticipated his enemy's moves. But the Scottish commander, Sir William Wallace, has further surprises in store. Even King Edward winces, albeit almost imperceptibly, as the Scots use fire-arrows to set light to carefully prepared lines of pitch, engulfing the next wave of Edward's soldiers in flames. Those who survive are brutally cut down, as the Scots counter the English attack with a ferocious assault of their own.

Sensing the entire English army is ready to break and run, Wallace signals his cavalry to enter the fray. But now it is Wallace's turn to look on with horror as his horsemen leave the field: the noble leaders of the cavalry have been bribed to take no part in the battle. King Edward allows himself a grim smile of satisfaction. Then, with the threat of the Scottish cavalry neutralised, he calls for his archers to unleash their arrows.

In the king's mind, checkmate is near, but one of his subordinates has the temerity to question his order: 'I beg pardon, Sire, but won't we hit our own troops?'

'Yes,' retorts King Edward, 'but we'll hit theirs as well.'

Watching as the archers carry out their bloody work, fighting off a brief cough that betrays his failing health, he also orders that his hidden reserves should be committed to the struggle.

Now supremely confident of success, he instructs one of his officers to 'bring us news of our victory' – and also to bring him Wallace, whether dead or alive. Then he turns back to his personal bodyguard: a mysterious figure, dressed all in black, who will soon be revealed as another traitor to Wallace's cause. 'Shall we retire?' Edward enquires briskly, in his clipped tones. But it is clear this is a command, not a question.

*   *   *   *

Many readers will have recognised this abridged description of Edward I in the film *Braveheart*, as portrayed by the late Patrick MacGoohan, commanding his troops at the battle of Falkirk. *Braveheart*, as is well known, has perpetuated a number of historical inaccuracies and is full of anachronisms. Nevertheless, the characterisation of Edward in the film – stubborn, unfeeling, cruel and duplicitous, yet also fiercely intelligent, resourceful and undeniably formidable – is one that can be traced in many other places. All of these elements can be found in medieval sources (although naturally there is a variety of emphasis within the different accounts), as well as in the work of many modern historians.

Braveheart has also helped to ensure that Edward's Scottish wars remain the most famous aspect of his career – although this, too, is not entirely due to Mel Gibson. While Edward has gained a number of *soubriquets* over the years – including 'the English Justinian' (after the Roman/Byzantine emperor who was famous for his laws) and 'Longshanks' (a contemporary nickname which requires no explanation) – the most enduring is the one inscribed on his austere black marble tomb at Westminster Abbey: *Edwardus Primus Scottorum Malleus hic est* – 'Here is Edward I: the Hammer of the Scots.'

It must be stressed, however, that Edward's Scottish wars form only a part, albeit a significant one, of his long, dramatic story. In the year 1286, when Scottish affairs first loomed large on his agenda,

Edward was already in his forties. He had been king of England for thirteen years, and had established a substantial reputation. At this time the English kings still held significant lands in south-west France – they were dukes of Aquitaine, often referred to as Gascony – and Edward was respected throughout Europe as a soldier and statesman. This chapter provides a brief insight into Edward's earlier life, with a particular focus on his military career, before moving on to examine his early relations with Scotland.

* * * *

Edward was born in 1239, the eldest son of King Henry III of England and his queen, Eleanor of Provence. Little is known about Edward's childhood, although by the time he reached adolescence it was clear that his character was very different from his father's. The difference was particularly marked in their respective attitudes towards war and violence. Henry was no saint (notwithstanding his dedicated patronage of Westminster Abbey), but he did not relish military activity, whereas his son was evidently keen to acquire and demonstrate the skills of a warrior.

The first indication of Edward's martial vocation came in the year 1253, when he was just fourteen years of age. A rebellion broke out in Gascony, and Henry III sought to raise an army in order to quell the revolt there. Desperate to raise funds for the approaching war, Henry resorted to an expedient, demanding the traditional levy to pay for the knighting of his eldest son. Edward might well have imagined, therefore, that he would be expected to join the campaign. But when Henry set out for France in the late summer, Edward was left behind in England. His dubbing as a knight, it might be added, had also been delayed. As the chronicler Matthew Paris tells the story, Edward watched the departing ships in anguish, sobbing uncontrollably, until their sails could no longer be seen on the horizon.[1]

Henry's Gascon war was one of his more successful endeavours. Edward did join his father in the following year, and may have gained his first glimpse of warfare as the royal army reduced the last of the rebel strongholds. But Henry's achievements in Gascony were largely based on diplomacy, and it was for this purpose that Edward had been summoned to southern France. The Gascon rebels had received Spanish support from King Alfonso X of Castile, who possessed a distant claim to the duchy of Aquitaine, but Henry and Alfonso were able to come to terms. Alfonso's price was a marriage alliance: it was agreed that Edward would marry Alfonso's half-sister Eleanor. This matter was out of his control, although the fifteen-year-old Edward gallantly praised his bride-to-be, making reference to reports of her beauty and other accomplishments. The marriage duly took place on 1 November at Burgos, where Edward was now also knighted by Alfonso.

The marriage of Edward and Eleanor (then aged just thirteen) would last for thirty-six years. Despite the couple's youth, Eleanor fell pregnant within the first year of marriage, although the child did not survive. It is one of the tragedies of Edward's life that so few of his many children lived to be adults (even given the prevailing rates of infant mortality), and no further children were born until the 1260s. Nevertheless, along with marriage and knighthood, the next few years would bring other responsibilities; these included a carefully supervised experience of administration and lordship in Gascony. But Edward was still a young man, who attracted other young men to his side, and he remained eager to test himself in combat. His late teens and early twenties did not provide an opportunity to engage in real war, but he became an enthusiastic participant in tournaments.

By the end of the Middle Ages tournaments had become showy spectacles (although they could still be dangerous): they were courtly rituals, involving complex allegories and featuring lavish settings and costumes. Some of these elements were also present in the thirteenth century, but at that time tournaments had fewer rules, and the chaotic *mêlées* that ensued were often bloody encounters. Edward made his *début* in 1256, at the age of seventeen, in a specially arranged tournament from which he fortunately emerged unscathed. In the early 1260s Edward made two trips across the channel to take part in tournaments in France, where chronicles suggest that he and his followers endured a more difficult time.[2] Edward suffered some minor injuries, as well as several defeats, though we might imagine that he emerged from this experience a tougher (albeit somewhat chastened) young man.

The behaviour of Edward and his young companions sometimes aroused disquiet, but amidst some examples of youthful high spirits, and perhaps even outright thuggery,[3] it seems clear that Edward was keen to identify himself with the prevailing ideals of *chivalry*: the warrior code of the medieval aristocracy. Chivalry is an evocative word, but it is not easy to define – perhaps not least because medieval people often held differing views about the subject. Modern scholars sometimes prefer to concentrate on isolated aspects – the traditions of courtly love, for example, or the ethics of war – but all of these must be situated within a larger whole. The most effective modern definition of chivalry remains that of the late Sir Maurice Keen, who described it as 'an ethos, in which martial, aristocratic and Christian elements were fused together'.[4]

With Keen's definition of chivalry in mind, it is evident that the most obvious of the prized chivalric virtues, *prowess*, was not enough in itself; the ideals of chivalry could also inspire other qualities, notably commitment to a cause, commitment to others (including people of both sexes) and generosity of spirit. Chivalry, of course, was a code of *honour*. Yet, as is the case in all 'honour societies', a strong emphasis on respect and reputation could sometimes induce irascible, arrogant behaviour. Moreover, as we shall see, exhortations to 'chivalrous' men to defend the weak did not always protect defenceless people from unspeakable horrors. Another modern writer has written eloquently of the 'ambivalent force of chivalry' during the Middle Ages,[5] and it is perhaps unsurprising that it played a similarly ambivalent role in the life of Edward I, a man who has provoked so much debate and curiosity – both in his own time and in ours.

* * * *

The later years of the reign of Henry III were marred by dissension in England, at the very heart of his realm. Dissatisfaction with various aspects of his rule, notably his patronage of the queen's relatives, led to demands for reform. The opposition found an effective leader in Simon de Montfort, earl of Leicester – a charismatic and determined figure, albeit somewhat egotistical.

Edward's relationship with his father was often difficult, and for a time Edward fell under the influence of Montfort (who was, incidentally, his uncle by marriage). When civil war broke out, however, in the mid-1260s, Edward fought hard on Henry's behalf. He took part in his first battle on 14 May 1264 at Lewes, yet this would prove to be another humbling experience. Edward led his own division in a successful cavalry charge, but he then allowed his men to indulge themselves in pursuit of the enemy. By the time his cavalry returned to the battlefield, the royal army had already been defeated.

Edward subsequently endured a period of captivity (as did his wife), while Montfort acted as *de facto* ruler of England on King Henry's behalf. But Edward was able to effect a daring escape from Gloucester with the help of some devoted companions. On 4 August 1265, by which time he was twenty-six, he led the army that defeated and killed Montfort at Evesham. As is often the case in civil wars (when loyalties are uncertain and both sides eager to settle the matter), Edward's tactics employed speed and guile. In order to ensure that Montfort could not escape from Evesham, for example, Edward advanced under banners that had been captured from Montfort's son (who had been expected to bring reinforcements to his father). Montfort therefore found himself trapped and outnumbered, and he was specifically targeted for elimination: one medieval writer referred to 'the murder of Evesham, for battle it was none'.[6]

It is unlikely that Edward's use of subterfuge would have unduly worried his contemporaries. Medieval authors, especially those concerned with chivalric values, often adopted an ambiguous attitude towards the *ruse de guerre*; many accounts do show a sneaking admiration for the use of cunning in warfare. However, some contemporary writers appear to have believed that Edward was too ready to break his word, and this was more damaging to his reputation than his use of military guile. In taking flight from Gloucester, for instance, Edward had broken his sworn promise that he would not try to escape. The author of the *Song of Lewes* compared Edward to a leopard (*leopardus*), because he combined the merits of a lion with the flaws of a panther; the lion (*leo*) was widely admired for its pride and ferocity, whereas the panther (*pardus*) was thought to have a deceitful and unreliable character.[7]

Despite the criticisms of some contemporary writers, the Lord Edward (as he was then known) had emerged as a person of substance. By the mid-1260s he had proved himself in warfare, in spite of some disquiet about his methods, and there are also some indications of growing wisdom; the battle of Evesham was not quite the end of the civil war, and it is possible that Edward's reputation began to improve as a result of his subsequent attempts to bring about reconciliation. One former rebel, for example, John de Vescy, would become one of Edward's most devoted servants. Doubtless there were some who began to look forward to Edward's coronation as king, although his father remained in robust health. Henry III was now in his early sixties, but he would reign for several more years. In the meantime Edward sought a new purpose. Eventually he found an outlet for his talents and restless energy as a crusader.

Most readers will be aware that the medieval Crusades were holy wars, which were thought to bring rewards in the next life. Originally conceived in the later eleventh century as wars against Islam, with the city of Jerusalem as the primary target, they were later unleashed against pagans and some considered heretics. Edward's was a traditional form of Crusade, in that it was directed against the Muslims. After what must have seemed like endless difficulties and delays (Edward 'took the cross' in 1268), he finally set out from England in August 1270. He himself would surely have seen this as the most significant moment of his career so far; at this time the Crusade was still widely thought of as the highest calling available to a European noble warrior. Moreover, Edward was following in the footsteps of a celebrated ancestor, Richard the Lionheart, with whom he quickly began to be compared. This, it might have been argued, was truly chivalry in action.

Edward was accompanied on his great adventure by his wife, as well as by several other characters who would go on to become important figures during his kingship, including the Savoyard knight Otto de Grandson. When Edward set out, his intention was to join Louis IX of France, who had been persuaded to launch an attack on the North African city of Tunis, but the French king's death from illness brought an end to this aspect of the Crusade. Edward therefore decided to push on to the Holy Land, arriving at the port of Acre in

May 1271. In the wake of the spectacularly successful First Crusade, the Latin kingdom of Jerusalem had been established. The Muslims had retaken Jerusalem in the 1180s, but the 'kings of Jerusalem' maintained a precarious hold on other parts of the Holy Land. Now Edward hoped to help save what was left of the crusader kingdom, although in truth, with a force of less than a thousand men, he was never likely to make the decisive impact he craved.

Edward remained in the Holy Land for around a year, during which time he engaged in limited operations against the Muslims, although the crusader state was now in a desperate position. In May 1272 the titular king of Jerusalem, Hugh de Lusignan, agreed a long-term truce with the famous Muslim Sultan Baybars. Edward, disgusted, began to make preparations to leave. But Edward had been identified as a determined enemy of Islam, and an assassin was despatched, armed with a poisoned dagger, to take him by surprise and kill him. The assassin gained access to Edward's personal apartments and attacked. But in a dramatic display of personal prowess, Edward was somehow able to overpower the assassin, killing him with his own weapon. We might imagine a brief moment of relief, before it became clear that Edward had been wounded in the struggle. It is said that Edward's wife Eleanor was the first to react, saving his life by sucking the poison out of the wound.

There is more than one version of the tale of Edward and the assassin (in another account it is Otto de Grandson who saves Edward's life), and it has taken on a legendary quality.[8] Even so, it must also be said that Edward and Eleanor were clearly devoted to each other. In an age when the marriages of great men and women were almost always determined by political rather than personal factors, Edward and Eleanor do seem to have formed a particularly strong bond. Moreover, the extraordinary episode with the assassin is only one of several occasions when Edward came close to death over the years: he appears to have led a remarkably charmed life, and this doubtless added to the popular notion that he was destined for great things.

* * * *

Henry III died in November 1272, when Edward was still abroad. His succession as king was accepted without question, but he did not return to England until the summer of 1274. He spent time in Italy and at the court of France, as well as staying for almost a year in Gascony. Once he did return to England, however, it quickly became clear that the new king would be a monarch to be reckoned with. Thirteenth-century England was already one of the most centralised and intensively governed kingdoms in Europe – there was an extensive bureaucracy – and Edward was determined to build on this legacy. Early in his reign he launched a substantial inquiry into landholding in England – an initiative that rivalled the more famous Domesday survey in its scope and ambition. Then the *Quo Warranto* proceedings (from the Latin for 'By what warrant?') called for men to provide proof of their rights to exercise various jurisdictions. He also passed a succession of new laws, which clarified and developed the work of previous statutes.

Much of this activity was undoubtedly designed to consolidate Edward's own power – he was determined to avoid the difficulties of his father's reign – but what did it mean for his subjects? Edward has emerged from one recent study as a ruler with a more sophisticated and responsible attitude towards governance than is sometimes allowed.[9] While he jealously guarded and promoted his own rights (and this was almost certainly the spur behind the *Quo Warranto* proceedings), there is evidence to suggest that he was genuinely committed to providing order and justice throughout his realm.[10] It has also been argued that Edward's relations with the nobility – a vital aspect of medieval kingship – were generally more positive and constructive than was previously thought. Rather than simply attempting to terrorise his barons into submission, it has been suggested that Edward employed a judicious balance of 'carrot and stick'.[11]

An element of compromise could be vital, because the king's power was not unchecked: whilst ideas derived from Roman law helped to justify an exalted conception of royal authority, there was simultaneously a growing perception that rulers were obliged to *consult* their subjects. Parliament was still a limited institution by modern standards; it was by no means truly representative, and an assembly would only come into being when it was summoned by the king. Nevertheless, parliament became more firmly established during Edward's reign as the most appropriate forum for debate. Edward inherited a tacit acceptance that the king should seek approval when he wished to levy taxation, and this could provide an opportunity for parliaments to extract concessions in return.

The king's actions could also be restricted in other ways. One important factor was the pervasive influence of religion in the medieval world, at a time when virtually every person in medieval Europe was a practising Christian – at least in theory. The structures of the Church ran in parallel to secular institutions, and religion permeated every aspect of medieval life (including warfare, as we have seen). Moreover, all of the kingdoms of Western Europe could still be perceived as part of a larger whole, known as Christendom. Important figures in the Church – notably, of course, the Pope in Rome – could not be easily ignored, and the lines between secular and spiritual authority could sometimes become blurred.

A medieval king, then, faced a variety of challenges. His role was complex and wide-ranging. Nevertheless, it is also clear that leadership in war was commonly regarded as the ultimate test of a medieval ruler, and this was undoubtedly a crucial aspect of Edward's own conception of kingship. Whereas his father was at heart a peaceable man, who chose an unusual *exemplar* in Edward the Confessor (after whom Edward I was named), his son would seek to prove himself as a true warrior king.

*   *   *   *

The first decade of Edward's reign witnessed substantial military activity in Wales. Anglo-Norman colonists had taken control of much of Wales, and the kings of England had established a loose form of authority over the whole country, but the thirteenth century saw a remarkable resurgence of native power. Two outstanding princes of Gwynedd, Llywelyn ap Iorweth and Llywelyn ap Gruffydd, successfully gained hegemony over other native lords. For long periods they ruled large parts of Wales as *de facto* independent rulers. In 1267, via the Treaty of Montgomery, Henry III acknowledged

Llywelyn ap Gruffydd's status by granting him the title prince of Wales. Edward himself had been forced to give up lands as a result of the treaty; this followed earlier clashes between Edward's men and Llywelyn, in which the prince had gained the upper hand. But the Treaty of Montgomery would prove to be the high point of Llywelyn's career.

When Edward returned to England in 1274 he called on Llywelyn ap Gruffydd to acknowledge his superior lordship (this was a stipulation of the 1267 treaty), but the Welsh prince failed to answer the summons. Perhaps Llywelyn simply over-estimated his strength, although he may genuinely have feared for his safety if he were to meet with Edward; there had also been disagreements between Llywelyn and the English government about various matters while Edward was still abroad.[12] The situation was further complicated by the fact that a number of Welsh exiles were then maintained at the English court. These men included Llywelyn's own brother Dafydd, from whom he had become estranged. Llywelyn also infuriated Edward by pursuing a marriage with Eleanor de Montfort, Earl Simon's daughter, although she was intercepted on her way to join Llywelyn in Wales. These, as well as other issues, eventually made conflict inevitable, and Edward's first Welsh campaign ensued in 1277.

Victory in the mountainous terrain of Gwynedd would not be achieved by exuberant charges on a battlefield; rather, warfare in Wales would provide a test of Edward's management of logistics. In some ways precedents were set for later efforts, although Edward also encountered a number of challenges. His officials found it particularly difficult to procure sufficient victuals to feed his troops – a constant theme in Edward's wars. On this occasion the problem was partly solved when a seaborne English force, led by Otto de Grandson and John de Vescy, captured Anglesey. A party of around 300 harvesters was put ashore to gather in the grain, and thus Edward's army gained vital supplies, whereas the Welsh now faced starvation. Terms were agreed for Llywelyn's surrender, and in the subsequent treaty his power was severely curtailed. Llywelyn was also compelled to restore his rebellious brothers, including Dafydd, to lands in Gwynedd.

But tensions continued between the English and the Welsh. There were complaints about the behaviour of English officials in various parts of Wales, and a number of Welsh lords became embroiled in complicated legal disputes which soon raised greater issues. In the case of Arwystli, which involved Prince Llywelyn himself, there was a protracted debate about whether the matter should be resolved according to Welsh or English law. Somewhat ironically, however, it was *Dafydd* ap Gruffydd who first took up arms against the English in 1282, although his elder brother also quickly became involved in the struggle. A second Welsh campaign ensued, which was more bitter and protracted, in which the power of Gwynedd was finally destroyed. Llywelyn was killed in the fighting, and his head was impaled on a spike in London. Dafydd, who briefly claimed the title prince of Wales, was captured and horrifically executed at Shrewsbury.

Edward had released Eleanor de Montfort to marry Llywelyn after his submission in 1267, but she subsequently died in childbirth; their daughter Gwenllian lived out her life in an English convent. The young children of Prince Dafydd would also spend the rest of their lives in English prisons or convents. Many of Edward's supporters were granted lands in Wales, as a reward for their service, although the heartland of Gwynedd was retained by the crown. As Edward's Statute of Wales put it, Wales was now 'wholly and entirely transferred under our proper dominion'.[13] In order to cement his victory in Wales (quite literally), Edward ordered the construction of several remarkable castles. Whilst these were primarily intended to act as military and administrative structures, they were also designed to be representative of his triumph. This symbolism was particularly marked at Caernarfon, where the architects incorporated Arthurian and Roman imagery that was intended to point towards Edward's power and majesty.

*   *   *   *

Edward's rule must be judged largely on the basis of his policies and the outcome of his decisions, but can we gain a more intimate impression of the man behind them? While medieval sources can often be heavily stylised, there is surely enough to suggest that

Edward was a 'larger than life' figure: the sort of man about whom stories circulate widely. Many of these stories concerned his fearsome temper. This was something he shared with most of the Plantagenets (and we will encounter much of it in the pages that follow), although it will already have become apparent that it did not always dominate his character. Moreover, whilst Edward could undoubtedly be a hard and ruthless man, there were other sides to his personality.

One aspect of Edward's character that is sometimes overlooked, for instance, is his sense of humour. The Edward of *Braveheart* has an effective line in rather acerbic quips, and there is some basis for this in contemporary letters and chronicles, but the real Edward's humour was sometimes of a more exuberant variety. On one occasion, for example, Edward engaged in some playful banter with his laundress, Matilda de Waltham, betting one of his prized warhorses that she would not be able to ride it. When the spirited Matilda proved Edward wrong, the king cheerfully kept to his wager: records prove that he subsequently bought the horse back.[14]

The episode with the laundress (and others might also be cited) suggests an ability to engage with others that was somewhat at odds with his more imperious tendencies. Indeed, Edward's most recent modern biographer has concluded that one of his major virtues was a talent for friendship, often forged through a 'common experience in arms'.[15] His closest companions included Henry de Lacy, earl of Lincoln, who provided the king with valuable service in peace and war. As Edward's reign progressed, and he outlived most of his contemporaries, he was also able to forge effective relationships with younger men; these included his kinsmen John of Brittany and Aymer de Valence.

Contemporary accounts suggest that Edward had an impressive appearance. The friar and scholar Nicholas Trivet had close connections with the royal court, and one of his works provides us with an excellent pen portrait of the king. Trivet's description of Edward's looks and physique is fairly detailed, and deserves to be quoted extensively:

> In build he was handsome and of great stature, towering head and shoulders above the average. In boyhood his hair was silvery

with a touch of yellow; in manhood it turned to black, but later it beautified his old age by becoming as white as a swan. His brow was broad, and the rest of his face regular, though a drooping of the left eyelid recalled his father's expression.[16]

Medieval art was often rather abstract, and only rarely provided truly life-like representations of people, but the last feature mentioned – the drooping left eyelid, which was a family trait – was widely known and is represented in a contemporary illustration. Edward's great height is also attested by other evidence: his body was exhumed in the eighteenth century, and he was found to be 6 feet 2 inches tall.

Trivet goes on to explain how Edward's natural attributes made him well fitted for martial pursuits. He had a broad chest and long arms – 'their agile strength made them supremely fitted for the use of the sword' – while his long legs (i.e. long shanks) 'gave him a firm seat even when galloping and jumping on spirited horses'. Like many medieval kings, Edward enjoyed hawking and hunting; the latter was often seen by medieval writers as training for war. Apparently Edward took particular delight in hunting the stag, which, in a remarkable display of courage and skill, 'he used to pursue on a swift horse and slay with his sword, instead of using his hunting spear'.

Trivet's work also tells us a little more about Edward as a person. We learn that he was an eloquent and persuasive speaker, for example, in spite of the fact that he 'spoke with a stammer' (which is sometimes translated as 'lisp'). Significantly, Trivet adds that Edward 'was a man of strong character too, not willing to submit to injuries, and this made him forget danger when he wanted revenge'.

*   *   *   *

With the benefit of hindsight, it may seem that it was only a matter of time before this most assertive and warlike of English kings turned his gaze towards the north. Scotland's status as an independent kingdom was well established, but in the 1250s the minority of the Scots' king, Alexander III, provided the opportunity for Henry III to make a forceful intervention in Scottish political affairs. It might be argued that in this, if in little else, Edward saw his father's actions as an example to follow. Yet for much of Edward's life he did not seek to impose his power upon the Scots. Alexander III continued to rule Scotland during the first half of Edward's reign, and the two kings established an effective rapport. In part this was due to family connections: Alexander had married one of Edward's sisters, Margaret.

A number of sources suggest that Margaret's early years in Scotland were unhappy,[17] but eventually her marriage helped to provide a basis for cordial relations between Edward and Alexander. During his youth Edward made two visits to Scotland, in 1256 and 1267, where we can assume he was well received by his sister and her husband. On the first occasion he was accompanied by Eleanor, and the two young couples made a pilgrimage together to St Ninian's shrine at Whithorn. Alexander and Margaret also made several visits to the English court. In 1274, for example, Alexander and Margaret were in London to attend Edward's coronation.

The coronation was a lavish affair, but Alexander was keen to remind the world that he was also a king, and an entertaining tradition has been preserved about his contribution to the festivities.[18] A hundred of Alexander's knights suddenly appeared, dismounted from their horses and then released them, while Alexander called out that anybody who caught one of the horses could keep it. Not wishing to be upstaged by the king of Scots, a number of Edward's barons followed Alexander's example, ordering their attendants to release more horses. The result, unsurprisingly, was total mayhem – but the whole affair also provided great amusement for Edward's guests. We can assume that such a gift, and the manner of its giving, would surely have appealed to Edward himself.

Similar personal connections existed between members of the English and Scottish nobility. This was not least because many noblemen at this time held lands in *both* kingdoms, forming what is often described as a 'cross-border' aristocracy. This phenomenon owed much to David I, who was king of Scots between 1124 and 1153. He spent much of his youth in exile at the English court, and when he succeeded to the Scottish throne he encouraged Anglo-Norman settlers – including warriors, administrators, merchants and churchmen – to follow him north. This influx of people helped David to introduce a range of Anglo-Norman customs and processes, most notably 'feudal' patterns of landholding, although the long-term impact continues to be debated by historians.[19] Over time, most of the immigrants became more integrated into local areas, but their descendants often maintained important links with England and sometimes also with France.

Many of the great Scottish families we will encounter – including the Balliols, Bruces and Comyns – had Anglo-Norman ancestors, and this heritage was reflected in their landholdings: the Bruces, for example, held English lands near Hartlepool and in Essex. There is some debate about the preferred language of the thirteenth-century Scottish aristocracy (would they have mainly spoken French, like their English peers, or would they have preferred to speak Scots or Gaelic?[20]), but many Scottish nobles were clearly adept at operating in a range of settings. In terms of culture, lifestyle and outlook they shared a great deal with their peers from south of the border – and also throughout Europe.

The application of modern ideas of nationality – with their connotations of citizenship or ethnicity – is therefore problematic: the political decisions of medieval noblemen often hinged on the question of *allegiance*, rather than national identity. For others, we must assume, the importance of local and family connections – as well as a powerful instinct for self-preservation – would always trump more abstract considerations. Nevertheless, it is also very clear that the concept of a distinctive kingdom of Scotland was a real and powerful force in the thirteenth century. It was an idea for which many Scots, both high-born and low, would ultimately give up their lives.

* * * *

People did not have to face hard choices, as far as Anglo-Scottish relations were concerned, during the first part of Edward's reign. Yet in truth this period was something of an anomaly, as by this time there was already a long history of conflict between England and Scotland. Both kingdoms had emerged as coherent political entities in the wake of the Viking invasions, but the path taken thereafter by the British Isles was by no means inevitable. In the twelfth century, for example,

David I had taken advantage of English weakness during a civil war to take control of large parts of northern England. This Scottish occupation was short-lived, but David's successors continued to maintain that Northumberland should be part of the Scottish realm. Moreover, as the Middle Ages progressed, there was also potential for Anglo–Scottish conflict in the territories bounding the Irish Sea, as the kings of both kingdoms sought to expand their power to the west.

The Treaty of York (1237) settled the question of where the border should lie (it was remarkably close to the modern border), but another key issue concerned something less tangible: this was the assertion of superiority, sometimes referred to as overlordship, which was often put forward by English rulers.

By Edward I's time English claims were underpinned by a tenacious myth, which was popularised by Geoffrey of Monmouth in the twelfth century.[21] It was said that a British kingdom was founded in distant antiquity by Brutus, a descendant of the Trojan Aeneas, and that his realm was subsequently divided between his three sons – thereby explaining the existence of England, Scotland and Wales. Given that England (or *Loegria*) was inherited by the eldest son, Geoffrey's readers concluded, did this not offer proof that English superiority was both ancient and inevitable? Following Geoffrey, it was also widely believed that the fabled King Arthur had ruled over the whole of Britain, having subjugated the Scots, providing further inspiration for the English kings.

Geoffrey of Monmouth's 'history' was taken seriously in the Middle Ages (although his credibility was not accepted without question), but England's rulers could also point towards less esoteric evidence. There had been several occasions in earlier Anglo–Scottish wars when the greater resources of the English had proved decisive, and a number of earlier Scottish kings, including Malcolm 'Canmore' (meaning 'Great Chief') and William 'the Lion', had been forced to make abject submissions. Yet the Scottish kings appear to have regarded these submissions as temporary expedients, whereas the English kings saw these occasions as important precedents to be jealously remembered.

The situation was further complicated by the fact that Alexander III had inherited certain lands in England, although these were not regarded as part of his kingdom; this was a legacy of David I's time in England and his marriage to an English noblewoman, and it was perpetuated by the Treaty of York. More specifically, in the light of medieval conceptions of landholding, it should be said that he held these lands *from* the king of England. This meant that the king of Scots, like all great landowners, was expected to give *homage* for his lordships in England: this entailed a ceremonial act of submission whereby he offered service to the English king in return for acknowledgement of his title to his English lands.

As far as Alexander III was concerned, the ritual of homage was connected specifically and exclusively to his obligations as an English baron, with no bearing on his status as king of Scots: a somewhat odd state of affairs, although Alexander's position is not really difficult to understand. However, Edward I was always keen to define, clarify or expand his rights, and could Alexander's act of homage be interpreted as having a deeper significance?

Alexander was aware of the dangers that his situation might pose and therefore, when he rode south to pay homage to Edward in 1278, he demanded an escort of three English earls and two archbishops as an acknowledgement of his exalted status. But Alexander's fears were realised when one of Edward's councillors, the bishop of Lincoln, asserted explicitly that Alexander's homage should also apply to his kingdom. The response was fierce: 'Nobody but God', said Alexander, 'has the right to the homage of my realm of Scotland, and I hold it of nobody but God himself.'[22] This, at least, is how a later Scottish writer presented the episode; an alternative English source, also composed much later, offers a very different account.[23] Whatever the truth of the matter, there is no evidence to suggest that Edward pushed this point any further. Several years later, of course, his attitude towards another king of Scots would be very different.

On the whole, though, while Alexander III was still alive, war between England and Scotland must have appeared extremely unlikely. Peaceful relations with England provided Alexander with the space to establish himself as one of medieval Scotland's most effective kings. He fostered economic growth, as well as the continued development of royal government; his reign also saw the expansion of the kingdom, at the expense of Norway. In the thirteenth century the Western Isles and Orkney still owed allegiance to the Norwegian kings, and in 1263 King Hakon IV attempted to reassert his power in the west. Hakon's forces were confronted by a Scottish army at Largs, although the subsequent engagement was inconclusive. But Hakon then decided to withdraw, and he died of illness on his way home. In 1267 King Magnus of Norway formally ceded the Western Isles: a significant moment in Scottish history. Unfortunately, however, for the Scots and their king, there would be much less to celebrate during Alexander's final years.

In the first of several tragedies that beset the House of Canmore, Queen Margaret died in 1275, still only in her thirties. But she had left a legacy in her children, fulfilling what would have been seen as her primary duty as queen. She had given birth to three children who survived infancy: Alexander, Margaret and David. Alexander III's line seemed secure, in spite of the loss of his wife, although by 1284 all three of his children had followed their mother to the grave. The middle child, Margaret, married King Eric of Norway; she died in childbirth in 1283, although her daughter survived. This child, another Margaret (although perhaps better known as the Maid of Norway), subsequently became King Alexander's heir. Now acutely aware of his own mortality, Alexander convened a meeting of his nobles at which they swore to uphold the rights of the little Maid. Nevertheless, even though Alexander was now a widower, he still hoped to have more children of his own.

By this time King Alexander was in his early forties – a mature man by medieval standards, but scarcely in his dotage – and in the autumn of 1285 he married for the second time. His new queen was Yolande de Dreux, who came from a noble French family. The wedding was celebrated with great cheer, yet later sources suggest it was accompanied by evil portents.[24] On 19 March, despite a terrible storm, Alexander crossed the Forth by boat from South Queensferry on his way to visit Yolande at Kinghorn. The boat reached land safely, but the awful weather showed no sign of abating. Tradition tells us that the ferryman implored Alexander to go no further, but the king shrugged him aside: impatient to see his young bride, he rode off alone into the night. Somewhere on the Fife cliffs his horse must have slipped and fallen, throwing Alexander down onto the rocks below. In the morning the king's attendants found his body on the shore.

When any medieval king died without an adult male heir, it almost always led to a period of tension and instability, but Alexander's death would prove to be a seismic moment in the history of the British Isles. There is no reason to believe that Edward I desired Alexander's death, but the event must also be seen as a defining moment in his own life too. When the news reached Edward he was in France, fully engaged in wider European affairs. Yet in the years that followed Edward's gaze would be irresistibly drawn towards Scotland, with all that ultimately entailed.

Chapter 2

To Reduce the King and Kingdom of Scotland to His Rule

In April 1286, in the wake of Alexander III's death, the leading men of Scotland came together to discuss the future of the kingdom. Two assemblies met at Scone. In spite of the promises made to the late king, however, Margaret of Norway was not acclaimed as queen. The situation was complicated by the fact that Yolande de Dreux was thought to be pregnant with Alexander's child, thereby raising the possibility of a direct male heir – albeit an infant. In the absence of an acknowledged ruler it was essential to find *some* basis for effective governance and so at the end of the month it was decided that an oath of fealty should be sworn, somewhat ambiguously, to the heir 'who ought to inherit' (or words to that effect).[1] Seven[2] *custodes* or 'Guardians' were appointed – three bishops, two earls and two barons – who represented the political community, or 'commune', of the realm.

The Guardians were William Fraser, bishop of St Andrews; Robert Wishart, bishop of Glasgow; William, bishop of Dunkeld; Alexander Comyn, earl of Buchan; Duncan, earl of Fife; John Comyn, lord of Badenoch; and James the Steward (the ancestor of the Stewart kings). With the exception of the earl of Fife, who was still in his early twenties, all were experienced men. The appointment of the Guardians might therefore be seen as an expression of strength, demonstrating an enduring commitment to the kingdom and its institutions.[3] Understandably, however, there were limits to their authority, and in these uncertain times it is not surprising that other men began to dream they might take the throne. After the Maid of

Norway there were two obvious candidates, both of whom were adult males. Both were also descended from daughters of Earl David of Huntingdon, a grandson of King David I.

The first of the potential claimants was Robert Bruce, the grandfather of the famous future king. This Robert Bruce was the fifth member of his family to bear that name. He was also known as 'the Noble' and later as 'the Competitor': a reference to his tenacious pursuit of the throne. The Bruces, like much of the Scottish aristocracy, held lands in England but the main source of their power had long been their lordship of Annandale in south-west Scotland. By this time, though, the family had expanded its influence, because the son and heir of Robert the Noble, Robert Bruce VI, had gained the earldom of Carrick by marriage.

Bruce's likely rival was John Balliol, even though up to this point he had spent much of his time on his lands in England and France. Balliol was the heir to the great lordship of Galloway, but at this time his mother, Lady Devorgilla, still held Galloway in her own right. It was significant, though, that Balliol had a connection with the Comyn family, to whom he was related by marriage. The Comyns were the most powerful noble family in Scotland; they held lands throughout the kingdom (although especially north of the Forth), and were also extremely influential in political affairs. Two members of the Comyn family were appointed as Guardians in 1286, as we have seen. The earl of Buchan was the head of one branch of the family, holding the core of his lands in north-eastern Scotland, but the lord of Badenoch represented the senior branch (even though he was not an earl); his powerbase was in the central Highlands.

The Comyns' influence was partly based on their military capabilities and their control of significant lines of communication. The lord of Badenoch held the important fortress of Inverlochy, for example, whose defences are thought to have been strengthened and modernised during the 1270s and 1280s.[4] Inverlochy held a vitally strategic position because it gave its owner the key to the Great Glen. Also known as Glen Albyn (from the Gaelic *Gleann Albainn*, meaning the 'Glen of Scotland'), the Great Glen is in fact a series of glens, following the line of a geological fault that bisects the Highlands. The Great Glen therefore allows penetration into the heart of northern

Scotland, meaning that control of this area has been crucially important throughout the whole of Scottish history. Inverlochy and the Comyns' other great castles, such as Lochindorb and Slains, also served as administrative centres and as a focus of noble culture.

The Bruces also had powerful connections. In late September Robert the Noble met with a number of his closest associates, including James the Steward, at his son's castle of Turnberry in Ayrshire. All those present agreed a pact of mutual assistance, which is known as the Turnberry Band. In addition to a group of Scottish nobles, the arrangement included two powerful Irish lords: Richard de Burgh, earl of Ulster, and Thomas de Clare. It has sometimes been suggested, therefore, that the meeting was prompted by concerns about the potential for disorder in Ireland and the Western Isles, which could spill over onto the Scottish mainland; whilst it is often noted that the Bruce family had 'Anglo–Norman' origins, by this time they were also part of a wider world that encompassed the Irish Sea.[5] But the Turnberry Band must also have renewed Bruce's confidence in the strength of his position in Scotland. By November it was clear that Queen Yolande would not become the mother of a king of Scots (her child may have been still-born), and Bruce decided to act.

The Bruces swept through the south-west of Scotland, openly in arms and with banners displayed. They took control of the royal castles at Wigmore and Dumfries, and also captured the Balliol stronghold of Buittle. These actions must have been interpreted as the opening moves in a Bruce bid for the throne – possibly paving the way for assistance from Ireland – but in fact Bruce had overestimated the extent of his support. Crucially, for example, he received no encouragement from James the Steward, who stayed true to his wider responsibilities, and the Bruces were soon forced to seek terms with the Guardians. They were not punished for their actions, but were compelled to give up the castles they had taken – and also to swear fealty to Margaret of Norway as the 'Lady' of Scotland and future queen.

* * * *

Establishing the Maid of Norway's right to the throne of Scotland was one thing, but even her most stubborn adherents would have conceded that rule by a child – and a female one at that – was far from ideal. Moreover, her father, King Eric of Norway, was reluctant to give permission for Margaret to sail to Scotland unless her safety could be guaranteed. What little Margaret needed, then (from the medieval point of view), was a powerful protector: and was there a better candidate, it might have been argued, than Edward of England?

With the benefit of hindsight, it might be suggested that the Scots were mistaken to involve Edward in Scottish affairs. And was it really necessary? After all, it is clear that the Guardians were able to maintain a relatively effective administration, and even to face down the abortive rising of the Bruces. However, recent work has indicated that they found it increasingly difficult to stand apart from the aristocratic world of which they were still a part (and not only because of their connections to potential claimants to the throne).[6] Edward, by contrast, might have provided an impartial source of authority, much as his father had done, to a certain extent, in the 1250s. Later events would suggest the Guardians were not entirely naïve, and doubtless there must have been considerable debate before any appeal was made to England. Nevertheless, it is also very clear that the Scots (or at least some of them) were keen to open a dialogue with Edward.

Immediately after the death of Alexander III, two Franciscan friars were despatched to inform Edward of the sad news of the passing of the king of Scots. Their task was at least partly a matter of courtesy, but they were followed by two more high-powered embassies. The first of these, in May 1286, was led by Bishop Fraser of St Andrews – who appears to have particularly respected Edward – but it is not clear if the bishop was able to meet with Edward before the latter left England for France. The second embassy, led by William Comyn, bishop of Brechin and two others, pursued Edward to the continent; they were ushered into his presence at Saintes, north of Bordeaux. According to the testimony of Walter Bower, writing in the early fifteenth century, the Scots pleaded with Edward to give them his 'counsel and protection'.[7]

If the Scots truly hoped for great things from Edward, they would be sadly disappointed. He might well have given some vague assurances of his goodwill, but at this stage of his career he was concerned with much larger matters (as he would undoubtedly have understood the situation). As one modern historian has explained, 'as so often, [Edward's] plans seem to have been inflexibly set, and he was not to be diverted from them'.[8] But what were these plans? Edward had travelled to France in order to place himself at the heart of a complex dispute involving the Papacy, France and the kingdom of Aragon (part of modern Spain). On this occasion Edward sought to act as a peacemaker: it was hoped that the achievement of unity between the great powers of Europe would pave the way for the organisation of a new Crusade. For the next three years Edward would have little time for Scottish affairs.

The main source of conflict in Europe at this time was the kingdom of Sicily (which then encompassed much of southern Italy). In 1282 there was a major revolt in Sicily, the so-called 'Sicilian Vespers', which led to the expulsion of the French ruler, Charles of Anjou, from the island itself. The Sicilian rebels invited King Peter III of Aragon to take the crown in Charles's place, and Peter was pleased to accept their offer. Charles, in his turn, received financial and military backing from the king of France, Philip III, and he was determined to oust the Aragonese. The Pope at this time, Martin IV, who was also a Frenchman, provided stalwart support for the Angevin cause. A war ensued, including a series of naval engagements throughout the Mediterranean. In 1285, however, all the major players in the conflict passed away (including Martin IV). This left Edward, who was then in his mid-forties, as the senior statesman in western Europe, and it was hoped that he would be able to use his natural authority and experience to arbitrate between the various heirs.

England would have to do without its ruler until August 1289: the longest absence by one of its kings since the reign of Richard the Lionheart (who famously spent only around six months in England). Edward went first to Paris, where he met with the new king of France, Philip IV, and was obliged to pay homage to him for his duchy of Aquitaine – it is often noted that Edward does not appear to have appreciated the ironic parallel between his own situation and that of the king of Scots! – although he was also able to negotiate a truce between France and Aragon. From Paris Edward set out towards his own lands, visiting Fontevrault, the burial place of his Angevin ancestors, on his way south. He also took the opportunity to tour his lands in southern France, before he eventually reached Bordeaux in January 1287 (around which time he received the Scots envoys).

In addition to his efforts to resolve the Sicilian problem, Edward diverted himself with various other activities (such as hunting wolves). He also devoted considerable time to the governance of Gascony, as well as founding a number of new towns, known as *bastides*.⁹ (These followed similar developments in Wales.) The matter of Sicily remained his primary concern, however, although here he faced serious obstacles. The situation was complicated by the fact that Charles of Anjou's heir, Charles of Salerno, had been captured by the Aragonese. But this did not strengthen the Aragonese position as much as might be expected, because the new Pope, Honorius IV, continued to support the Angevins. It was therefore anticipated that the release of Charles of Salerno would set off a chain of events that would pave the way for lasting peace.

Edward's labours took on greater intensity after Easter Sunday in 1287, when he suffered another near-death experience. He was standing in a room in a tower when the floor suddenly collapsed, causing the king and his entourage to fall nearly eighty feet. Edward was lucky to escape with a broken collar-bone, although others were more seriously injured and three men were killed. One chronicle suggests the floor was dislodged by a bolt of lightning. This incident may therefore have been seen as divinely inspired, intended as a message for Edward. Perhaps he concurred: as soon as he was physically recovered, he once again 'took the cross'. Pope Honorius agreed to provide funds for Edward's enterprise, and nominated the archbishop of Ravenna to provide papal endorsement of his intentions. But unfortunately the Pope died in the meantime, rendering invalid the ensuing ceremony (as well as the financial negotiations that had preceded it).

Naturally the Pope's death had wider diplomatic implications, although Edward continued to press for Charles's release. Eventually he was able to bring this about, although the deal he brokered involved considerable costs for Edward; he himself paid part of Charles's ransom (as a loan, albeit one that was never repaid), and he also sent English hostages to act as temporary surety when Charles was freed.

However, in return Charles was expected to acknowledge the Aragonese hold on the island of Sicily (as was the Papacy). Whilst Charles offered profuse thanks to Edward, he swiftly reneged on his agreement with the Aragonese and further warfare ensued. Charles was later castigated for his dishonourable behaviour by Otto de Grandson, and this almost certainly reflected Edward's own attitude. But for the moment Edward believed he had done everything in his power, and he was now keen to return to England.

Writing in the summer of 1289, a clerk who had accompanied Edward to Gascony commented that 'the stay in these parts has seemed too long, both to him and his'.[10] Edward was deeply disturbed by reports he had received from England, and when he returned to his kingdom in June he became particularly concerned with the restoration of order. Several of Edward's officials in England were censured, as it was thought they had exploited the king's absence for their own gain. It was around this time, too, that Edward set in train the expulsion of England's Jews (probably inspired by a mixture of prejudice and financial motives): a policy that would not be reversed until the seventeenth century. But Edward was now also increasingly interested in Scotland: doubtless he had received reports about the unsettled nature of affairs there. By this time it appears that the authority of the Guardians, which was always precarious, had finally begun to fracture.

*   *   *   *

In September 1289 the youngest of the Guardians, Duncan, earl of Fife, was murdered near Brechin. Earl Duncan had made numerous enemies during his time as a Guardian (the *Lanercost Chronicle* describes him as 'cruel and greedy'[11]), yet even so this was a shocking event. The perpetrator, Hugh Abernethy, was quickly arrested and imprisoned,[12] notwithstanding his own considerable status and close ties to the Comyns, but Earl Duncan was not replaced as a Guardian. Indeed, the failure to replace any of the Guardians who died in office (by this time the earl of Buchan and the bishop of Dunkeld had also passed away) may well provide evidence of political disagreements and an increasing sense of factionalism. The Maid of Norway could potentially provide a focus for unity, given that all of the main political actors in Scotland had offered her their loyalty, although of course there was a limit to her appeal while she remained with her father across the sea.

It was therefore necessary to find a way to overcome King Eric's resistance to the notion that his daughter should leave Norway. Efforts had already been made to find a way out of the impasse before the alarming murder of the earl of Fife, and these efforts continued throughout the year 1289. An idea was mooted – although it is not clear where the suggestion originated – that Margaret should marry Edward I's son and heir, Edward of Caernarfon (so-named after the place of his birth). Naturally the theory was that, in time, Margaret's husband would serve as her protector and provide a guiding hand. Edward of Caernarfon was then still very young, but it was assumed that until he reached his majority his father would be happy to protect Margaret's interests.

From the point of view of Eric of Norway, a marriage alliance with England had considerable appeal. Much of the impetus appears to have come from the Norwegians and the Scots, and the initial round of diplomacy took place while Edward was still in France. Nevertheless, Edward did express enthusiasm for the projected match; he welcomed a Norwegian embassy at Condom in May 1289, and he also sought to obtain a dispensation for the marriage from the next Pope, Nicholas IV. (A dispensation would be necessary because the children in question were cousins once removed.) Even though Edward could indeed sometimes be inflexible, to the point of obstinacy and obsession, it seems his mind was constantly alive to the possibility of future opportunities. In this case, of course, Edward understood that the marriage held the potential to make Scotland part of the Plantagenet domains.

Whilst Margaret and Edward of Caernarfon were both still too young to marry, the papal dispensation was successfully obtained. A series of complex negotiations laid the groundwork for a future marriage to proceed. The Treaty of Salisbury (6 November 1289) imposed significant obligations on the Scots. The terms of the treaty suggested that Margaret might travel first to England, before moving on to Scotland, but the latter would not occur unless the Scots could prove to Edward I and King Eric's satisfaction that the realm was in a good state of order. However, the treaty also obliged Eric to send Margaret from Norway within the year.

In the coming months, ostensibly working on behalf of his son and prospective daughter-in-law, Edward began to assert himself in Scotland. He sought to gain control of Scottish royal castles in the name of the young couple; he also took the Isle of Man, which was then nominally part of the Scottish realm, under his 'protection'. Whilst the question of the castles became a thorny subject in subsequent discussions, the Guardians remained eager for the marriage plan to be confirmed as this would mean their 'lady' could at last come to Scotland and become their queen. But they were also determined to ensure that the status of the kingdom would be preserved.

Fresh talks between the English and Scots in July 1290 led to another agreement, at Birgham in southern Scotland, which must have helped to set the Scots' minds at rest.[13] Among other things it was specified that, after the young Edward and Margaret married, Scotland would remain 'separate, free in itself without any subjection to England'. The 'rights, laws, liberties and customs of the realm of Scotland' would all be retained. Whilst it was envisaged that the heir to the young couple would eventually inherit both of their thrones, future kings would be bound to maintain separate administrations in England and Scotland. The rights of the Scottish Church would be protected, because elections of its bishops would be held in Scotland, and the rulers of England and Scotland would also be expected to travel north of the border to receive the homage of their leading Scottish subjects.

Thus the agreement at Birgham held out the prospect of a peaceful union between the crowns of England and Scotland, more than 300 years before James VI of Scotland succeeded to the English throne. As Sir Walter Scott mused in his *Tales of a Grandfather*, had it come to pass then 'an immeasurable quantity of money and bloodshed would probably have been saved'.[14] Some readers might well take a less optimistic view of the projected marriage and its subsequent effects, although what it would have meant in practice remains one of the great 'what if's of British history. But tragedy once again intervened, striking yet another blow against the House of Canmore. The Scots had been promised at Salisbury that the Maid would reach the British Isles by 1 November. She did set out from Norway at some point in the autumn of 1290, but she never reached England or the Scottish mainland. Her ship put in to a harbour in Orkney, where little Margaret died of illness.

*   *   *   *

The death of the Maid of Norway once again raised the spectre of civil war in Scotland. Naturally Robert Bruce was keen to reassert his claim to the throne, but John Balliol's position was now somewhat stronger than it had been in 1286: Balliol had recently inherited the lordship of Galloway, following the death of his mother, and doubtless it was taken for granted that he could rely on his Comyn relatives in any power struggle to come. Writing in early October, when the news of the Maid's death was still uncertain, the bishop of St Andrews continued to see Edward as a potential source of neutral authority; in the event that the Maid had indeed passed away (as, of course, she had), he exhorted Edward to travel swiftly north, for 'the consolation of the Scottish people and for saving [preventing] the shedding of blood'.[15]

Unfortunately Edward's reply to Bishop Fraser has not survived. A later Scottish source asserts that he encouraged the Scots to delay any decisions about the succession until he could offer his advice in person, promising to help them as 'a friend and neighbour'.[16] But the death of the Maid of Norway was closely followed by a more personal tragedy for Edward: the passing of his beloved wife. Queen Eleanor fell ill, and died at Harby in Lincolnshire on 28 November 1290. Edward was distraught; writing to the abbot of Cluny in the New Year, he described Eleanor as the woman 'whom in life we dearly cherished, and whom in death we cannot cease to love'.[17] Eleanor's body was conveyed to London in a sad procession, and Edward later commissioned a monument at each of the places where the cortege rested for the evening: several of these 'Eleanor Crosses' still survive. Her tomb at Westminster was beautified by a splendid bronze effigy fashioned by William Torel, a celebrated goldsmith.

Eleanor's funeral took place at Westminster on 17 December. Thereafter, in the depths of winter, Edward retreated to Ashridge Priory in Buckinghamshire. Here, one must imagine, he spent a desolate Christmas. When he emerged from Ashridge, however, in January 1291, the matter of Scotland appeared to be very much on his mind. But he was no longer speaking of friendship with the Scots. At a gathering of the king and his nobles, which took place at some point in early 1291, a chronicle from Waverley Abbey tells us that Edward openly stated his intentions: he 'said that it was in his mind to reduce the king and kingdom of Scotland to his rule, as he had recently subjected Wales to his authority'.[18]

It seems Edward was not seriously contemplating military action at this time, although it is clear that he intended to exploit the situation in Scotland to his own advantage. What the Scots undoubtedly wanted was an arbitrated settlement between Robert Bruce and John Balliol: given Edward's previous experience in such negotiations, it might have been argued that he would be admirably suited to such a role. To this end, in May 1291 the great men of Scotland gathered in Berwick-upon-Tweed (then an important Scottish town), where they waited for Edward to join them. But then the Scottish Guardians were summoned to meet Edward across the border at Norham. Here they learned that Edward did not intend to help resolve the issue as a disinterested arbiter, but rather as a judge – and as the superior lord of Scotland.

Edward had already taken steps to prepare the ground: not only had he ordered his officials to scour the chronicles for evidence of his 'rights', he had also summoned a force of knights to join him at Norham. But the Guardians of Scotland were not easily cowed; with Bishop Robert Wishart of Glasgow taking the lead, they rejected Edward's position, acting with a poise and confidence that speaks highly of their courage and resolve.

The Guardians subsequently adopted a more conciliatory tone, but eventually Edward overcame their resistance by approaching the claimants directly. A number of candidates were encouraged to submit their claims – not only Bruce and Balliol – and ultimately all of them accepted that Edward had the right to make his decision between them as overlord of Scotland. Perhaps the candidates assumed that Edward would be satisfied with a theoretical acknowledgement of his superiority. Of course, it could also be argued, less charitably, that they simply feared being excluded from the succession if they did not accede to Edward's demands.

Once the claimants had given their submission – John Balliol, it should be noted, was the last to give way – the Guardians had little opportunity for any further protest. What followed was a lengthy and complex legal process, punctuated by numerous delays, which has become known as the 'Great Cause'.[19] In the meantime – with the grudging consent and cooperation of the Guardians – Edward took possession of the royal Scottish castles, as well as retaining the Isle of Man, and effectively gained custody of the Scottish realm. Two Englishmen, Anthony Bek, bishop of Durham, and Sir Brian FitzAlan, were appointed as Guardians to serve alongside the four Scots still in office. This state of affairs endured for well over a year, and perhaps surprisingly a precarious state of order appears to have been maintained. It has been observed that Edward 'moved softly' and 'was on his best behaviour'.[20] The people of Scotland, it might be suggested, collectively held their breath.

Edward's court, now based at Berwick, considered the arguments of a long series of candidates: fourteen in all. Most of the claims, including those of the king of Norway and Edward himself,[21] were never likely to be successful, and Bruce and Balliol were widely accepted as the most likely of the various claimants. As noted above, the two men were both descendants of Earl David of Huntingdon, a grandson of King David I. Balliol possessed the simplest and most coherent claim: he was the grandson of Earl David's eldest daughter Margaret, and he therefore argued that he should inherit by right of primogeniture. Bruce's case was derived from his mother Isabel, who was the next daughter of Earl David; he therefore argued that he should succeed because he was closer in *degree* to Earl David; he also asserted that King Alexander II had previously nominated him as his heir in the event of a failure in the main line.

At one point there was a significant pause in order to consult lawyers based in Paris, although the case was also complicated by various other factors, notably the dramatic emergence of Count Florence of Holland as a serious contender. Florence's claim was based on his assertion that Earl David had renounced his rights to the Scottish throne to his sister Ada, from whom the count was descended. However, Count Florence was unable to provide any documents to prove his case, despite being granted an adjournment of almost a year in which this evidence might be found.[22] But when the court convened for the final time, in October 1292, all the momentum was with Balliol. Bruce, now desperate, made a last-ditch plea that the realm should be divided between himself, Balliol and the Englishman John Hastings (a third descendant of Earl David), but this was rebuffed. On 17 November 1292 Edward finally announced that Balliol would be king.

*   *   *   *

Like previous Scottish kings, John Balliol was inaugurated at Scone, and he was able to take possession of the Scottish castles and crown lands that had recently been under Edward's control. This provides a telling reminder that Edward had not completely lost sight of the rights of others, nor had he forgotten his own obligations. Yet when John did homage to Edward on Boxing Day, the realities of his position became clear. The ceremony took place in England, at Newcastle, and there was no ambiguity whatsoever about his relationship with the English king. John spoke the words: 'My lord, Lord Edward, lord superior of the realm of Scotland, I, John Balliol, king of Scots, hereby become your liegeman for the whole realm of Scotland.'[23]

By this time John Balliol was a mature man, probably in his early forties, but in many respects he was an unlikely king. It was remarkable that he had inherited his father's lands, never mind the throne of Scotland. As a youth, before the premature deaths of his three elder brothers, he was probably destined for a career in the Church. Moreover, as we have seen, he did not know Scotland particularly well. Obviously the support of his Comyn relatives was extremely valuable – if potentially restrictive – although he would presumably have faced a steep learning curve even if he had been given time and space to consolidate his rule.[24] But John's main problem, of course, was Edward, who seized every opportunity to assert what he saw as his own rights in Scotland. In particular, Scotsmen who objected to King John's judgements were encouraged to appeal to Edward as their 'superior lord'; this gave Edward a pretext to summon John to the English court to answer for his actions.

There were a number of appeals, the most significant of which involved a Scottish nobleman by the name of Macduff, an uncle of the late earl of Fife, who claimed he had been wrongly deprived of some of his lands. Macduff occupied two disputed manors, but was evicted by agents of the bishop of St Andrews (who was then administering the earldom of Fife on behalf of the new earl, who was then still an infant). Denied justice by King John, as Macduff would have seen it, he was also temporarily imprisoned, and he therefore decided to appeal to Edward. It was impressed on King John that he would be expected to appear in person to answer the charges against him, and after some prevarication he duly presented himself in England.

It is quite possible that Balliol believed he was honour-bound to respond to Edward's summons, rather than simply acting out of weakness, but he must have been aware of the significance of the situation. Thus when Macduff's case was discussed in England, at the November Parliament of 1293, John came well prepared. Called upon to speak, he argued that 'he dare not and cannot answer here on any matter touching his realm without consulting the people of his realm'.[25]

John's statement at the parliament gained him a little time, but he was subsequently threatened with the loss of three important castles (including Berwick) as a punishment for his tardy response to Edward's summons. Doubtless more subtle forms of intimidation were also brought to bear, and the king of Scots was compelled to reaffirm his homage and his acceptance of Edward's lordship. Macduff's case was adjourned, but John promised to return to the English parliament in the following year, where he would 'report' to Edward on the advice he had received.[26]

*   *   *   *

Ultimately the Macduff case was overtaken by other events, and it was never concluded, but from Edward's point of view another important precedent had been set. Nevertheless, it might be argued that Edward's uncompromising attitude towards the king of Scots was counter-productive: another European conflict was brewing while he was seeking to impose his will on John Balliol – and this time the king of England would not be able to stand apart. The most pressing issue on Edward's agenda throughout the early 1290s was his deteriorating relationship with Philip IV of France. Philip was famously handsome and was known as 'the Fair' (*le Bel*), although he is best known today for his savage persecution of the Knights Templar. He was surely one of the most ruthless men ever to sit on the French throne.

Tensions between the kings of England and France were nothing new, but the particular problems at this time were due to an escalation of disputes at sea: there had been a number of violent altercations between English and French seamen. As we have seen, Edward owed Philip homage for his lands in France (although not for his kingdom of England), and Edward was summoned to the French court in an attempt to resolve the matter. Unlike John Balliol, however, Edward did not feel compelled to answer a summons from his liege-lord in person. He responded by sending his younger brother Edmund, and soon it appeared that a compromise had been reached: it was agreed that Edward would temporarily surrender to Philip a number of key towns, including Bordeaux, but then the duchy of Acquitaine would be formally regranted on more favourable terms in a lavish ceremony.

It may not seem immediately obvious why the agreement negotiated by Edmund should have resolved the matters at issue, but it appears to have been understood that this would mark a fresh start in relations between England and France. The renewed sense of accord between the kings of England and France was to be symbolised by a marriage between Edward (now, of course, a widower) and Princess Margaret, Philip's sister. Edward kept his side of the bargain: his officials in Gascony were ordered to surrender Bordeaux and the other towns to the French. Once he had the towns in his possession, though, Philip reneged on the deal: Edward was now deemed to be in default because he had not obeyed the French king's summons to court, and all his lands in France were declared forfeit.

Upon hearing this news, apparently Edward 'went red, and became very afraid, because he had acted less than wisely'.[27] But why had Edward been so easily deceived? There were suggestions that Edward's judgement had been clouded by the prospect of marriage to a young Frenchwoman,[28] but it is more likely that he was sincerely committed to fostering peace with France at this time. Within the British Isles Edward sought mastery, but in Europe he continued to seek harmony. Behind his seemingly rather naïve approach to foreign relations (also demonstrated in his dealings with Charles of Salerno), there remained the dream of the Crusade. To lead another Crusade was still Edward's most deeply held ambition: one that was expressed in correspondence to a diverse set of foreign rulers, including the king of Hungary and the *Il-Khan* of the Mongols. From 1291 onwards the fall of Acre – the last Christian outpost in the Holy Land – had lent this a new urgency.

Unsurprisingly Philip's machinations led to war between England and France, and as French troops prepared to entrench themselves in Gascony, the scales fell from Edward's eyes. He made plans to lead an army to Flanders, and the Scottish nobility were summoned to serve him in this enterprise, but the campaign had to be delayed. The initial problems were financial. Edward was let down by his long-time creditors, the Riccardi of Lucca,[29] and his increasingly aggressive pursuit of money caused discontent at all levels of society. His demands caused great anger in Wales, where simmering resentments soon burst into flame.

The Welsh rebels found a leader in Madog ap Llywelyn, who was distantly related to the princes of Gwynedd and now declared himself prince of Wales. Edward's energies were therefore diverted to the west, as the king led the response to the Welsh uprising in person. Eventually Edward's superior resources proved too much for the Welsh: Madog was captured (although, strangely, he was not executed, and appears to have died much later in English captivity), and the revolt was crushed. But the campaign was hard-fought and dangerous. Madog was a talented soldier, and he had enjoyed some early successes. The great chain of fortresses that Edward had ordered to be built in North Wales was still not complete, and his most cherished new castle, at Caernarfon, was all but destroyed. At one point Edward was himself pinned down at Conwy, with his men bereft of supplies.

Edward's various difficulties appeared to offer an opportunity for the Scots to throw off the shackles of English overlordship. By the autumn of 1295 King John's activities were formally supported by a Council of Twelve; some accounts suggest he had been replaced altogether. We can therefore assume that his policies had wider approval – and were quite possibly driven by others. Following the natural principle that 'my enemy's enemy is my friend', the Scots made representations to Philip the Fair. Bishop Fraser of St Andrews, who by this time was thoroughly disillusioned with Edward, was a leading member of the Scottish embassy. On 23 October 1295 terms were agreed for a treaty, committing the Scots to an alliance with France. This was the beginning of the so-called 'Auld Alliance', which ensured that England, Scotland and France would be locked together in a diplomatic triangle for the rest of the Middle Ages. In Edward's mind, of course, this was the action of a group of rebellious vassals. War between the kings of England and Scotland had now become inevitable.

Chapter 3

The Bodies Fell Like Autumn Leaves

Both sides mustered their forces in early March 1296, with Edward's nobles instructed to gather at Newcastle at the beginning of the month. On this occasion the ultimate size of Edward's army is not clear, but it is well known that he had ordered the exchequer to ensure that 1,000 men-at-arms (i.e. heavy cavalry) and an incredible 60,000 infantry would join him.[1] The latter is clearly an impossible figure: this *may* suggest that Edward was generally wise to delegate administration to others, although it also provides an indication of the extraordinary demands he placed on his officials. Nevertheless, even if Edward's ambitions for the host were ultimately unrealistic, it is generally accepted that the army raised was a large one – almost certainly over 20,000 strong – supported by a fleet.[2]

Whilst Edward's invasion of Scotland in 1296 is not the best documented of his military endeavours, academic historians have used a wide range of sources to reconstruct the composition of his armies in considerable detail. The relevant evidence includes pay rolls and horse lists (which were used to provide compensation for horses lost in the course of operations), as well as various other documents. Administrative records for this period are by no means complete, but we are extremely fortunate that so much evidence has survived. Other sources can provide useful information about military equipment, and a range of other matters.

A theoretical Edwardian army can largely be broken down into two components: cavalry and infantry. To a certain extent this can be misleading – sometimes the cavalry might dismount to fight, while infantry might sometimes ride to battle – although it does accord with the contemporary approach to army organisation. This chapter offers an introduction to military life at the time of Edward I, before moving on to provide an account of Edward's first Scottish campaign.

* * * *

Edward's mounted forces included the members of the highest nobility, although below this rank there were also numerous knights.[3] However, the bulk of the cavalry was made up of men of significant but less exalted status, variously described as esquires (*scutifers*), sergeants (*servientes*), valets (*valletti*) or *soldarii*. (Medieval scribes were not always consistent in their definitions, so these designations should not be regarded as ranks in the modern sense.) A certain level of wealth was necessary in order to afford appropriate weapons and armour, although of course the quality of the equipment would vary. Acquiring suitable horses could be particularly expensive, not least because several different horses might be needed during the course of a campaign.

By the end of the fourteenth century the military elite almost always dismounted to fight in battle (due to the increasing tactical importance of the longbow), but in the Edwardian era they still preferred to fight on horseback whenever possible. For combat, a special breed of horse was desirable (one which no longer exists today), which was known as a *destrier*. Contemporary sources show that destriers had upright necks and large buttocks – clearly such horses needed to be large and powerful if they were to carry armoured men into battle – but the popular notion that destriers were the ancestors of shire horses was long ago discredited. Only stallions would be used in battle, as they were thought to be braver and more aggressive than mares. Some of the best horses were imported from abroad, notably from Spain: destriers were sometimes described more generically as 'Spanish'.

As one might expect, destriers were particularly expensive to buy. Edward himself, as a keen rider and sportsman, spent large sums of money on horses of all kinds, but his war horses were particularly valuable. In 1297, for example, in the midst of a period of intensive military activity, Edward sold one of his destriers for £33 6s 8d, which he then replaced for the staggering sum of £66 13s 4d.⁴ To put this into perspective, both sums would have exceeded the annual income of many of his knights (and, of course, this expenditure did not include the subsequent cost of caring for the animal). Few other Englishmen could have afforded horses of such quality, but all destriers would have represented a considerable investment. The horse lists present some difficulties of interpretation,⁵ but they do provide a broader sense of valuations. During the period from 1282 to 1339 it has been estimated that the mean value fluctuated between £8 10s and £16 8s.⁶

In the late thirteenth century an elite warrior would have worn various kinds of protective clothing,⁷ although medieval armour was still some way from the peak of its development. Effective body armour has always relied on *layers* of protection, and medieval soldiers could choose from a range of options. Protective clothing during Edward I's era was made from various materials, including quilted fabric, whalebone (often used to make gauntlets) and *cour bouilli* (hardened leather), as well as from metal. Men made their choices on the basis of a wide range of factors, including cost, personal experience and changing fashion – although, of course, new developments would not be adopted *en masse*.

A coat of chain-mail was a fairly standard piece of equipment, worn over an *aketon* (padded tunic), with *chausses* (mail stockings) to protect the legs. Chain-mail was widely used throughout much of the Middle Ages. An item more distinctive to Edward's period was the *poleyn*, a piece of armour, often made from *cour bouilli*, designed to protect the knee. The poleyn was often attached to a *gamboised cuisse*, a quilted tube providing additional protection for the thigh. Poleyns were sometimes made of metal, and more substantial forms of plate armour were also starting to appear. During his prolonged stay in Gascony, for example, in the late 1280s, Edward bought a pair of *jambers* (shin-guards) in Toulouse.⁸ Nevertheless, body armour of this type does not appear to have been widely available, probably because the production process was still experimental, and therefore relatively expensive. For the head, a conical or sugarloaf-shaped *great helm* would offer the most effective protection at this time, although it could be extremely hot to wear in combat and restricted the wearer's vision. Contemporary illustrations also depict other types of headgear, including the egg-shaped *bascinet* and the *chapel de fer* (kettle hat).[9]

When fighting on horseback, an elite soldier carried a lance or spear, but this would likely shatter on impact during the course of a charge. At this, the man would usually drop the stump and draw his sword – surely one of the most treasured and important of his possessions – although others might also have wielded a mace or a horseman's axe. A mounted warrior would also have carried a triangular wooden shield, painted with the device of its owner. *Aillettes* – square or rectangular pieces of wood attached to the shoulder, perhaps originally to provide additional protection for the neck – were also painted with heraldic images.

The reference to heraldry provides a reminder that not everything a man wore or carried into combat was solely designed for his protection – at least not in an obvious sense. During this period a noble warrior would still have worn an embroidered surcoat over his armour (split at the front and back for ease of movement), which would have borne the same device as that on his shield. Of course, this would have helped others to identify the man in question. However, as there was a strong correlation between heraldic devices and personal or family honour, this might also have offered a source of pride and inspiration in the field. Many horses, when they appeared on the battlefield, would have been similarly decked out with colourful heraldic imagery; they were often covered with *caparisons*, made of decorated cloth. There are also indications, moreover, that horses could be armoured like their riders, protected by mail or *cour bouilli*.

* * * *

How was the cavalry recruited to Edward's standard? An important component was provided by the royal household. By this time the household was a large and complex organisation, comprising several hundred people, which offered personal service to the king during peace and war. From a military perspective, the knights of the household naturally played a particularly important role. These men did not always reside with the king, but they were permanently retained: they received fees and robes on an annual basis. ('Robes' were lengths of expensive cloth, sometimes lined with fur, which would be made into lavish garments.) The knights of the household were not only selected for their martial qualities; they also served the king as diplomats, for example, and in a variety of other roles. Many of them were, however, experienced warriors.

Numbers within the royal household fluctuated, but in 1300 Edward retained fifty knights and thirty *knights banneret*.[10] The latter were senior knights, whose status was marked by their right to display a square banner; the bannerets received a higher rate of pay and acted as officers during war. In addition to the knights, the king's household also included 'sergeants-at-arms' and esquires, and each of the knights would be supported by his own small retinue. During a campaign the military capacity of the household might be expanded, and new members (known as 'forinsec' troops) could be temporarily enrolled. At the battle of Falkirk in 1298, for example, the household made up one of the four battalions of cavalry, with a fighting strength of around 800 men.[11]

Much ink has been spilt over the question of how Edward recruited the rest of his cavalry. This is a complex subject, of which only a brief overview can be given here. In traditional accounts of post-Conquest England, it is often stated that the king stood at the apex of a 'feudal pyramid', constituting an elaborate military system; theoretically the king's subjects provided military service, for a specified period of time, in return for the tenure of their lands (or sometimes in return for the delegation of other privileges). As we shall see, 'feudal' service could encompass a range of obligations, although the most significant of these was *knight service*. Quotas were determined for the numbers of knights that were expected to appear when a summons was issued, and the king's greatest subjects would each provide a force of mounted warriors. However, by a process that remains opaque, these quotas had been negotiated downwards by the start of Edward's reign.

Given Edward's evident need for large numbers of effective fighting men on a regular basis, it used to be thought that Edward set in train a significant transition from a 'feudal' host to a more 'professional' royal army. In reality, it is unlikely that the specified feudal quotas had *ever* provided the kings of England with a force of cavalry that met their needs, and it is now well established that the novelty of Edward's reign has been somewhat exaggerated. As early as 1100, for example, it is clear that military obligations might be commuted in return for cash payments (known as *scutage*), and the Norman and Angevin kings also appear to have recruited large numbers of paid warriors.[12] Nevertheless, as far as the recruitment of the cavalry is concerned, Edward did attempt to make some changes.

We have already seen that Edward was willing to provide payment for military service (assuming he had sufficient funds at his disposal), but on several occasions he also sought to widen the military obligations of the landed classes on the basis of their own wealth. The traditional means to summon the host was to issue writs to the *tenants-in-chief*: those who held land directly from the crown. However, in 1296 and 1300 Edward made a direct appeal to all those who held lands worth in excess of £40 *per annum*, at which point a man was expected to take on the office of knighthood, requesting their service in Scotland. Royal pay was offered to those who appeared – the standard rate of pay for a knight was 2s per day – although Edward probably hoped to exact fines from those who did not attend. But unsurprisingly the unprecedented nature of Edward's demands was deeply unpopular, and this experiment was abandoned after 1300.

It must be stressed that there were some occasions, notably in 1298, when there was an enthusiastic response to Edward's call to arms. Many of the aristocracy shared their king's values and relished the opportunity to provide leadership in war, and there was a broader sense of obligation as a result of the fealty they owed him. The greatest lords often served *voluntarily*, nominating members of their retinues to carry out feudal service on their behalf, as well as bringing forces that were massively in excess of the feudal quotas. Moreover, whereas we might assume that the lesser aristocracy were always acutely conscious of the costs of campaigning, the great magnates were sometimes actively hostile to the idea that they should receive royal wages in return for their service. In the build-up to Edward's second Welsh war, for example, the earls ostentatiously rejected

Edward's offer of pay, which ultimately compelled him to issue a more traditional feudal summons.

The magnates' reluctance to accept royal wages was partly a matter of pride, although other factors were also important. The great nobles were probably wary of royal interference in the organisation of their retinues (from Edward's point of view, of course, increased control would have been the key advantage of recruiting an entirely paid force), and it might be added that the tenants-in-chief had the right to levy *scutage* payments from their own tenants who did not serve in person. In 1300, for example, the earl of Lincoln was able to levy the sizeable sum of £125 from his tenants in the honour of Pontefract.[13]

There were a number of reasons, then, why the aristocracy might have resisted the 'professionalisation' of the English royal army. As Edward's reign progressed, however, it has been suggested that the nobility began to resent the financial difficulties that gratuitous service could entail. Most of the warriors recruited to the banners of Edward's great captains would surely have expected to be paid. For the majority of those who served with the cavalry, we can assume that the distinctions between paid, 'feudal' and 'voluntary' service had little practical impact.[14]

* * * *

The heavy cavalry – with superior weapons, armour and (sometimes) long years of martial training – could exert a disproportionate influence in the field. As we shall see, however, successful military operations required the effective combination of various different units (as has always been the case, and doubtless always will be). The numbers demanded fell as time went on – perhaps due to straitened financial circumstances as much as tactical considerations – but all of Edward's armies included large infantry contingents. In Edward's earliest campaigns in Scotland, before 1300, the forces he raised were enormous by the standards of the time. In terms of size at least, these armies would rarely be matched again until the seventeenth century.

Infantry soldiers were recruited by means of *commissions of array*. This process evolved throughout Edward's reign; by the 1300s the commissioners appointed were increasingly men with military experience, including members of the household. However, local communities also had an important part to play in the assembly of the foot; each village or *hundred* would be expected to provide a specified number of men, whose suitability would then be assessed by the relevant commissioner. Those who were selected to serve received wages on campaign, the basic pay of an infantryman being 2d per day. Whilst this might seem to be a derisory amount of money, not least because soldiers were usually obliged to pay for their own provisions, an unskilled man could rarely have hoped to earn much more. For some men, as has been the case throughout the ages, joining the infantry represented a new start: there were several occasions when Edward offered pardons to convicted criminals in return for military service.

According to Edward's Statute of Winchester (1285), every man aged between sixteen and sixty was expected to have weapons ready appropriate to his station, but in practice it would often fall upon the men's communities to provide the equipment for the infantry. According to the chronicler Bartholomew Cotton, writing about a muster in East Anglia in 1295, this equipment consisted of white tunics, knives and swords,[15] although many of the infantry would have been equipped with bows or spears. Once mustered, the infantry was organised into groups of twenty, with each group commanded by a *vintenar*. Five such groups, forming a hundred men, were commanded by a *centenar*. The centenars would in turn defer to a more senior officer, a *millenar*, who was responsible for the direction of a thousand men.

Edward recruited infantry from throughout his domains, including soldiers from Ireland, although the Welsh made a particularly important contribution: they fought in their thousands. Given that Edward had destroyed the power of the Welsh hero Llywelyn ap Gruffydd, and had only recently suppressed a popular rebellion in Wales, perhaps it may seem strange that so much of his army was made up of Welshmen. But it is important to realise that substantial numbers of the Welsh prince's countrymen had fought *against* Llywelyn, and that Welshmen had served in large numbers during virtually all of Edward's campaigns. It is clear that the king valued their service highly, and it is also very striking that Welshmen formed part of his personal bodyguard.

As infantry, the Welsh had gained an impressive reputation, for a number of reasons. First, they were widely renowned for their courage and ferocity in battle. Moreover, whilst we are still some way from the golden age of the longbow, when the 'arrowstorms' of Welsh archers rained death upon the nobility of France, the bowmen of Wales were already famous for their skill. Writing somewhat earlier in the Middle Ages, for example, Gerald of Wales had praised the men of Gwent in particular for their great strength and accuracy (although at this time their bows were made of elm, rather than yew).[16] Gerald relates an anecdote in which Welsh archers loosed arrows with such speed and force that they were able to penetrate an oak door the width of a man's palm.

The Welshmen were also renowned for their agility and hardiness: one Flemish chronicler, who witnessed Welsh soldiers on campaign, was shocked to see them still 'running about bare-legged' in the depths of winter.[17] Born and bred in a land of hills and mountains, it is understandable that men with such physical attributes would be valuable additions to Edward's armies in Scotland. Later events will show that Edward was conscious of the potential of his Welsh infantry to pursue an elusive enemy – as the Scots would often prove to be.

It is well known that several medieval kings enacted statutes that were designed to encourage ordinary people to hone and maintain their military skills; most famously there were laws passed, albeit somewhat later in the Middle Ages, to enforce archery practice, and also to ban distracting activities such as football. Naturally this would suggest that medieval commanders recognised the importance of infantry, but there remains a tendency to dismiss the footmen as little more than a rabble – notwithstanding the qualities of the Welshmen described above. Certainly infantry were prone to desertion (this was also sometimes true of their more exalted colleagues), although in fairness this could be seen as understandable when pay was so often delayed.

The infantry could also be ill-disciplined during the course of a campaign. Nevertheless, whilst medieval infantry would surely have fallen a long way short of modern standards of training and discipline, recent research has shown the existence of a cadre of professional soldiers amongst the infantry of Edward's reign.[18] These men have been described as an 'officer-class', able to provide an element of direction, experience and resolve amidst the larger mass of semi-trained levies.

The careers of several veterans, such as the wonderfully named John Bagepus, can be reconstructed in some detail; he was a highly experienced officer, though he also served on some occasions as a *soldarius* in the cavalry. Such men offered repeated service during Edward's Scottish wars. During major campaigns they played a vital role as officers of the infantry, but they might also provide more extensive service as members of garrisons. Robert Lankerdaunce, for example, was the *vintenar* of a force of crossbowmen from Cheshire; he and his men provided almost continuous service in the garrisons of Berwick and Lochmaben between 1298 and 1301. Skilled crossbowmen, incidentally, were highly valued, and were often equipped at royal expense.[19]

In addition to the cavalry and infantry, the important role of auxiliaries – such as woodcutters, carpenters, smiths and engineers – should also be remembered. We have already witnessed the vital contribution of a group of reapers during Edward's first Welsh war, and huge teams of woodcutters were also employed to hack a road through the dense Welsh forest. Auxiliaries were respected for their skills, and this was reflected in their pay.[20] It has been noted that the infantry received 2d per day, whereas woodcutters and ditchers received 3d. Smiths, masons, carpenters and miners all received 4d per day. Naturally foremen or particularly skilled craftsmen (known as 'masters') would be paid a little more. At 9d per day, the pay of a master engineer approached that of a knight. Such experts were responsible for complex operations, notably (though not exclusively) during sieges. Several of these men, such as Master Richard of Chester, will appear more prominently later.

* * * *

The previous sections have offered an introduction to the armies that Edward I led in his Scottish wars, but what of the forces that opposed them? We know much less about Scottish armies in this period than we do about the English, for the simple reason that much less evidence survives. However, scholars have assembled enough material to provide a rough sketch of Scottish military organisation in the late thirteenth and early fourteenth centuries, even if specific details are often lacking.[21]

One key difference between the two armies is that the Scots were rarely able to field significant numbers of heavy cavalry. Funeral monuments (together with some other evidence) seem to imply that members of the Scottish elite were often equipped in a similar fashion to their English counterparts,[22] but the numbers who fought on horseback, in the English style, were substantially smaller. Some Scots did have a 'feudal' relationship with their king, specifically holding land in return for military service, but in the thirteenth century the kings of Scotland were more concerned to develop their economic resources.[23] The Scots nobility would surely have been accompanied on campaign by personal retinues, much as was the case in England, but Scottish armies in the Middle Ages were primarily composed of infantry. Scottish tactics on the battlefield were heavily dependent on massed ranks of spearmen, supported by smaller groups of archers and light horse.

Recruitment processes in Scotland remain somewhat obscure. However, the bulk of Scottish medieval troops appear to have been recruited according to the tradition of 'Scottish Service' (as it was specifically termed north of the Forth), forming a 'common army' (*communis exercitus*). Theoretically, all able-bodied free men owed military service to the king, and each area was expected to provide a quota of men. Command was usually delegated to the earls, whose titles were more closely aligned with real territorial power than was often the case in England.

It is generally believed that the rank and file of the Scottish common army were unpaid (although they were entitled to keep a proportion of any plunder that might be acquired), but their service was limited to forty days. There is scattered evidence, though, of payments made to Scottish soldiers (for example in the mid-1260s).[24] It might therefore be argued that at least some Scots must have received financial inducements to encourage them to serve in the more prolonged campaigns of the Wars of Independence.

There was a major disparity between the English and Scottish armies, it is often suggested, in terms of their experience. Many (though by no means all) of Edward's troops who served in 1296 would have been veterans of previous campaigns in Wales or France, whereas the last few years had provided few chances for Scottish warriors to demonstrate their mettle on behalf of their king. A dramatic Norwegian account of the battle of Largs incorporates a respectful depiction of Scottish knights,[25] but few of those who fought at Largs would still have been active in the coming campaign. Somewhat ironically, however, Scottish connections with England had provided some Scotsmen with more recent opportunities. Some Scots had fought alongside Edward in his earlier wars in England and Wales; others (including Robert Bruce 'the Noble') had previously joined Edward on his Crusade. Many Scottish nobles, of course, were also English landholders, and as such they were sometimes called upon to meet an *obligation* to contribute to Edward's military endeavours.

It is very clear, though, as they encountered the first serious English military threat for more than a hundred years, that the Scottish commanders were facing a daunting challenge. They would eventually find effective ways to negate the English advantages in the field – not least, as implied above, by exploiting their knowledge of the rugged Scottish terrain. But in the spring of 1296, as the Scots encountered Edward's formidable war machine for the first time, their experience would be a difficult one.

The Scots' efforts were also to be hindered because of divisions within their ranks: Edward was supported in the campaign by a section of the Scottish nobility. In part this might be seen as a function of the complexities of cross-border landholding, but there were some, notably the Bruces, who had never been reconciled to John Balliol's kingship. Robert the Bruce 'the Noble' had recently died, and the new head of the family, Robert Bruce VI, chose to adhere to Edward, even though this decision led to the temporary loss of his lordship of Annandale. The death of Bruce's wife Marjory also meant that he was obliged to give up the earldom of Carrick to his eldest son, Robert Bruce VII, although at this time the youngest Bruce still followed his father's lead. Others who chose to support Edward included Patrick, earl of March, who remained consistently loyal to

Edward for the rest of his reign, and Gilbert de Umfraville, earl of
Angus.

* * * *

Edward appeared to hold the advantage, but as his army left
Newcastle on 5 March 1296 the Scots were already making the first
moves. The first flashpoint occurred near Wark, then an important
border stronghold. This incident provides further evidence of the
difficult choices that men had to make at this time. The English lord
of Wark, Robert de Ros, was in love with a Scottish woman, Christine
de Mowbray, and for this reason he resolved to change sides.[26]
However, when Robert admitted his plans to his brother William, the
younger man, outraged, sent word to Edward, requesting his support,
and Edward duly dispatched a small group of men. Robert, now in
command of a Scottish force, surprised Edward's men while they
were camped for the evening, although his attack failed. The Scots
had arranged a password – 'tabard' – to avoid confusion, but when the
English overheard this they were able to use it to their own advantage.
Robert's treachery (as Edward would have seen it) was ultimately in
vain: he made his way to Scotland, but Christine rejected him and he
died within the year.

Apparently Edward was unperturbed by the actions of Robert de
Ros, perhaps because he could now depict the Scots as the aggressors –
and of what the Scots had begun, he is said to have exclaimed, he
would in due course make an end. But more significant events
occurred in the west, where a substantial Scottish army, including
seven earls, invaded England and threatened Carlisle. A Scottish spy
had been captured and imprisoned by the city's inhabitants, but when
the Scottish army approached he somehow broke loose and started a
fire. Mayhem ensued. In the confusion the Scots came close to taking
the city, as the panicked defenders sought to extinguish the flames, but
the attack was foiled by the city's women. 'Acting like men', as the
chronicler Walter of Guisborough put it, the women beat off the Scots
by hurling stones and pouring boiling water.[27]

The Scots' failure to take Carlisle meant their incursion was
ultimately no more than a distraction, and Edward had no need to

alter his own plans. On 25 March he celebrated Easter at Wark, which was now back securely under English control. Here he welcomed the Bruces, along with the earls of Angus and March, and these Scottish magnates renewed their homage and fealty. Three days later Edward and his army crossed the Tweed near Coldstream, *en route* to his first major target: Berwick-upon-Tweed.

At this time Berwick was a thriving settlement. The years of relative harmony between England and Scotland had enabled the town to exploit its considerable natural advantages, not least as the closest Scottish port to Flanders. (This was significant because Flanders provided the key market for Scotland's most valuable commodity: wool.) By the late thirteenth century much of Scotland's overseas trade was carried through Berwick, and it became the richest town in the kingdom. As such it was a valuable prize, and naturally the Scots had taken steps to prepare its defence. In the spring of 1296 the population of Berwick was swollen by an influx of armed men. The town's castle was garrisoned by a force under Sir William Douglas; the town itself was defended by men from Fife.

Edward sent messages to the town from Coldstream, formally calling for Berwick's surrender. On 29 March the English army advanced to Hatton, six miles from Berwick, from where Edward himself pushed on to make an appeal in person. It is said that Edward offered generous terms if Berwick would capitulate – guaranteeing the lives and property of all those within – but the king was greeted with scorn.[28] The defenders taunted him with various insults, and invited him to try and dig his way in. Just in case he should fail to hear and understand their meaning, they also bared their buttocks. We can safely assume that Edward retired in a fury.

*   *   *   *

On the following day Edward's army made ready to assault the town. How can we reconstruct the events that subsequently occurred? Record sources can provide important insights into other aspects of military life, but our knowledge of military engagements is almost always based on chronicles: medieval historical narratives. Some chronicles were written almost contemporaneously with the events they describe, but it is well known that these sources offer various difficulties. Perhaps most significantly, the mental approach of the medieval chronicler was very different from that of the modern historian; medieval writers tended to adopt a providential scheme, often seeking to explain historical outcomes by reference to a divine plan.

Chronicles must always be used with caution, therefore, not least because their authors' preoccupations did not always match our own. Nevertheless, it should also be remembered that many medieval writers were intelligent people who worked hard to incorporate useful material. The chronicle of Walter of Guisborough, who provided one of the fullest near-contemporary accounts of Edward's Scottish campaigns, provides a good example. Walter was a member of a religious community; he was an Augustinian canon. As he was based at Guisborough Priory in North Yorkshire, it is extremely unlikely that he could offer first-hand information about events in Scotland. Yet he appears to have acquired information from local men who took part in the Scottish wars. He also made use of written documents that came into his possession, in some cases copying them whole.

Most medieval chronicles were at least partly based on other written sources – especially if they were produced in religious foundations, which were centres of literacy. For instance, whilst the so-called *Lanercost Chronicle* was certainly *compiled* at Lanercost Priory, near Carlisle, it is largely based on the work of two Franciscan friars who lived elsewhere. Both were northern Englishmen, however, and understandably this colours the outlook of the work as a whole. It is unfortunate that few Scottish chronicles have survived to provide a balancing narrative from the other side of the border. A notable exception, which has its origins in fourteenth-century St Andrews, is now referred to by historians as *Gesta Annalia* II. This is preserved as part of a larger compilation, and was formerly attributed to John of Fordun.

One of the most colourful sources for Edward's Scottish wars is the *Scalacronica*, which is the work of Sir Thomas Gray. A knight from Northumberland, Sir Thomas appears to have taken to writing history when he was captured by the Scots in the 1350s; he was subsequently imprisoned for some time in Edinburgh. In writing the

Scalacronica, he could therefore draw upon direct personal experience of warfare – a very unusual advantage. In truth, much of Gray's work is based heavily on earlier written sources, but he also took the opportunity to recount the experiences of his father (another Sir Thomas), who was a veteran of the Wars of Independence. Other chronicles will be discussed in passing as the narrative moves forward.[29]

*　*　*　*

As the English royal army massed outside Berwick, Edward marked the formal opening of hostilities by knighting several young men. (The recipients of this honour included Henry Percy, a nobleman from Yorkshire who would become the ancestor of one of medieval England's most powerful and famous northern families.) However, the commanders of Edward's fleet, which was shadowing the army, misunderstood the meaning of this ceremony. Seeing 'an army in arms and many banners displayed', the seamen assumed the attack had already begun.[30] They moved to support the king, sailing into the harbour, but the leading ship ran aground. It was quickly surrounded by Berwick's defenders, who set the ship on fire and killed the crew; two other vessels suffered a similar fate. The *Lanercost Chronicle* tells us that Berwick's women became involved in the action (much like the women of Carlisle), assisting their menfolk as they set light to the English ships.

From his own position, Edward could see smoke rising from the harbour, and once he understood what had happened his response was fierce and decisive. The chivalric pageantry was brought to an abrupt halt, and Edward launched his men into the fray. Berwick did not have stone walls at this time, and the town's ditch and palisade provided little obstacle to the English advance. The castle remained defiant – at least for the moment – but the English found a weak point in the urban defences and poured into the town. The only serious resistance was offered at the Red Hall, the headquarters of Berwick's Flemish merchants, whose owners had promised to defend it on behalf of the king of Scots. Eventually, however, the hall was set on fire, and the Flemings perished in the flames. Now Edward's soldiers ran amok through the streets, and a massacre ensued. In the words of William Rishanger, a monastic chronicler based at St Albans Abbey, 'the bodies fell like Autumn leaves'.[31]

The chronicles suggest that as many as 15,000 people died, although this figure has (rightly) been rejected by modern historians.[32] Nevertheless, given that it is beyond any doubt that a slaughter of defenceless people took place at Berwick, the question of numbers is not the only issue worth considering here. In particular, whilst a certain amount of looting, rape and killing was surely inevitable, is it significant that Edward himself is said to have been motivated by a desire for personal vengeance? According to Rishanger, he was enraged by the death of his young kinsman Richard of Cornwall, who was killed during the assault on the Red Hall: the chronicler goes on to tell us that, 'angry like a boar pursued by wolves', Edward urged his men on.[33]

Edward was supposedly moved to halt the killing by the intervention of a group of clerics, who processed through the town carrying relics – although this last addition to the story has a distinctly formulaic quality. It is intriguing, nevertheless, that when the men of the castle's garrison subsequently surrendered they were treated with much greater respect than was shown to the people in the town. The commander, Douglas, was taken into Edward's custody, but the soldiers of the garrison were allowed to depart unharmed (albeit on the specific understanding that they would take no further part in the campaign). True, it was common for different terms to be offered if a siege proceeded in stages, but the contemporary conventions of warfare did not oblige a victorious commander to be merciful, even if the defenders had surrendered.

Without seeking to dismiss the importance of earlier events, it has been suggested that Edward was attempting to distance himself from the bloodshed in the town; his treatment of the garrison could be viewed as an example of *franchise* – the nobility of spirit that was so admired by 'chivalric' writers.[34] It also sent out a clear message that Edward was willing to treat his enemies with honour if they submitted and sought his grace. Yet doubtless there were many others in Berwick who would have submitted had they been given the opportunity to do so, and this reminds us that 'chivalric' courtesies were always extended selectively in war – and often only to the elite.[35] Moreover, whilst it should be noted that Edward was sometimes criticised by contemporary English writers for being *too merciful,* he was not always consistent in his approach – and his attitude towards defeated enemies would change and harden as the Scottish wars progressed.

*   *   *   *

Berwick was a prize that Edward was determined to hold, and his men now faced the grim task of clearing the bodies from the streets. The halt at Berwick also provided an opportunity to hold a court-martial; a 'plea roll' has been preserved from this campaign, providing some interesting evidence of attempts to maintain discipline within the army.[36] Many of the cases that came before the court were much as might be expected: there were numerous instances of theft, squabbles over plunder and disputes concerning debts. But the roll also demonstrates that men could be punished for failing to carry out allotted tasks, suggesting that medieval commanders had greater expectations of their forces than is sometimes allowed. The centenar Richard le Taillur [*sic*] was fined one mark because he and his men had failed to perform 'watch and ward'. Similar proceedings subsequently took place at Roxburgh, Edinburgh, Perth and various other places.

Edward was still at Berwick on 5 April 1296 when he received John Balliol's *diffidatio,* or defiance: a formal renunciation of his homage and fealty, filled with indignation. As well as outlining the 'grievous and intolerable injuries' that Edward had inflicted against the Scots and their king, carried out 'in a manner which offends against God and against justice', John's letter also argues that his homage had been extorted by 'extreme coercion'.[37] In Edward's eyes, naturally John's words had no validity. But it was characteristic of Edward that he ordered his notary John of Caen to make a careful copy of the letter, 'as fuller evidence of the matters aforesaid'.

The Scots also made a more tangible response to Edward's sack of Berwick, as their forces were once again in action south of the border. The earls of Mar, Ross and Menteith by-passed Edward's great army and rampaged through Northumberland. Several English chroniclers assert that their forces committed terrible atrocities, suggesting that the English did not have a monopoly in brutality. The *Lanercost Chronicle* provides a particularly graphic account.[38] Proving themselves 'apt scholars in atrocity', it is said, the Scots 'raised aloft little children pierced on pikes, to expire thus and fly away to the heavens'. The author claims that the Scots raped and killed nuns and other women in consecrated churches, which were then destroyed. This raid also became notorious for the story that the Scots burned alive a group of schoolboys at Corbridge (or Hexham, according to the Lanercost account), and Edward made much of this in later propaganda.[39]

It is not easy to determine how to interpret such evidence. There are comparable descriptions (in fact, in some cases, almost word for word) of earlier Scottish raids. When David I invaded England in 1138, for example, it was reported that his troops from Galloway (notorious for their savagery) had indulged in a similar range of gruesome activities.[40] But does this mean that the various chroniclers were recording terrible events that genuinely reoccurred? Or were these writers, perhaps influenced by biblical imagery (such as Herod's Massacre of the Innocents), drawing upon a cultural reservoir, deliberately constructing an image of the Scots as bloodthirsty barbarians? Perhaps it can be difficult for historians to accept that human beings can treat others with such sickening cruelty. Yet before we dismiss the chronicle accounts as rhetoric, we might consider evidence from our own times that should probably make us pause.

On their return to Scotland the Scottish earls captured Dunbar Castle, which belonged to the earl of March. In another interesting case of divided loyalties, whilst the earl had given his allegiance to Edward, his countess had opened the gates to the Scottish commanders. Edward dispatched one of his most committed supporters, his old companion-in-arms John de Warenne, earl of Surrey (often referred to as the Earl Warenne), with a significant detachment to besiege Dunbar. Surrey, it might be noted, was John Balliol's father-in-law, yet he does not appear to have suffered any conflict of loyalties. Reacting in his turn, King John sent a Scottish force from Haddington to relieve the besieged garrison.

At noon on 27 April the relief force appeared near Spott, on the high ground overlooking Dunbar, on the edge of the Lammermuir Hills. Now the Scottish garrison disparaged Surrey's forces from the walls of Dunbar castle, threatening to cut off their tails.[41] The bizarre notion that the English had tails was frequently asserted by their enemies (including both the Scots and the French), although it might be argued that the Scots' bravado would once again prove to be misplaced. The English turned to confront the new threat, but the commanders of the relieving army misinterpreted Surrey's subsequent manoeuvres as preparations for flight. With cries of 'They flee! They flee!', the Scots launched a ragged charge, but their attack was a dismal failure.[42] The English quickly gained the advantage, and the Scottish force was defeated. In the words of one English chronicler, now the Scots 'fled headlong all together, hunted by the English like wild beasts amid general derision'.[43]

The English exulted in their victory: snatches of popular songs, which must have circulated widely, have been preserved in various places. Some were included in the chronicle of Peter Langtoft, a canon from Bridlington who is justly notorious for his hostility towards the Scots. One of these rhymes been translated into modern English as follows:

> For those Scots,
> I rate 'em as sots,
> What a sorry shower!
> Whose utter lack
> In the Attack
> Lost 'em at Dunbar.[44]

Edward was later informed that over 10,000 Scots had been killed at Dunbar, but it has often been argued that the scale of the fighting has been exaggerated.[45] It is not at all clear that the entire Scottish host was engaged, as is sometimes suggested, because King John and the Comyns remained in arms to the north. Nevertheless, the effect on Scottish morale was profound.

Edward and the rest of his army arrived at Dunbar the following day, and he was able to accept the surrender of the castle in person. Again he showed mercy to the leaders (and there is no suggestion of any reprisals against the rest of the garrison), but the earls of Mar and Ross,[46] together with many other knights and esquires, were later taken south as prisoners. Others had already surrendered after the battle. On this occasion there was little honour in defeat; the Scots, to the number of over a hundred, were transported to England in shameful conditions. Langtoft tells us they were conveyed 'by two and two together mounted on a hackney, some in carts, with fetters on the feet'.[47] References to these men are plentiful in English records, because many of them languished in English captivity for several years; a large proportion eventually died there.

*   *   *   *

After the battle of Dunbar Edward's campaign became more like a procession, as his army was virtually unopposed. James, hereditary steward of Scotland, surrendered Roxburgh Castle to Edward's representatives, and many other Scottish commanders followed suit. Short sieges were necessary at Edinburgh and Linlithgow, but the garrison of Stirling abandoned the castle, apparently leaving the keys hanging above the gates.[48] Some Scots in Edward's allegiance were also active on his (and their own) behalf. The Bruces, for example, were able to re-establish control of their lands in Annandale and Carrick. Edward himself, in pursuit of King John and his Comyn allies, and accepting the submissions of local leaders as he went, ultimately marched as far north as Elgin.

John Balliol's proud words had proved to be nothing more than hot air. The defeats at Berwick and Dunbar should not have been decisive, yet Balliol's resolve had crumbled almost immediately in the face of adversity. It is difficult to escape the conclusion that on this occasion the collapse of Scottish resistance owed rather more to John's failure of leadership than it did to Edward's qualities of command. Indeed, John was now quick to seek terms, and there were some negotiations towards that end. But Edward, ruthlessly exploiting Balliol's abject position, would ultimately accept nothing less than total surrender. John's life was spared, but he was forced to undergo a humiliating ceremony at Montrose, where the royal arms were ritually torn from his person; thus he gained the nickname 'toom tabard' ('empty surcoat'). He was then taken south to captivity in England, no longer a king in Edward's eyes. John Balliol would never set foot in Scotland again.

Edward attempted to consolidate his triumph by symbolic and political means. The famous Stone of Destiny – on which the Scottish kings sat at their inauguration – was removed from Scone to Westminster Abbey, where it joined other precious items taken previously from the Welsh.[49] The submissions of leading Scottish landowners – to the number of over 1,500 – were recorded in the so-called 'Ragman Roll'. Edward did not adopt any new titles, and there was no official statement about a change in status of the kingdom of Scotland, but the implications were clear. Peter Langtoft took up the subject with enthusiasm, connecting Edward's new mastery of the British Isles with a reputed prophecy of Merlin:

Now are the two waters united in one.
Which have been separated by great mountains.
. . . Now are the islanders all joined together.
. . . There is neither king nor prince of all the countries
Except King Edward, who has thus united them;
Arthur had never the fiefs so fully.[50]

Despite his advancing years, Edward had once again demonstrated his ability to lead his armies to victory. Ten years of rising tensions between England and Scotland had culminated in a military conquest that was accomplished with almost embarrassing ease. Delegating authority in Scotland to the earl of Surrey, we find Edward in a relieved but contemptuous mood: 'He does good business', he quipped, 'who rids himself of shit.'[51] Yet the extent of Edward's success was deceptive. To be fair to John Balliol, fate had dealt him a difficult hand, but the Scots would find more resolute and effective leaders in the coming years. Moreover, whilst it might be anachronistic to talk of 'nationalism' in the thirteenth century, the independent kingdom of Scotland was an ancient and tenacious concept – and it would take more than the removal of symbolic artefacts to erase this idea from men's hearts and minds. In short, Edward's Scottish wars had only just begun.

Chapter 4

He Lifted Up His Head

Edward had achieved an easy victory, and his coarse jest appears to testify to his contemptuous, complacent attitude towards Scotland. Chroniclers' accounts of direct speech cannot always be trusted, but in this case it is conceivable that the *Scalacronica* has preserved a genuine exchange between Edward and Surrey; the author's father served under Surrey later in the Scottish wars and it is therefore quite possible that the earl himself was the source of this story.[1] Edward's actions spoke louder than words: he was now confident that he would be able to give priority to his struggle with Philip of France. Edward again planned to campaign against Philip in person, and he fully anticipated that a cowed Scotland would provide him with money and men to assist in this enterprise. His focus quickly shifted away from Scotland, and the governance of his latest conquest was delegated to others.

A new administration needed to be put in place, because the success of Edward's whirlwind campaign had created a vacuum in Scottish politics. A number of Scottish magnates, including James the Steward and Earl Malise of Strathearn, were able to make their peace with Edward. However, along with John Balliol and those who had been taken at Dunbar, a large number of other Scottish aristocrats were taken south to prisons in England. The most significant captives, after John Balliol, were eight members of the Comyn family, but there were also many others who held extensive influence and important offices (such as sheriffdoms); these included members of families such as the Murrays, Randolphs and Cheynes, all of whom were prominent in the Scottish administrations of the later thirteenth century.

Naturally the removal of so many powerful Scots gave great hope to the faction within the Scottish nobility which had opposed Balliol and supported Edward. Robert Bruce 'the Competitor' may have passed away, but his eldest son, Robert Bruce VI, had inherited his ambitions. The family had been restored to their lands in Scotland, but this was not enough for Bruce: he hoped he would be installed as a new client king. When he tentatively approached Edward towards this end, however, the hapless Bruce was given short shrift: 'Have we nothing else to do', exploded Edward, 'but to win kingdoms for you?'[2] Edward had no intention of creating another Balliol.

Edward's own solution to the problems of governance in Scotland was rather different from the one envisaged by Bruce and his supporters. North of the River Forth English garrisons were installed at key strongpoints (including Urquhart and Aberdeen), and significant responsibilities were delegated to a mixture of English and Scottish officials. Doubtless many Scotsmen were ready to bend with the wind, although others were possibly intimidated into collaborating with the new regime because their relatives were held captive in England; the latter group included, for example, Reginald Cheyne, sheriff of Inverness. South of the Forth a more intensively English administration was put in place, where the majority of key office-holders were men with no prior connections to Scotland; these included Henry Percy (Warden of Ayr and Galloway) and William of Ormesby (Justiciar of Lothian).

Edward's Scottish administration, with its headquarters at Berwick, was headed by a triumvirate of key officials: the earl of Surrey (who became Lieutenant), Walter Amersham (Chancellor) and Hugh Cressingham (Treasurer). All three had served Edward well in the past, but Surrey and Cressingham would soon become notorious for their performance in Scotland.

As Lieutenant, Surrey theoretically became the most powerful man in Scotland after Edward himself, with responsibility for the administration of justice and military affairs. But Surrey was an ageing man – by this point he was in his sixties – and he had little enthusiasm for his office. He spent as little time in Scotland as possible; at one point he apparently claimed the Scottish weather was bad for his health! Cressingham, by contrast, was both diligent and efficient, but as the man most closely associated with Edward's incessant financial demands he soon became hated throughout Scotland. Some Englishmen shared the Scots' feelings. Walter of Guisborough particularly disliked Cressingham, denouncing him on the basis of his obesity, avarice and inordinate pride. Theoretically Cressingham was a churchman – although he showed little evidence of any inclination towards religion – and one of his 'livings', the parish of Rudby, was very close to Guisborough Priory.[3]

Edward's new regime has often been described as 'colonial', and it was perhaps at the local level where the changes were most keenly felt. Notwithstanding the shared elements of culture between the elite members of society on both sides of the border, it is surely significant that few of Edward's English officials had any previous experience of Scotland. There must have been communication difficulties in some areas, because the inhabitants of many regions – particularly in the west – were still largely Gaelic-speaking at this time. (It is generally assumed that many Scottish noblemen would have spoken at least some Gaelic.) It is not easy to account for the effects on ordinary people, but memories were preserved of English brutality. John Barbour's later poem *The Bruce* accuses the English of rape and theft.[4] Certainly there is an indication that English officials adopted an over-zealous attitude towards potential dissidents: Guisborough singled out William Ormesby in this respect.

Edward's insatiable thirst for money was also a great source of resentment. Throughout the course of the thirteenth century the Scottish kings had increasingly sought to exploit potential sources of revenue, but there was no tradition, as yet, of extensive and systematic taxation. By contrast, regular taxation had become a part of life in England, and Edward's subjects in Ireland and Wales were also expected to make substantial contributions as his reign progressed. Previous demands had led to a dangerous rebellion in Wales, as we have seen, but Edward's officials in Scotland had learned nothing from this experience. With Cressingham as the driving force – and evidently his zeal to serve his exacting master was great indeed – large sums were raised at first. Shortly after Cressingham's appointment, more than £5,000 was sent from Scotland to the count of Bar, whom Edward was effectively bribing in order to gain his support against the French.

Some of this revenue was derived from the confiscation and sale of wool; this happened, for example, at Melrose and Sweetheart Abbeys, which were then economic powerhouses as well as centres of religion. Given that wool was Scotland's main source of economic wealth, this would have been a particular source of anger. It must also have been a source of fear, as people became deeply concerned about the possibility of similar exactions in the future. There were also growing fears that Scotsmen – and not just the nobility and their retinues – would be forced to serve in Edward's armies overseas. It was later asserted that Edward had already made plans to call upon '*le menzane*' (or 'middling' people), 'to their great damage and destruction'.[5]

Many (though by no means all) of the traditional leaders of society had been removed from the Scottish political scene, but it has been well observed that 'the Scots named on the Ragman Roll and their peers and neighbours were not a formless mass beneath the king and his barons'.[6] Naturally this wider group – including lesser knights, prosperous farmers, burgesses and local clergy – possessed considerable influence and status within their own communities. Such men had just as much cause as their lords to take offence as English officials trampled on local customs and dismissed the importance of long-established networks; it was this section of society that would initially provide the backbone of resistance to Edward's rule. Doubtless the tipping point was different for each individual, and men were motivated by a wide range of factors, but by the spring of 1297 large numbers of Scotsmen were openly in armed rebellion.

* * * *

The first serious disturbances occurred in the north-west of Scotland, where the MacDougalls of Lorn took the lead. The MacDougalls were descended from Somerled, the first and greatest of the Lords of the Isles, and they were now the most prominent family in the Argyll region. Local politics was undoubtedly important in this area – the MacDougalls' main rivals, the MacDonalds, were now acting as agents for Edward I – but the impact of the Scottish Wars of

Independence on the Gaelic world can be unduly neglected. Somewhat ironically, the MacDougalls eventually became stalwart supporters of the English kings, and they later suffered greatly for their opposition to Robert Bruce VII (after he made his bid for the Scottish throne).

Other rebels – perhaps better referred to from here on as patriots – were also active north of the Forth, especially in the region of Moray. The most dynamic leader here was Andrew Murray, a dashing young nobleman who remains one of Scotland's least appreciated heroes. Murray fought at Dunbar, where he was captured alongside his father. He was imprisoned in Carlisle, but somehow managed to escape. Making his way back to his family's lands near Inverness, he immediately rejoined the struggle against Edward's regime. An early attack on Urquhart Castle was unsuccessful, but thereafter the patriots won a series of victories under Murray's command.

Murray, it should be stressed, was very much a member of the Scottish elite. Whilst his family was not quite as powerful as the Comyns, for example, the Murrays had risen faster and further than most. His father, also called Andrew, was Justiciar of Scotia (Scotland north of the Forth); this was one of the most important crown offices. His Uncle William (to whom Murray was heir) was known as 'the rich'; he was the lord of Bothwell in the Clyde valley, where he constructed a remarkable castle. Other members of the Murray family were prominent in the church. In spite of this aristocratic background, Murray successfully attracted supporters from other sections of society. Evidently a charismatic man, he also demonstrated a flair for unconventional warfare that pre-dates the exploits of the more famous Robert Bruce.

This period also marks the emergence of Robert Bruce VII, now well established as earl of Carrick, as a substantial figure in his own right. His father had retired to his estates in England, but Bruce gathered his family's retainers in Annandale, hoping to inspire them to join him in rebellion. He had previously sworn an oath to the bishop of Carlisle that he would remain faithful to Edward, but he now explained that he had been forced to do so – and thus the oath could not be binding. Finally, as reported by Walter of Guisborough, he made a passionate appeal to their sense of patriotism: 'No man holds his own flesh and blood in hatred and I am no exception. I must join my own people and the nation in which I was born.'[7] This is stirring stuff, but at this time the young Bruce (now in his early twenties) was still something of an unknown quantity. As these men saw it, their primary loyalty was still owed to Bruce's father, who consistently remained in Edward's allegiance, and so the young Bruce received an evasive answer.

The following morning Bruce found that the men had stolen away in the night, yet he resolved to travel north, where he was able to raise an army in his own lands of Carrick. Leaving aside his rousing words, it is intriguing to consider Bruce's motivations. Even if he was driven by youthful idealism (and perhaps anger, following his father's humiliation by Edward), it is difficult to imagine that he was inspired by the prospect of John Balliol's restoration. Guisborough offered a simple explanation: he believed that Bruce was already aiming for the crown. Many years would need to pass, however, before Bruce's personal cause would become inextricably linked with a powerful concept of Scottish freedom – and he had not yet gained the steely determination for which he is rightly renowned today.

Bruce was joined in his enterprise by James the Steward. As we have seen, the Steward had long-standing connections with the Bruce family, but he remains an elusive, enigmatic figure; events would show that James (like Bruce?) offset any patriotic impulses with more personal, pragmatic considerations, as had already been demonstrated at Roxburgh. Nevertheless, it should not be forgotten that he was one of the first Scottish nobles to raise his banner in defiance of Edward at this time. Bruce and the Steward received spiritual guidance (and doubtless more practical advice) from another former Guardian, Bishop Robert Wishart of Glasgow, whom we have already encountered as a stalwart defender of Scottish liberties.

At this time, then, the English in Scotland faced a plethora of enemies, many of whom were acting independently, and none of whom exercised clear authority over the others. Eventually, however, Scottish resistance in this period would come to be associated, above all, with the personal story of one man: William Wallace.

* * * *

William Wallace was 'a shunned, deceitful criminal, a hater of piety, a sacrilegious plunderer, an arsonist, and a murderer crueller than Herod and madder than Nero'.[8] Or so the English chronicles tell us. Later Scottish sources have presented a rather more attractive portrait. For instance, Walter Bower tells us that, in addition to possessing great height and strength, Wallace was 'cheerful in appearance with agreeable features'.[9] He goes on to say that Wallace was a 'most skilful counsellor, very patient when suffering' – and a man who comforted others. With God's help, apparently, Wallace became 'a man successful in everything'. In the later fifteenth century the various stories about Wallace's life were brought together in Blind Harry's epic poem *The Wallace*, which eventually provided the inspiration for a more modern epic: *Braveheart*.

In the spring of 1297, as the Scottish continuator of *Gesta Annalia* tells us, Wallace 'lifted up his head'.[10] This is an apt phrase, suggesting a sudden emergence, because little is known for certain about Wallace's life before this point. This is not for want of trying, however, and generations of historians have worked hard to provide insights into Wallace's background and early career.[11]

The surname Wallace is often rendered in medieval sources as 'le Waleys', meaning 'the Welshman', and it is likely that Wallace's family originally came from Shropshire. It is also known that members of the Wallace kin-group established connections with the Stewarts, though Wallace's closest relations have left little trace in the records. Even so, an old tradition derived from Blind Harry, that Wallace was the son of Sir Malcolm Wallace of Elderslie, has been proved to be false. We can now be sure that Wallace's father was a man called Alan; this information is derived from a cast of Wallace's seal, the significance of which was not fully recognised until the 1990s.[12] Further research has identified Alan as a tenant farmer from Ayrshire. Wallace's father was not a knight then, but if he was the Alan Wallace named on the Ragman Roll, he was evidently a man of some local standing. Wallace's elder brother Malcolm was a knight, although it is not clear when he achieved his promotion.[13]

Wallace also later became a knight, and shortly afterwards he certainly held lands, but did he own any property before he achieved fame? As a younger son he surely needed to make his own way in the world. His seal – which included an image of a bow and arrow – provides a clue as to how he earned his living. This choice of emblem may suggest he was a skilled archer, although we cannot know whether the young Wallace was a skilled hunter, a poacher or a soldier – or perhaps all three. English chronicles consistently describe him as a 'robber' and there is other evidence to suggest he sometimes lived outside the law. In early August 1296 a certain Matthew of York (an Englishman?) was indicted for stealing ale from a Perth woman. Matthew was said to be in the gang of 'a thief, William le Waleys'.[14] It has been noted, however, that Edward's army was then in the Perth area: was Wallace already engaged in guerrilla activity against the English, and was he perhaps requisitioning supplies?[15]

Wallace's first significant exploit against the English, both in fact and fiction, was the murder of William Hazelrigg, the sheriff of Lanark. Blind Harry's poem tells us that Wallace fell upon Hazelrigg by night, having slipped past his armed guards, and cut him into pieces.[16] Then he set fire to the sheriff's lodgings, and all those left within were consumed by the flames. Harry paints a dramatic picture, but the savage nature of the attack and Wallace's brutal treatment of Hazelrigg are attested in more contemporary sources.[17] Tradition tells us that Wallace was now fighting to avenge a lost love, Marion Braidfute, who was cruelly murdered by the English in order to spite him. Harry was the first to give the woman a name, and in *The Wallace* she becomes the hero's wife, but the story first appears in the work of Andrew Wyntoun, who was writing somewhat earlier.

Wallace followed up the events at Lanark with a lightning mounted raid on Scone, nearly eighty miles away. His main target here was the hated William Ormesby. This time Wallace was not quite as successful, although Walter of Guisborough implies that Ormesby was lucky to escape alive.[18] By July Wallace had established himself in the wild country around Selkirk, as 'one who holds himself against [Edward's] peace'.[19] Selkirk (now Ettrick) Forest, often simply known as *the* Forest, would soon become famous as a haven for patriots.

Many readers will have noted the intriguing parallels between the career of William Wallace and the tales of Robin Hood (a similarly ambiguous figure). On the one hand, it is easy to understand why Wallace has been sometimes characterised as a romantic outsider, contemptuous of authority. On the other, it is generally accepted that Wallace was a political conservative, who was committed to the restoration of John Balliol. Moreover, whilst there is an enduring tradition that Wallace provoked the hostility of the Scottish aristocracy, who were jealous of his success, he was evidently capable of working effectively with noblemen: recent research has shown that, during his attack on Hazelrigg, Wallace fought alongside a knight, Richard Lundie.[20] During his attack on Scone Wallace was accompanied by Sir William Douglas, whom we have already met as the commander of the Scottish garrison at Berwick; Douglas was a hard and reckless man, but he was indisputably of noble blood.

* * * *

Edward was now somewhat distanced from events in Scotland, but information reached him from a number of sources. News from northern Scotland was brought to Edward by Andrew Rait, a Scotsman in English allegiance; Rait would subsequently spend a great deal of time engaged in carrying correspondence between England and Scotland. On 4 June commands were issued in the king's name to restore order.[21] Somewhat vaguely, the targets were 'many persons who disturb our peace and quietness of our kingdom'. Henry Percy and Robert Clifford, another young northerner, were instructed to 'arrest, imprison and justify [*sic*] all disturbers of the peace in Scotland'. They were to receive support from the sheriffs of several northern counties, including Lancaster, Cumberland and Westmorland (where they quickly recruited troops), as well as 'personal aid and counsel' from Cressingham.

All this activity required funds, of course, although Edward was reluctant to commit significant resources to Scotland. The sum of £2000 was advanced to the administration at Berwick, but it was given on the strict understanding that it should be regarded as a loan; the money was expected to be repaid from Scottish revenues by 1 August.[22] In the event this proved impossible, but it reminds us that Edward's main focus was elsewhere. Expediency may also explain Edward's decision to release two of the greatest Scottish magnates, John Comyn, lord of Badenoch, and John Comyn, earl of Buchan (the son of the former Guardian). It was originally envisaged that they would earn their rehabilitation by joining the planned expedition to Flanders, and a number of Scottish noblemen did later serve with Edward there. However, the two Comyns were now set free on the understanding that they would assist the English to restore order in the north of Scotland.

Ultimately, the risings led by Wallace and Murray would prove to be the most significant, yet it is perhaps understandable that Percy and Clifford chose to focus their energies upon the seemingly greater threat posed by Bruce, the Steward and Wishart. Percy and Clifford advanced rapidly into south-west Scotland, confronting the patriots at Irvine in Ayrshire. For reasons that are unclear (there is no indication, for example, of the size of the respective forces), the Scottish leaders immediately offered their surrender, on terms to be agreed. Even so, the subsequent negotiations were protracted: were the Scots playing a canny hand, allowing Wallace (and others) to continue to make gains while the English forces were occupied elsewhere? But if that was the case, then the secret appears to have been well kept. Sir Richard Lundie – Wallace's former companion – was in the patriot army at Irvine, and he was reportedly so disgusted by the leaders' capitulation that he decided to change sides.[23]

Wishart was eventually taken into captivity alongside Sir William Douglas (who later died in prison), but Bruce and the Steward were allowed to return to their lands; Bruce was expected to present himself at Berwick in order to renew his homage to Edward, but it seems unlikely that he ever had any intention of doing so. It is also clear that Percy and Clifford underestimated Wallace, who was left to wreak havoc from his forest lair. As Wallace's confidence grew, so did his ambition. He increased the scope and scale of his operations as summer progressed, with an ever-growing army at his back. The patriots also continued to gain ground north of the Forth. The English position in north-east Scotland became so precarious that one of Edward's English sheriffs, Henry de Latham, decided to join the patriots: perhaps he was mindful of the fate of William Hazelrigg?

If the loyalties of English officials were tested, it is little wonder that Scotsmen still in Edward's allegiance began to reconsider their position. From Edward's point of view, his policy towards the Comyns was a complete failure. The earl of Buchan did make a gesture towards the suppression of the revolt, but when he encountered Murray's army he declined to offer battle. A letter from the bishop of Aberdeen excused this on the basis that Murray had retreated into a woody bog and his position was impenetrable,[24] but Buchan's true inclinations are clear; within a few months he had openly joined the patriots. The lord of Badenoch adopted a more cautious approach, possibly because his eldest son, yet another John Comyn, was serving with the English army in Flanders. He did not offer tangible assistance to either side, although it is difficult to believe that Murray's forces could have operated in Moray with impunity if Comyn had been minded to stop them.

* * * *

On the English side Hugh Cressingham became increasingly prominent, as he attempted to take matters into his own hands. In July he raised a sizeable army, consisting of 300 horse and 10,000 foot,[25] but he was unable to commit this force against the Scots. The army was instructed to muster at Roxburgh, where Cressingham met with Percy and Clifford. Buoyed by their easy 'victory' at Irvine, the two young noblemen claimed to have entirely restored order south of the Forth – although this, of course, was far from the case – and argued that Cressingham's plans for further operations were unnecessary at this time. In the absence of Surrey, it was unclear who should have the last word, and it was eventually agreed that any further action should be delayed until the earl himself came north. 'And thus', as Cressingham complained to Edward in a particularly telling phrase, 'matters have gone to sleep.'[26]

Cressingham kept up a steady flow of correspondence, and this is one of the best sources for events in Scotland at this time. The treasurer was still greatly concerned with financial matters (he was not able to repay the money advanced to him earlier in the summer, and took pains to explain and justify his position), but his letters also provide a wider view of the collapse of the English administration. From our perspective it is clear that Cressingham's pessimistic assessment of the situation was entirely justified, at a time when others remained extraordinarily complacent. He was deeply suspicious of the Scottish lords in Edward's allegiance, for instance, encouraging Edward to be wary of news from north of the Forth: 'Sir Andrew de Rathe [Andrew Rait] is going to you with a [letter of] credence, which he has shown to me, and which is false in many points, and obscure, as will be known hereafter, as I fear.'[27]

Cressingham's best known letter to Edward, dated 24 July, outlines a desperate situation:

> Sire, let it not displease you [!], by far the greater part of the counties of the realm [of Scotland] are still unprovided with keepers, as well by death, sieges or imprisonment; and some have given up their bailiwicks [jurisdictions], and others neither will nor dare return; and in some counties the Scots have established and placed bailiffs and ministers, so that no county is in its proper order excepting Berwick and Roxburgh, and this only lately.[28]

This letter was also written to warn Edward that 'not a penny could be raised in your realm [Scotland] until my lord the earl of Warenne [Surrey] shall enter the land and compel the people of your country by force and sentence of law'.

Cressingham was not without faults, but his appraisal of the situation deserves respect; even if he exaggerated somewhat, it was surely to inspire action. We do not have a direct record of Edward's response, but in the event the treasurer did not have to wait long for Surrey's arrival in Scotland. The earl's presence at Berwick had little impact, however. Doubtless Surrey hoped that his stay in Scotland would be a short one, and that he would be able to join Edward when he waged war in France. Edward had belatedly decided, possibly with Surrey's active encouragement, that the earl should now be relieved of his office. Another nobleman, Brian FitzAlan, lord of Bedale in Yorkshire, was invited to take the role in Surrey's place.

FitzAlan had a strong record of service to Edward. He was a veteran of the Welsh wars, and was one of the two Guardians of Scotland appointed by Edward in 1291. He was also conveniently placed, as he had recently taken on responsibility for the defences of Northumberland. Crucially, however, FitzAlan was offered a somewhat lower salary than Surrey had received up to that point, and therefore was extremely reluctant to take on the new position. A letter to Edward made his position clear: 'In my poverty, I could not keep the land in peace to your profit and honour, when such a lord as the earl cannot hold it in peace with what he receives from you.'[29]

In fairness to FitzAlan, his personal income was dwarfed by Surrey's, but this was almost certainly intended as the opening move in a negotiation for better terms. Cressingham was convinced that FitzAlan would become more amenable if Edward would match the existing salary,[30] but no further offer was forthcoming and Surrey remained in post.

* * * *

By the end of the summer of 1297 Edward's control of Scotland appeared to be in serious jeopardy. If Edward appeared to be neglecting Scotland, however, it should be remembered that he was now fighting a war on two fronts: his war with Philip of France was still on-going, and it was a considerable drain on the crown's resources. In order to put events in Scotland into better context, therefore, it is also necessary to understand what was happening in the rest of Edward's world.

Whilst the numbers involved were limited, compared to the army he led against the Scots, Edward had despatched several expeditionary forces to Gascony; here they were joined by Gascons who remained loyal to Edward, as well as by Spanish mercenaries. The French remained entrenched in a number of strongpoints that had previously been under Edward's control, notably Bordeaux, but the English were able to reassert their presence in the region. In the past year, though, the English had suffered a number of reverses in Gascony. Edward had delegated command there to his brother Edmund, but he had fallen ill and died in June 1296. In January 1297 an English force was surprised and defeated near Bellegarde, and one of Edward's most talented commanders, John de St John, was captured.

Edward decided upon a two-pronged response, planning a new expedition to Gascony whilst also threatening Philip from the north.

He had established an alliance with the count of Flanders, a region still effectively independent from France, and he continued to solicit the assistance of other northern powers, partly by means of substantial financial inducements, the largest of which was offered to Albert of Nassau, the king of the Romans (i.e. Germany). Now, at last, Edward intended to cross in person to Flanders, from where he would launch an invasion of France at the head of a grand coalition of Philip's enemies.

Edward's strategy was not particularly original – King John had followed the same path before his fateful defeat at Bouvines, and his father had also attempted something similar at one point in his career – but the main obstacle to achieving his ambitions on the continent was opposition at home. In the past three years Edward's armies had fought wars in Scotland, Wales and Gascony. The costs were enormous, and would continue to rise: it has been estimated that in the period from 1294 to early 1298 Edward's administration spent around £750,000 on diplomacy and military operations.[31] Much of this money was raised by taxation. Even if England was not (yet) on the verge of armed rebellion, some of the same issues that had provoked revolts in Scotland and Wales were also causing resentment in the very heart of Edward's domains.

Edward drew his revenues from a wide range of sources, but there were three main types of taxation in England: first, taxes on the movable wealth of lay people (although, as we have seen, there was tacit acceptance that consent was required via parliament); second, clerical taxes (funds provided by the church); and third, customs duties. In addition, there was the *prise*, or compulsory seizure, of foodstuffs and other commodities; in theory, financial compensation would be provided later, but in practice this was far less certain. By the end of the thirteenth century all of these exactions were familiar to English people, and resentment was rising as a result of the scale and frequency of Edward's demands.

Resistance might be expressed in covert ways. It is striking that taxes on lay wealth brought in diminishing returns; this may be due to tax avoidance, although it may also be an indication of genuine impoverishment during a period of poor harvests.[32] But probably the most hated tax was the so-called *maltolt*, or 'bad tax', a swingeing duty on the export of wool. Merchants passed on the tax to customers and suppliers (as is their wont), meaning that the latter received a much lower price.

Edward called for huge sums from the clergy as a contribution to the war effort – no less than half of their income in 1294 – but in 1297 he faced overt opposition led by Robert Winchelsey, archbishop of Canterbury, whose temper and tenacity could sometimes match Edward's own. Winchelsey argued, on the basis of a recent statement from the latest Pope, Boniface VIII, that papal approval was necessary in advance.[33] But on this occasion Edward cynically circumvented the issue by withdrawing his protection for church property, and many churchmen considered it prudent to regain this by paying a substantial fee.

In many respects a storm was brewing, and Edward's demands for military service were another cause of controversy. As we have seen, it was beyond doubt that the king's leading subjects owed him military service, but the precise form this should take was perhaps more open to question. This subject was debated at Salisbury, where a parliament convened in February 1297. Edward had requested that certain magnates should join the projected expedition to Gascony, but Roger Bigod, earl of Norfolk, contended they were not bound to serve overseas unless they were campaigning with the king in person.

The earl was careful in his arguments, making reference to precedent, but according to Walter of Guisborough Edward lost his temper with Norfolk, snarling 'By God, Sir Earl, either go or hang!' But Norfolk calmly stood his ground: 'By the same oath, O King, I shall neither go nor hang.'[34] Ultimately Norfolk did not go, but nor did he hang. Whilst Edward was acutely aware of the rights of a medieval king, he also understood there were limits – although in the coming months he would push closer to these boundaries than he had ever done before.

The more subtle aspects of Edward's character became apparent later in July, when a temporary reconciliation was effected with Archbishop Winchelsey, but his critics amongst the laity were less easily mollified. By this time Norfolk had emerged as the clear leader of the opposition, along with Humphrey de Bohun, earl of Hereford. Both Norfolk and Hereford had personal grievances that might have been significant: Norfolk owed substantial debts to the crown, and Hereford was still smarting at his treatment by Edward in a dispute from some years before. Nevertheless, it is generally accepted that they were aware of wider points of principle, advocating a programme of reform that drew upon much broader concerns. As Walter of Guisborough put it, 'the cause they were striving for was not only their own, but also that of the whole community'.[35]

A manifesto known as The Remonstrances was drawn up on behalf of the two earls and their supporters. In time-honoured fashion the document stressed its authors' loyalty to the king, but requested that recent abuses should be corrected in accordance with established laws and tradition (particular reference is made to Magna Carta). The Remonstrances covers all of the issues that had become contentious, including the king's financial exactions (which were denounced as excessive) and his demands for military service overseas. The document also encompasses other long-standing grievances, calling for a review of the administration and boundaries of the Royal Forest – a point that would take on increasing significance. Almost in passing, it is suggested that Edward's French campaign was ill-advised, given the situation in Scotland. The Remonstrances has been described as 'an able document',[36] but Edward was unimpressed.

Not everyone was opposed to Edward's war in France, and he was able to recruit an army of modest size for his forthcoming campaign; the strength of this force is estimated at around 9,000 men (including 895 cavalry).[37] He also pressed on with his demands for money. On 30 July officials were instructed to assess and collect new taxes on the laity, which Edward asserted had been agreed by a new parliament – although his critics derided this assembly as 'people standing around in his chamber'.[38] Prises of foodstuffs continued and a prise of wool was also ordered, although of the latter only 799 sacks were collected out of a projected 8,000.[39] A letter issued in the king's name stressed the danger he was about to face, asserting the extraordinary nature of the situation, and urging his subjects to remember their duty.[40] Edward, then, was perfectly aware that these measures would be unpopular. Even so, it is unlikely that his words were well received.

The king's single-mindedness – one might well say obstinacy – was remarkable. It can only be concluded that Edward was gambling heavily on a victory against the French, which he believed would also improve his position in England, because he left the country on the verge of civil war; on the very day that Edward embarked on board his ship at Winchelsea, 22 August, Norfolk and Hereford appeared at the exchequer in arms to prevent the collection of taxes.

Edward left his son Edward of Caernarfon as regent, even though he was still only fourteen years old. At that time the boundaries between childhood and adulthood were somewhat more malleable than they are today, but it is generally accepted that real decision-making power rested with the prince's council. A series of meetings was subsequently arranged between the council and the disaffected magnates, but at the same time it is clear that both sides were preparing for war. At the royal fortress of Tickhill, for example, steps were taken to improve the defences, and a force of crossbowmen and archers was hired to garrison the castle. There is also some evidence of disorder in the Welsh Marches, where the earl of Norfolk was taking steps to strengthen his great castle at Chepstow.

*   *   *   *

With so many other matters to divert his attention, Edward devoted little time to the problems in Scotland, but towards the end of August the earl of Surrey roused himself to action at last, launching an expedition into southern Scotland, accompanied by Cressingham. Presumably Surrey's army consisted largely of men recruited by Cressingham earlier in the summer, if the earl had been able to retain their service, supplemented by his own personal retinue. Walter of Guisborough estimated the size of the army to have been over 50,000, but medieval chroniclers were almost always prone to great exaggeration. It is more likely that Surrey's army was closer to 10,000, and it may conceivably have been somewhat smaller than this.

By this time Murray and Wallace were no longer skulking in woods and bogs. Murray had successfully taken a number of important towns and castles, including Aberdeen, Elgin and Inverness, and Wallace could now be found some distance from the Forest. The two men joined forces for a siege of Dundee, quickly gaining access to the town. Murray and Wallace formed a formidable partnership. Despite their different backgrounds, they shared a common purpose – as well as broad agreement about the methods that should be employed.[41] After receiving intelligence that Surrey intended to march into northern Scotland, where the patriots had now established control over most of the country, they took steps to prevent him from crossing the Forth. Delegating the siege of Dundee Castle to local people (apparently they were ordered to continue on pain of death), Murray and Wallace moved south.

Today thousands of commuters cross and recross the River Forth on a daily basis, by road or rail; the two spectacular bridges north of Edinburgh now form one of Scotland's best known landmarks, and there is another road bridge further west, at Kincardine. In medieval times the Forth was a far more formidable obstacle: it was often referred to as 'the Scottish Sea' and is depicted in medieval maps as cutting Scotland in half.[42] In the thirteenth century the first bridge across the river was at Stirling, almost forty miles inland from the modern crossings of the Firth of Forth. Stirling Bridge was overlooked by Stirling Castle on its mighty rock, and it is almost impossible to overemphasise the strategic importance of this site.

When the earl of Surrey arrived at Stirling Bridge, therefore, on 10 September, he found a hostile Scottish army assembled on the opposite bank of the river. Stirling Castle (on the English side of the Forth) remained in English hands, but the patriots had taken up a strong position on rising ground to the south of the Abbey Craig (an imposing volcanic plug). Before the English could engage the Scots, of course, they would need to cross the river: a laborious process, during which they would be dangerously exposed. The bridge itself was narrow – barely wide enough for a horse and cart – before a causeway carried the road across fields and meadows. The presence of the causeway implies that this was soft ground, unsuitable for heavy cavalry. Murray and Wallace had set Surrey a considerable problem. Surrey, however, appears to have underestimated the two young Scottish commanders, and was not even convinced that the Scots would fight at all.

From this point onwards most historians rely heavily on Walter of Guisborough.[43] His account is almost always the most detailed of the narrative sources we possess for this period, although it should also be noted that he was a colourful writer with a flair for the dramatic. That said, it has been mentioned above that Guisborough was well informed, and on this occasion he was probably influenced by eyewitness testimony: his work gives particular attention to the role of Sir Marmaduke Thweng, whose lands bordered those of Guisborough Priory.

Presumably it was quite late in the day when Surrey arrived at Stirling, because both armies set up camp for the evening. On the following morning the English prepared to cross the river, but the situation became farcical. A substantial number of soldiers had already crossed when it became apparent that Surrey had overslept, so they were swiftly recalled. Another crossing was halted when James the Steward rode into the English camp, accompanied by the earl of Lennox. Both of these men were now technically in Edward's allegiance, although they held their forces apart from both armies. The Scottish lords had previously offered their service as mediators, and Surrey had accepted, but their efforts (which were probably somewhat half-hearted) had been rebuffed by the patriots.

Perhaps Surrey was simply observing the form, but on hearing of this setback he despatched another embassy to the Scots: two Dominican friars crossed the river and called on the patriots to surrender. Wallace's magnificent reply, as reported by Guisborough, has resonated through the ages: 'Tell your commander that we are not here to make peace but to do battle to defend ourselves and liberate our kingdom. Let them come on, and we shall prove this in their very beards.'[44] Battle was now inevitable.

Meanwhile, Surrey had belatedly convened a council of war. The boldest voices urged an immediate attack, although Sir Richard Lundie (who obviously knew of Wallace's abilities) advocated more considered tactics; he suggested that a detachment should first be separated from the main English force, outflanking the Scots by means of a ford further up-river. But Lundie was brusquely interrupted by Cressingham, who would accept no further delays, and Surrey ordered the more direct approach. Whatever else Cressingham may have been, he was certainly no coward, and himself led the English vanguard across the bridge. As the troops crossed the river for the third time, Murray and Wallace realised that the English were finally in earnest. It was an opportunity they were determined to take.

When the Scottish commanders judged the time was right (probably when around a third of the English army had crossed the bridge), they unleashed their forces in a wild charge. Whereas the English had easily repelled the Scots at Dunbar, on this occasion their experience would be very different. The sudden assault meant that the English were thrust onto the defensive, forced back within a natural loop formed by the river. A fierce struggle ensued, in which the Scots quickly gained the upper hand. They also gained control of the bridge and the causeway, so that the English vanguard was cut off. Sir Marmaduke Thweng and his men were able to fight their way out, temporarily regaining control of the bridge, and some of the lightly armed Welshmen were able to swim back to the other side of the river. Many of their companions faced a worse fate.

Much of Surrey's army had not engaged, but the men who were still on the other bank were forced to look on while their companions were cut to pieces. Soon they lost any heart for the struggle. In desperation Surrey ordered that the wooden bridge should be burnt on his side, in order to hinder pursuit, as his forces began to melt away. Having destroyed the English vanguard, the Scots were left in possession of the field; the remainder of the English army retreated southwards. Many of the English and Welsh soldiers must have found their way to safety, but the stragglers were harried by mounted followers of Lennox and the Steward (who also looted the English baggage train); now that victory was certain, the two nobles had openly espoused the patriot cause.

There was no escape for Hugh Cressingham, who was trapped on the Scottish side of the Forth. His last moments must surely have been horrific, as he was engulfed in a sea of hatred, but he suffered a knightly death in combat. Nevertheless, although Guisborough's account does convey a suitably patriotic anger at the English defeat, he reported the gruesome fate of Cresssingham's body with evident relish: the corpse was flayed, and many Scotsmen took pieces of his skin as grisly symbols of their victory. *The Lanercost Chronicle* tells us that Wallace used Cressingham's skin to make a sword belt.[45]

Surrey survived the battle, having failed to cross the river, but he fled the field in ignominy. Entrusting the defence of Stirling Castle to Sir Marmaduke Thweng (who was shortly afterwards forced to surrender), Surrey now rode hard for Berwick. He continued to take part in military campaigns until his death in 1304, perhaps in conscious pursuit of his lost honour, but his reputation has never recovered.

One modern historian has characterised the earl of Surrey as 'an ordinary, stupid and arrogant feudal chief'.[46] Other writers have offered more measured judgements, and one recent study has emphasised some mitigating factors in his defence.[47] There is circumstantial evidence to suggest that Surrey may have been genuinely unwell, which may explain his late rising on the morning of the battle (although it should be noted that it did not prevent him from making an effective escape). It must also be stressed that Edward's own sense of complacency about Scottish affairs, and his obsession with the French campaign, had undoubtedly hindered his administration's efforts in Scotland. Yet the most widely held view is that Surrey was a mediocrity, despite the great advantages of his birth.[48] In short, although the earl could be an effective subordinate, he lacked the aptitude for high command. Edward's faith in Surrey was misplaced, and on this occasion he had chosen poorly.

* * * *

The defeat at Stirling sent shockwaves throughout England. The Scottish victory owed much to the brilliant opportunism shown by Murray and Wallace, as well as to English ineptitude, but it must have seemed incredible that an English army, including heavy cavalry, could be defeated by a force of Scottish infantry. What is more, the Scots had not achieved a battlefield victory such as this against the English since the early eleventh century. From the English point of view, the disaster at Stirling could be seen as a vindication of the position taken by the authors of The Remonstrances – although surely even the most pessimistic Englishman could not have predicted such an outcome.

Meanwhile, Edward had landed safely in Flanders, but his position there was increasingly alarming. His chief ally, the king of the

Romans, made no move to join the English host, and the Flemish had already suffered defeats at the hands of the French. Edward received a cool welcome – it was very different from what he had expected – and his soldiers did not endear themselves to the local people. He was forced to move from Bruges because of rumours that the Flemish had planned to change sides. At Ghent, increasing antagonism between Edward's forces and the citizens (who were supposedly Edward's allies) exploded into a short burst of savage fighting. Eventually the English army established control of the city, but there were fatalities on both sides. According to the *Chronicle of Bury St Edmunds*, Edward took a leading role: at one point he 'trampled down a huge chain stretched across a street by clapping his spurs to his charger and rushing at it', heedless of the danger to himself and his horse.[49]

The regency government in England was aware of the disaster at Stirling within ten days, and probably earlier, but understandably the news took a little longer to reach Edward in Flanders. On 5 October it appears that he was still not aware of what had happened in Scotland; a letter from the king makes reference to Hugh Cressingham in such nonchalant terms that it is difficult to believe that Edward knew his faithful servant was already dead. But events from the next few days would suggest that Edward learned about the battle shortly afterwards: on 9 October terms were agreed for an Anglo-French truce, and it has been argued that the news from Stirling provided the catalyst.[50] Perhaps Edward was fortunate that Philip did not fully appreciate the weakness of his position, but this would have provided little consolation. The year 1297 was surely Edward's *annus horribilis*. In the following year the Scots would feel the full force of his rage.

Chapter 5

The Road to Falkirk

Once he had received the news from Stirling, we may presume that Edward immediately swore vengeance against the Scots. His revenge, however, would be a dish served cold. For the moment he stayed in Flanders, where he would remain for the next six months. The truce agreed with the French was for two months only, so Edward concluded that his presence in Flanders was necessary to maintain pressure on the French. This might imply that he now wished to force Philip to accept more lasting terms of peace, although he continued to hope in vain for the arrival of his ally Albert of Nassau. In many ways Edward shared the outlook and inclinations of his Plantagenet ancestors (and successors), and he could never have contemplated the prospect of entirely abandoning his ambitions on the continent – in spite of the disaster his army had suffered in Scotland.

In England, meanwhile, the regency government was striving hard to restore unity – but this would come at a price. Reconciliation was achieved with the most trenchant critics of Edward's policies in return for the so-called 'Confirmation of the Charters', the charters in question being Magna Carta and the Charter of the Forest. In fact the agreement went beyond this, because it was also explicitly promised that any future prises and taxation would only be possible 'with the common assent of the realm'.[1] A document to that end was drawn up on 10 October 1297, but of course Edward's acceptance of the contents was still necessary if it were to have any real meaning. Edward subsequently endorsed the agreement on 5 November; we might imagine it gave him little pleasure to do so.

It was envisaged that the Confirmation of the Charters would pave the way for a new English campaign in Scotland. For the moment, though, the political wrangling in England provided an opportunity for the Scottish patriot leaders to consolidate their gains. Wallace had pursued Surrey as far as Berwick, but thereafter he returned north to bring the siege of Dundee Castle to a close. Now completely isolated, without any hope of relief, the garrison surrendered. A number of English garrisons held out throughout the winter – notably at Edinburgh and Roxburgh – but most of Scotland slipped beyond Edward's control.

*   *   *   *

All of the momentum was against the English in Scotland. They could take a little comfort, however, from the knowledge that one of their most dangerous enemies had fallen. Andrew Murray had been mortally wounded in the course of the fighting at Stirling, on the cusp of his greatest triumph. For some time afterwards letters were issued on behalf of both Murray and Wallace, as joint commanders of 'the Army of Scotland',[2] but Murray's active role had come to an end. The precise date of his death is uncertain, but we can assume he passed away before the end of the year.[3] He left an unborn son as his heir, another Andrew Murray, who would later prove to be another indefatigable champion of Scottish independence.

The death of Murray left Wallace as the outstanding military commander in Scotland, but other Scots also continued to take action against the English. By the end of September the earl of Surrey had withdrawn as far south as York, and the town of Berwick (but not the castle) fell to Henry de Haliburton. The knowledge of this latest setback would have particularly irked Edward, because Hugh Cressingham had failed to complete the new defences that the king had ordered to be constructed. By mid-October Scottish raiders began to appear south of the border, and for several weeks the northern counties of England were harried by the Scots. Walter of Guisborough reported that 'in all the monasteries and churches between Newcastle and Carlisle the service of God totally ceased, for all the canons, monks and priests fled before the Scots, as did nearly all the people'.[4]

The impetus behind these raids was probably spontaneous. Euphoria in the wake of Stirling Bridge was offset by economic hardship and widespread hunger in Scotland: bad weather had led to poor harvests, leading to a shortage of grain and other foodstuffs. Many Scots who crossed the border were almost certainly motivated by the prospect of plunder. But in early November Wallace himself arrived in Northumberland to provide a greater focus for the raids. *Gesta Annalia* II implies that Wallace was determined to maintain his army at the expense of the English.[5] It might also be suggested that Wallace's own position could only be maintained if he were able to deliver continued military success.

In Blind Harry's poem Wallace sacks York and rampages south as far as St Albans. In truth, his achievements were rather more modest. He sent a cleric to demand the surrender of Carlisle, in the name of 'William the Conqueror', but this was refused;[6] once Wallace had surveyed the city's defences, he thought better of an assault. The Scots also threatened Newcastle, yet this endeavour also came to nothing. Once again, though, there are reports of appalling atrocities: a number of chroniclers provide testimony of the cruel effects of the Scottish invasion on people who were not able to find safety in the towns. According to the *Flores Historiarum*, a chronicle compiled at Westminster Abbey, captured English men and women were humiliated and tortured by the Scots: they were first stripped naked and forced to sing for Wallace, before they suffered various torments.[7]

A more positive view of Wallace does emerge, at least on one occasion, in the account of Walter of Guisborough.[8] When Wallace arrived at Hexham Priory, we are told that he piously asked to hear mass, before going outside to remove his weapons. Unfortunately a number of his men took advantage of their leader's temporary absence to steal the holy vessels from the altar. Apparently Wallace was incensed by this act of sacrilege, and ordered that the culprits be taken and hanged. Intriguingly this proved to be impossible; Guisborough tells us that attempts to apprehend the thieves were rather half-hearted, although Wallace did offer the priory a letter of protection against further outrages. Guisborough obtained a copy of this document (which is dated 7 November 1297, and was issued in the names of both Murray and Wallace), and the text of the letter is preserved in his chronicle.

To a certain extent, then, the anecdotal evidence of the chronicles can also be complemented by other sources.[9] A particularly detailed picture has emerged of the devastation wrought by the Scots in Cumberland. Rents and other sources of income were badly affected, and other, more telling details can also sometimes be gleaned. At Bolton in Allerdale, for example, the Scots burnt the mill, the fulling mill and the grange (an agricultural complex that belonged to the monks of nearby Holm Cultram). By the end of November, however, the fury of the Scots was spent. The English believed that St Cuthbert unleashed blizzards against the Scots in order to protect the people of Durham; certainly this winter was exceptionally hard. Doubtless the Scots were now happy to return home, laden with plunder.

By this time, too, the English had begun to regroup, and there were reprisals before the end of the year. Robert Clifford led a counter-raid into Annandale. But the main action was planned to take place in the east. A massive English army – 18,500 strong at its peak – was mustered at Newcastle. Many of the great magnates who had not joined Edward in Flanders were present on this campaign, which seems to suggest a renewed sense of common purpose.[10] Early in the New Year the army advanced into Scotland. English control of Berwick was reasserted, and the besieged garrison at Roxburgh was relieved. Soon afterwards, however, the English commanders received orders from Edward that any further operations should be suspended. The Scottish 'rebels' were not to escape chastisement, but any further punishment would be directed by the king himself.

*   *   *   *

Edward returned to England in March 1298. He had now established a year-long truce with the French (the terms were agreed at Tournai on 31 January), bringing his disappointing time in Flanders to a close. The suspension of the winter campaign in Scotland led to a waste of resources, but Edward's decision to focus on the Scottish problem – finally – was surely a popular move. Further evidence of the king's renewed sense of intent lies in the fact that the English Exchequer, the heart of the royal administration, was moved to York, where it would remain for the next six years. The remnants of the separate Scottish Exchequer, under Walter Amersham, were incorporated into a wider network. Much of the responsibility for the day-to-day administration of Edward's military efforts in Scotland now fell to the Wardrobe (a department of the Household that was theoretically subordinate to the Exchequer), whose officials played a vital role in all the king's affairs.

The bulk of the English forces raised in the winter had been disbanded, but the leaders of the army remained at Berwick with their retinues. On 8 April Edward summoned them to a parliament at York, which was scheduled to take place on 24 May, along with representatives from the shires and important towns. The more detailed instructions in Edward's message to the earls suggest that he had abandoned the insouciant attitude displayed at the end of the 1296 campaign. They were warned to travel as secretly as possible, ensuring that they left a sufficient force to hold Berwick in the event of a new Scottish incursion. At around the same time general orders were sent out for the recruitment of a new army, which was ultimately expected to muster at Roxburgh on 25 June.

As always, the core of Edward's army was provided by the heavy cavalry. Many of those who had recently shown commitment to their lord by joining the king's expedition to Flanders served again on this Scottish campaign. These included Edward's young kinsman Aymer de Valence, the future earl of Pembroke, who was accompanied by a large following. Edward was increasingly impressed by Valence, recognising his nascent qualities of leadership; indeed, Valence would hold a succession of important commands in Scotland in the years to come. Of course, Valence was joined by many of the other great magnates, including the earls of Hereford, Norfolk and Surrey, who were already present in the north. The bellicose bishop of Durham, Anthony Bek, would also feature prominently. The names and heraldic devices of over a hundred of the most prominent leaders are recorded in the *Falkirk Roll of Arms*, which was probably composed for Henry Percy.[11]

Edward did not issue a formal feudal summons for this campaign, but the service of the English ruling classes was requested on account of the fealty and respect they owed to their king. They responded in large numbers. It has been estimated that the total strength of the cavalry was around 3,000.[12] Recent research, based on a sample of 140 men, has provided fresh insights into the experience of the knights who took part in this campaign.[13] One of the most interesting aspects of the findings is the broad range of ages. One knight, for example, John de Claron, was thought to have been forty years old when he died in 1324, making him just fourteen when he served in 1298. At the other end of the spectrum we find William de Mere, a knight from Staffordshire, who was probably around fifty-five years old at the time of the campaign. Mere was around the same age, then, as Edward himself.

A knight's age was not always a clear indicator of his military experience. Some of the older men were veterans of the Welsh wars, and even of Edward's crusade, but many established knights were serving for the first time. This was also true, of course, of many of the younger knights, and some of this group would go on to pursue long military careers. For example, the Hampshire knight John de Scures served in Scotland on four more occasions during Edward's reign, as well as taking part in the ill-fated Bannockburn campaign. Below this rank, of course, there were the 'sergeants' or 'esquires', who made up the majority of Edward's mounted warriors. Serving at this level was not necessarily a path to further advancement, but a number of those who served as *valetti* did go on to greater things. These included, for instance, Giles de Argentin,[14] who later became known as the 'third best knight in the world', eventually meeting a heroic death at the battle of Bannockburn.

In addition to the cavalry, Edward was also keen to recruit another huge force of infantry.[15] Accounts recording payments to the infantry have been preserved, and show that more than 20,000 footsoldiers mustered at Carlisle. Of these, more than 12,000 were Welsh. To put this into perspective, the entire population of Wales at this time is estimated to have been around 200,000. It has therefore been calculated, on this basis, that over half of the Welshmen of fighting age took part in this campaign. If so, this was an extraordinary commitment, but the scale of the numbers involved was not entirely exceptional: in Edward's recent expedition to Flanders, for example, over 5,000 Welshmen served, out of around 8,000 infantry in total.

The Welsh had once again impressed Edward with their bravery in Flanders. Whilst there was little fighting in Edward's continental campaign, the conflict with the people of Ghent was a notable exception. This provided an opportunity for one intrepid Welshman (unfortunately unnamed) to display his martial skills. Apparently he swam across a river, climbed the city's palisade and killed three men before nonchalantly returning to his companions. He is said to have received 100 shillings from Edward as a reward for his reckless courage.[16] Doubtless Edward was hoping to witness similar exploits in the weeks to come. But if the king relied heavily on the Welsh, it should also be stressed that he drew support from every corner of his domains; the presence of Gascon troops amidst Edward's subjects from across the British Isles provides a telling reminder of the diverse nature of his lordship.

✳ ✳ ✳ ✳

Edward's army was one of the largest ever raised by a medieval English king, and naturally a force of this size was dependent on a phenomenal logistical effort. Napoleon once famously remarked that 'an army marches on its stomach', and obviously this was just as true during the Middle Ages as it was in the eighteenth and nineteenth centuries. It has often been observed that a medieval army resembled a great city on the move, not least because armies always attracted a large number of non-combatants: priests, cooks, physicians, entertainers, even prostitutes.[17] On this occasion Edward's army was larger than the population at that time of any city in the British Isles, with the notable exception of London.

Logistical arrangements had evolved throughout the course of Edward's reign, and the king and his officials were able to draw upon past experience of waging war, in particular in Wales. Some medieval armies lived off the land – although this was not always possible or desirable – and in any case local supplies were often insufficient. In his earliest campaigns Edward had relied heavily on independent merchants to provide his armies with supplies, and enterprising businessmen did continue to play a role, but a more centralised approach was adopted in the early stages of his Scottish wars. Much of the responsibility for the collection of supplies lay with the sheriffs, supported by other royal officials delegated to assist them; at this time the sheriffs acted as the crown's deputies in each county, with a wide range of duties encompassing military, legal and financial affairs.

Sometimes the instructions provided to the sheriffs could be extremely detailed, not only in terms of the quantities that should be collected but also in terms of how the provisions should be packaged or transported. Towards the end of the year 1298, for example, Edward wrote to the sheriff of York concerning supplies of flour that had been requested: 'You shall have the said wheat well ground and properly sifted, so that there is no bran in it, and you shall put the flour into strong clean casks, so that the flour can be closely packed and pressed down, and in each tun [cask] you should put three sticks of hazel, and some salt at the bottom of each, to prevent the flour from going bad.'[18]

Supplies were conveyed by water whenever possible. Medieval roads were not quite as bad as later tradition would suggest, but water transport was cheaper and faster. It has been estimated that transporting goods by road at this time cost twice as much as river transport, and eight times more than transport by sea.[19] As Edward's Scottish wars progressed, Berwick and Carlisle became increasingly important as supply depots which could be restocked by sea. (Carlisle's port was at nearby Skinburness, which provided access to the sea via the River Eden.) In eastern Scotland supplies could be moved further inland by means of the Rivers Tweed, Forth and Tay. But, of course, transportation by land was sometimes unavoidable, so it also fell on the sheriffs, as well as the receiving officials, to organise large fleets of vehicles and animals. On 12 June 1298, for example, the sheriff of Northumberland was ordered to assemble horses and carts for the use of Edward's army.[20]

Transportation by water was necessary because Edward had requested provisions from the length and breadth of England. Bread was the staple food of the English medieval soldier, so large amounts of grain were needed; on this occasion the burden fell heavily on Yorkshire and Lincolnshire, although in later campaigns the southern counties were expected to contribute more. Vast quantities of oats were also required (to provide fodder for horses), and wine and ale were much in demand because water supplies were often unreliable.

Medieval people might not have understood that bacteria cause disease, but they were evidently able to observe the effects of drinking contaminated water.

Edward's lordship of Ireland was also expected to contribute to the war effort. During the campaign of 1296 some 3,000 Irishmen are thought to have served in Edward's army, although he also expected the Irish to contribute in other ways. The treasurer of Ireland eventually paid out over £4,000 for goods that were requisitioned for the 1298 campaign, accounting for more than 70 per cent of the Irish Exchequer's expenditure in this year.[21]

Compulsory purchase, or *prise*, continued, although Edward and his advisers were now increasingly sensitive to the resentment it could cause. In fairness to Edward, it appears that he was keen to ensure that payments should be made quickly. When the sheriff of Gloucester passed on concerns about payment, for example, Edward assured him that purveyance would be carried out 'in the best way and to the least grievance' of anybody affected.[22] It must be added, though, that no payments would be made until the goods had been received on behalf of the king; even if the system was operating as efficiently as possible, the payment process was likely to take several weeks, and probably months.

The efforts to provision the army may seem impressive, but later events would reveal major defects in the supply chain. Besides, man cannot live on bread alone, so before the campaign started in earnest Edward visited a number of religious sites. These included the shrine of St John of Beverley in Yorkshire, and Edward took the saint's banner with him to be flown alongside the royal standard. It is possible that he was consciously trying to imitate the formidable Anglo-Saxon king Athelstan, who also visited Beverley *en route* to his great victory at *Brunanburh* in 937. The true site of *Brunanburh* remains uncertain and contested, yet it was one of the most decisive battles in British history. Athelstan triumphed there over a remarkable alliance led by the Scottish king Constantine, which also encompassed Celtic and Norse rulers. Athelstan subsequently extracted submissions from a number of British leaders, and was described by a contemporary scribe as 'raised by the favour of the All-Accomplishing One on the throne of the whole kingdom of Britain'.[23]

It has been argued that Edward, 'a propagandist of no little skill if no exceptional honesty, would be content to let the parallel between himself and his successful predecessor be remarked among those he commanded'.[24] We should be wary, though, of assuming that Edward's motives were entirely cynical. At a time when there was widespread belief that saints remained active in the world, John was thought to be a particularly powerful saint whose support was often sought. For Edward, though, the protection of John of Beverley was not sufficient. He also acquired another potent symbol, indeed perhaps one that was even more potent: the banner of St Cuthbert, who was still revered on both sides of the border. As we have seen, it was widely believed that he had recently favoured the English, unleashing his terrible power to protect them against the depredations of William Wallace.

What Edward himself thought of Wallace can only be imagined, but doubtless he was eager to crush the rebellion and bring his opponent to heel. Having said that, the popular notion that the pursuit of Wallace's destruction became a dark obsession for Edward, and that the conflict had become truly *personal*, is difficult to credit – at least at this point in his career. Walter Bower's account does tell us that Edward had already sent a letter to Wallace, presumably in early 1298, admonishing the Scottish leader that 'if he dared to invade England again, he would at once realise that the avenging hands of the king himself were seeking retribution on him and his men for their presumption'.[25] Apparently Wallace responded in similar vein, promising to revisit England before Easter. Regrettably, however, no such letters have survived.

*   *   *   *

Meanwhile, in Scotland William Wallace had reached the high point of his career. At some point over the winter he was knighted, presumably by one of the Scottish earls, several of whom, such as Malise of Strathearn, had by now thrown off any pretence of allegiance to Edward. The elevation in Wallace's status was necessary because he was also appointed sole Guardian, serving in the name of John Balliol (who remained in captivity in England). Wallace was not simply a military figure; as early as November 1297, after the death of

Bishop Fraser, he had intervened in the election of a new bishop of St Andrews, helping to secure the role for William Lamberton (of whom more shall be heard). Even so, with the impending English invasion in mind, it is likely that Wallace's thoughts – like those of many Scots – were almost entirely focused on war.

While Edward gathered his power during the spring and early summer of 1298, Wallace made his own preparations. As Guardian he possessed considerable authority, and his 'Army of Scotland' represented the community of the realm. The documents that survive in Wallace's name demonstrate that he (or perhaps those around him) understood the importance of the written word. It was also later stated by the English that Wallace had called parliaments and sought to renew links with the French. If this is so, then it is likely that Wallace would also have sought to restore the machinery of Scottish royal government in order to recruit men to his cause.

Unfortunately we must rely on anecdotal evidence to gain an insight into the administration of Wallace's army, but Walter Bower's chronicle provides an intriguingly detailed portrait of its organisation:

> One man was always to be chosen out of five from all the groups of five to be over the four and called a quaternion; his commands were to be obeyed by them in all matters, and whoever did not obey was to be killed. In a similar manner moving up to the men who were more robust and effective there was always to be a tenth man over each nine, and a twentieth over each nineteen, and so on moving up to each thousand and beyond to the top [i.e. Wallace himself].[26]

Historians are often suspicious of this account, noting the clear parallels with classical and biblical sources that Bower would have known,[27] although it might be noted there are similarities to how the English organised their infantry.

Bower's account also stresses the importance of discipline to Wallace, and there is other evidence to suggest he sought to control his army through harsh measures. We have already seen that Wallace threatened to hang thieves in Northumberland (although on that occasion the threat was not carried out), and it was said that he had gallows constructed in other places in order to intimidate people into doing his bidding.[28] It is also possible that Wallace was forced to press men into service. Much later, in 1306, a certain Michael de Miggel, indicted by the English on account of his earlier support for Wallace, argued that he 'remained with Wallace through fear of death and not of his own will'.[29] He claimed that he had escaped three times, but was brought back by Wallace's men, and on the final occasion it was made clear that if he tried to leave again he would be killed.

It might be questioned, however, whether Wallace's methods were at all draconian by the standards of the time. Surviving military ordinances from England also promise dire penalties for breaches of discipline (although it must be said that Edward sought to fine and imprison deserters, rather than hanging them), and many commanders, including military leaders from more recent times, would not have given Miggel three chances to prove his worth. Moreover, given everything he achieved, surely it is reasonable to assume that Wallace possessed the ability to inspire, as well as to command? It is certainly difficult to conclude, on the basis of such scanty evidence, that the majority of men who served in Wallace's army did so unwillingly.

Another issue that is difficult to quantify is the role of the Scottish nobility. Wallace could never have achieved the office of Guardian without a certain amount of support from the Scottish elite, and it has already been shown that he was quite capable of establishing effective links with noblemen. Nevertheless, while many Scottish nobles had now thrown off their allegiance to Edward, it is not clear how much active support they provided to Wallace; nor is it entirely clear how many of them were willing to serve under his command in person. We can be certain, however, that a number of Scottish aristocrats did join Wallace's army; these included Sir John Stewart (the younger brother of James the Steward) and Macduff of Fife (the same man, ironically, who had previously sought Edward's support against John Balliol). A number of Scottish knights later had their lands declared forfeit by Edward, as a specific punishment for their participation in the coming campaign.[30]

* * * *

When Edward crossed the border into Scotland on 3 July, the stage
was set for a titanic clash between the English army and the Scots.
The following account of the ensuing campaign draws upon various
sources, but the fullest contemporary narrative is once again provided
by the chronicle of Walter of Guisborough.[31]

Edward's army marched north following the natural route used by
invading English armies in eastern Scotland, through Lauderdale
towards Edinburgh. Edward himself reached Edinburgh on 11 July.
On the way, it is said that Edward's soldiers ravaged the land. The
intention behind this was almost certainly to provoke Wallace into
offering battle; given that the Scottish leader had recruited a large
number of men from the Lothian region, it is possible that he came
under pressure to do so. However, Wallace, who had probably massed
his forces in the Torwood near Stirling, was happy to draw Edward
on. This would prove to be a sound decision, at least initially, because
Edward quickly ran into difficulties.

Edward's main problem, in spite of all the efforts described above,
was a shortage of supplies. How had this come to pass? One issue was
the weather – contrary winds prevented many of the grain ships from
reaching their destination at Berwick – but the king increasingly came
to believe (perhaps with good reason) that negligence on the part of
his officials was also greatly to blame.

Presumably there were provisions available to the army when
Edward crossed into Scotland, otherwise it is difficult to understand
the policy of systematic destruction. We have seen that supplies were
sent from Ireland, and a number of resourceful local merchants also
appear to have negotiated payments to make up for part of any
shortfall. But Edward was aware as early as the first week of July that
he did not have sufficient supplies for the duration of the campaign.
A series of increasingly furious messages were dispatched to England,
complaining about the sluggish nature of the supply chain and
threatening dire penalties if the expected provisions did not arrive.
Peter Draycote, the sheriff of Lincoln, and Peter Mollington, a royal
official delegated to help him, were the particular targets of Edward's
ire.[32]

From 15 to 20 July Edward was based at Kirkliston, close to the
Firth of Forth, where he hoped to receive the delayed provisions by

sea from Berwick. (Presumably the plan was for supplies to be landed at South Queensferry, about two miles to the north.) Around the same time a detachment under the bishop of Durham had been sent to reduce the castle of Dirleton, thirty miles to the east, as well as two others (possibly Yester and Hailes).[33] An initial attack on Dirleton was repulsed, however, and soon the bishop's men were reduced to eating beans and peas from the fields. We can assume that Bek was in command of a fast-moving mounted force – Guisborough tells us they were not hindered by siege equipment – and with morale already low he was reluctant to order another assault. He sent one of his subordinates, a fierce knight by the name of John FitzMarmaduke, to explain the situation to Edward and to ask for fresh instructions.

Guisborough's chronicle provides us with Edward's response: 'Go back and tell the bishop that as a bishop he is a man of Christian piety, but Christian piety has no place in what he is now doing'.[34] Then Edward had words for FitzMarmaduke himself, clapping a hand on the knight's shoulder: 'And as for you, you are a bloodthirsty man, and I have often had to rebuke you for being too cruel. But now be off, use all your cruelty, and instead of rebuking you I shall praise you. Take care you don't see me until all three castles are burned'. When the knight expressed doubts, asking for more detailed advice of how to proceed, Edward was unsympathetic: 'That you will know when you have done it, and you shall give me a pledge that you shall do it.'

Guisborough has almost certainly given his imagination a fairly free rein here, but this episode does have an authentic feeling. In the event we are told that three English supply ships fortuitously arrived, providing much-needed sustenance for the bishop and his men (although the chronicle does not explain where these provisions were landed, or how they were conveyed from there). Thus revitalized, apparently Bek's force succeeded in taking Dirleton. The other two castles, now abandoned, were also 'put to the flames', and Bek rejoined the main army.

Guisborough's account reports that other ships reached Edward, but unfortunately these vessels contained more wine than anything else. Perhaps Edward remembered an experience in North Wales; at one point he had raised morale by ostentatiously rejecting the final share of alcohol, ordering instead that it should be shared among his men. However, on this occasion, in Scotland, some of the Welshmen became excessively drunk and disorderly, and an ugly fracas ensued. A number of priests sought to calm the situation, but some of them were struck and killed by the intoxicated Welshmen. A force of cavalry was brought in to restore order, and eighty of the Welsh were killed. It is said that the Welsh then sullenly drew apart from the rest of the army, and that they even threatened to join the Scots (if circumstances would make this possible). But when news of this reached Edward he was apparently unmoved: even if his 'enemies' did join together, with God's help he would defeat them all!

It truth it is unlikely that all of the Welsh infantry were involved in the mutiny: clannish, regional loyalties were often just as important to the Welsh as their broader national identity at this time, and internal divisions might well have prevented them from acting *en masse*. Presumably the majority of Edward's army remained loyal, and much of the bravado on the king's part would have been intended for their benefit. Edward may have been an intensely driven man but he was surely no fool, and in private he must have begun to doubt his chances of success. As a result, it seems, Edward decided to curtail his advance.

The planned move to Edinburgh was envisaged as a prelude to a general retreat, and it is intriguing to consider the implications if Edward had withdrawn – not only in Scotland, but also in England. Leaving aside his many wars in Scotland, Wales and France, Edward was the first king of England since the Norman Conquest who did not have to face an armed rebellion from his *English* subjects. Given the difficulties that his son later experienced as king, in the wake of defeats against the Scots, would this have remained the case if Edward had failed in Scotland in 1298? We have seen that England had already come perilously close to civil war in the summer of 1297.

Edward's position at this time was made all the worse because he still had no idea of the whereabouts of Wallace and the Scottish army. In the light of the tactics employed by the Scots during the Dunbar campaign, it was even thought possible that Wallace might have planned to slip over the border in a diversionary raid. Such an attack was certainly feared in northern England. As late as 18 July the sheriffs of the northern counties received orders from York that they should investigate 'as secretly and circumspectly as possible' whether the Scots were planning an invasion. If so, messengers were to be sent 'riding day and night' to York, so that preparations could be made for resistance and warning: Scotsmen still living in the northern counties (perhaps as a legacy of more peaceful times) were to be arrested; wood and turf would be assembled to make beacon fires; and troops (such as were available) would be swiftly recruited.[35]

In the event the fears of the northerners were groundless, because Wallace had no plans to leave Scotland. Edward's reconnaissance operations appear to have been delegated to the two most faithful 'Scottish' earls in his allegiance – the earls of Angus and March – who we can assume were able to call upon men with local knowledge. On 21 July they brought news that the Scottish host had, at last, been sighted. It appears that Wallace was now prepared to confront the English army. As reported by Guisborough, Edward's sense of relief was profound: 'May God be praised, for he has solved all my problems. The Scots will have no need to follow me, for I will march to meet them at once.'[36]

A scout passed on information that Wallace's army was now encamped near Falkirk, and Edward ordered his army west, notwithstanding the continued difficulties in obtaining adequate supplies. As one modern writer has commented, 'from this point we hear no more of hunger, only marching and battle'.[37] But Edward's boldness did mask other concerns, because the scout (sometimes described as a spy) had also revealed that Wallace was planning to surprise the English and fall upon their camp; this, indeed, is surely the best explanation of the Scottish leader's abrupt change in strategy.

On the evening of 21 July the English made camp near Linlithgow, on the Burgh Muir to the east of the town. Wary now of the prospect of a surprise assault, the English spent the night arrayed for battle. The lords and men-at-arms apparently wore their armour, with their horses tethered by their sides. However, one of Edward's squires was careless in his duties, and Edward's own horse stepped on the king, injuring his ribs. In the resulting commotion the English came to believe they were under attack, and panic could easily have ensued. But Edward was able to calm the situation. Doubtless through gritted teeth, he also successfully conveyed the impression that he was not seriously hurt – even though he must surely have been in considerable pain.

On the next day, 22 July, the feast of Mary Magdalene, conflict would become inevitable. The Scots' victory at Stirling had showed that the English were not invincible; assuming his intelligence was good, Wallace would also have taken some heart from the various troubles that the English had suffered. But, of course, the army that Edward had brought to Scotland this time was vastly more formidable than the force that had been defeated at Stirling Bridge. Edward was about to exert the full might of the king of England in the field.

* * * *

Military historians have sometimes displayed a tendency to focus excessively on battles, to the exclusion of other elements of warfare that can be equally significant. This is understandable. A battle is undeniably an extraordinarily traumatic, dramatic event, characterised by an intensity of experience that is rare in human existence. It is therefore hardly surprising that battles can very easily – and sometimes very quickly – become totemic events to be celebrated or mourned. Moreover, while the strategic impact of battlefield victories can sometimes be overstated, battles had a heightened meaning in the Middle Ages because their outcomes could be interpreted as the judgement of God. It is important to remember, nevertheless, that battles were comparatively rare in medieval warfare.

The exceptional nature of battles is borne out by the career of Edward himself. Whilst he was a veteran of many campaigns, the battle of Falkirk would be only the third set-piece battle of his long career – and it would also prove to be his last. As a young man, Edward had taken part in numerous tournaments (and, as we have seen, these were much more violent and dangerous than the stylised combats of the later medieval period), but the only previous time he had commanded an entire army in a real battle – at Evesham in 1265 – was now more than thirty years ago. The Welsh of Gwynedd had avoided battle, preferring to trust in the formidable natural fortress of Snowdon, and there had been no real engagements of note during his recent campaign in Flanders. We should be cautious, therefore, in assuming that Edward's greater experience would give him a marked advantage over Wallace. Both men must have felt they had much to prove in the battle to come.

On the morning of 22 July the English left their camp at dawn. Their route to Falkirk from Linlithgow would have taken them across the River Avon close to Manuel Priory (near the village of Whitecross), before taking the higher ground towards Redding Muir. It was probably on Redding Muir that, according to Guisborough, the English vanguard encountered a force of spearmen. Evidently this was not the main Scottish army, as the English initially supposed, because when Edward's vanguard advanced up the hill the Scots quickly melted away. Guisborough's account does not explain how the Scots effected this mysterious disappearance, but in truth the force of 'many spearmen' was more likely to have been a small party of scouts (probably mounted), who had been stationed there to provide warning of the English advance. It appears that Wallace had already received the news – doubtless extremely alarming – that Edward's army was now close at hand.

When Edward himself reached the crest of the hill a tent was pitched so that he could pause to hear mass. From this vantage point the English could now truly see the Scottish army, hurriedly engaging in manoeuvres as the Scots prepared for battle. In the absence of archaeological evidence, our knowledge of the ensuing events is again derived largely from the chronicles.[38] The location of the Scottish position has not been determined with certainty – the site of the battle is still not marked on modern Ordnance Survey maps – but it is generally accepted that the Scottish army was drawn up to the south of Falkirk, about a mile to the north-west of Redding Muir.[39] Guisborough tells us that the Scots took up a position on a hill, which has been identified as the ridge to the south of Callendar Wood (an area now occupied by Woodend Farm Riding School). The Glen and Westquarter Burns flow through the valley below. At the time of the battle the confluence of the two burns appears to have formed a boggy loch, at first undetected by the English, which then covered part of the valley floor.

Denied the advantage of surprise by Edward's unexpected

advance, Wallace adopted defensive tactics. According to Guisborough he drew up his spearmen (the bulk of his army) in four large circles called *schiltroms*. (The origin of the word 'schiltrom' is uncertain, but it probably approximates to something close to 'shield wall'.) Each of the four circles was 'made up wholly of spearmen, standing shoulder to shoulder in deep ranks and facing towards the circumference of the circle, with their spears slanted outwards at an oblique angle'.[40] This seems to suggest that the Scots' flanks were not protected by geographical features, and that Wallace was expecting attacks from all sides. Rishanger adds the detail that the Scots attempted to fortify their position by means of ropes and stakes, although this is not corroborated by Guisborough's more detailed account.

It should not be assumed that Scottish spearmen adopted circular formations on every occasion (as is sometimes supposed), but this was obviously a sensible disposition for dismounted soldiers to take up when they were likely to face attacks from waves of cavalry; contemporary Flemish armies adopted similar tactics when fighting defensive battles against the French.[41] But, of course, Wallace's spearmen were not the only troops at his disposal. He also had a contingent of bowmen (though probably not as numerous as he would have liked), and a small force of cavalry (which was presumably made up of noblemen and their retinues). Guisborough's narrative tells us that the archers were positioned in the spaces between the schiltroms, while groups of cavalry were stationed on the flanks, to the rear.

It appears that the mood in the Scottish camp was grim, but stoically determined. Wallace's quip to his men, as recorded by William Rishanger, has justly become famous: 'I have brought you to the ring; hop [dance] if you can.'[42] Rishanger was clearly reluctant to give Wallace any credit – for him, these were the words of a 'seducer' who quickly abandoned his men – but this speech was evidently well known. Amidst a sea of Latin text, these words stand out immediately because they are written in English (albeit in archaic spelling), which is described as Wallace's 'own language'; this might suggest that they had reached the scriptorium at St Albans by common report.

On surveying the Scottish dispositions, Edward's attitude became cautious. Initially, his orders were that the English should make camp, so that his men could take sustenance and further rest. The English, it should be remembered, had been on the road since early in the morning, covering a distance of several miles, and Guisborough tells us that Edward was mindful that his men had not eaten since the previous day (which suggests that food supplies were strictly rationed). But Edward's barons were apprehensive about the possibility that the Scots could attack and take the English unawares. In truth, assuming that the battlefield has been correctly identified, Wallace's position on this occasion was not really suited to making unexpected rapid manoeuvres. Perhaps surprisingly, however, Edward deferred to his subordinates' concerns. Invoking the Holy Trinity, he ordered an immediate assault.

Edward himself would also have ridden towards the Scots, surrounded and protected by carefully chosen members of his household. We cannot know whether the king's hair had yet turned to the swanlike white that 'beautified his age' (perhaps we might imagine an iron grey?), but he must have been increasingly conscious of his advancing years. With hunger gnawing at his belly, and excruciating pain in his ribs, it would have taken a great deal of energy to convey a regal, confident demeanour. But, in fact, Edward did not lead the advance in person. Judging from Guisborough's account, which can be partly corroborated by the *Falkirk Roll of Arms*, it appears that Edward led the third of four battalions of cavalry in column, with Surrey commanding the reserve. Edward's banner would provide a point of focus and inspiration on the field, but it was common for a medieval general to hold himself somewhat aloof in a battle – at least at first.[43]

The first battalion of cavalry was commanded by the earls of Norfolk, Hereford and Lincoln; the second was led by the bishop of Durham. Guisborough tells us that the vanguard encountered the loch and was forced to make a substantial detour, but the bishop of Durham's battalion took a more direct route across the Westquarter Burn. It is said that the bishop, feeling dangerously exposed, sought to restrain his men, instructing them to wait for the king's division; presumably the infantry forces were also following some way behind. However, one of Bek's knights, a Yorkshireman by the name of Sir Ralph Basset, was scornful of the bishop's caution. Taunting Bek, he urged the bishop to return to his mass, while Basset and his companions would do all that was necessary to prove their knightly courage. At this, the bishop's men pushed on towards the Scottish army.

The mounted knight, resplendent on his charger, remains the most enduring image of the Middle Ages. Nevertheless, modern historians have (rightly) stressed that heavy cavalry only very rarely won battles without the effective support of other units – even during this period, when the military status of the mounted warrior was possibly at its height.[44] That said, it appears that Edward's cavalry now led the attack. As the first wave of cavalry neared the target, we might have seen Edward looking on, sitting taut in the saddle, anticipating the shock of impact. As a much younger man, he had led a successful cavalry charge at the battle of Lewes, and he must surely have remembered the tumult of emotions as the moment of impact came closer.

* * * *

The psychological aspect of medieval warfare – including the impulse towards courage, as well as its opposite, fear – is a subject that increasingly interests medieval historians.[45] It can be difficult, however, to find sources that provide a truly effective insight into the mindset of medieval warriors. Historians of later periods are often able to make good use of personal testimony by soldiers, but this sort of evidence is only very rarely available to medievalists.

One medieval writer who did address the question of emotion in war was the fifteenth-century Frenchman Jean de Bueil, whose work describes the mental state that some men could achieve in combat:

> When one feels that one's cause is just, and one's blood is ready for the fight, tears come to the eye. A warm feeling of loyalty and pity comes into the heart on seeing one's friend expose his body with such courage . . . and one makes up one's mind to go and die or live with him . . . Do you think that a man who acts in this way will fear death? Not at all; for he is so comforted, so much carried away that he doesn't realise where he is. He simply does not fear anything.[46]

Beuil's work suggests, then, that medieval warriors could draw courage through strong bonds with others or belief in a cause, although other medieval writers did acknowledge the presence of fear on the battlefield.

A rather different approach can be found in *The Vows of the Heron*, a fourteenth-century work which is often described as a satirical romance. Its characters were real people, and the Frenchman Jean de Beaumont is given an interesting speech that subverts traditional 'chivalric' values. It is said that young men, intoxicated by strong wine and seeking to impress 'ladies with white throats and tight bodices', are often given to making extravagant promises to prove their prowess in battle: 'Then we could defeat Yaumont and Agoulant [two Saracen warriors that were often featured in medieval romances], and others Roland and Oliver'. But when the moment of truth draws near, however, the author suggests that reality dawns: 'But when we are in the field, on our trotting warhorses, shields hung around our necks and lances lowered, a great frost numbing us, limbs crushed before and behind, and our enemies advancing on us, then we would like to be in a great cellar, and never make a vow again.'[47]

Of course it is quite possible that some men – with adrenaline pumping through their veins – felt a strange fusion of both the emotions described in the sources quoted above: a mixture of terror and exultation. As they prepared to receive their English enemies, might we have discerned the same heady mixture of fear and excitement among the Scottish spearmen? Almost certainly – and even though the English cavalry had stout protection, doubtless the efforts of the Scottish archers to bring down the horsemen would have been celebrated with roars of approval and defiance. But the Scots archers were too few to halt the English advance. As the English cavalry finally broke into a true charge, from less than a hundred metres away, one could well imagine that for many Scots the overriding feeling was a compulsion to run. We have already seen, though, that Wallace had attempted to instil discipline in his men through a mixture of terror, inspiration and (perhaps) training. Evidently he had been successful in this, because – whatever else may or may not have happened during the battle – the spearmen held their ground.

The clash between the heavy cavalry and the spearmen was a crucial episode in almost every battle of this period, throughout the whole of western Europe.[48] As the cavalry swept towards the ranks of the schiltroms, riding in a tightly packed formation, the Scottish archers would have unleashed a last desperate volley of arrows – but there is no indication to suggest the English attack was stalled. The spearmen themselves, with the butts of their twelve-foot weapons thrust firmly into the ground, presented more formidable opposition. If the ranks of spearmen had wavered, however, then this would have provided an opportunity for the cavalry to drive their horses into any gaps that appeared, thereby breaking up the Scottish formations. But Guisborough's description of the fighting makes it clear that the horsemen were unable to find any weak points – at least not at this stage.

Of course, horses are intelligent animals and will not willingly impale themselves, but the momentum of the English charge must have driven some of the horses onto the spear-points of the Scots; there would have been sickening collisions, breaking weapons as well as killing horses, accompanied by a cacophony of shrieks from men and beasts. This is an occasion, perhaps, when the records can provide useful information to complement the chronicles, as the horse lists demonstrate that more than a hundred men claimed compensation for horses killed at the battle of Falkirk.

It is generally assumed that the initial English attack on the schiltroms was repulsed, but most of the sources indicate that the Scottish cavalry proved much less brave than the spearmen. The role envisaged by Wallace is unclear, but it is implied in several of the chronicles that the Scottish horse fled the field almost immediately in the face of the English advance. But not all of the Scottish nobles fled with the cavalry, and at least some remained to fight on with the infantry. Rather confusingly, Guisborough's account seems to suggest that some of them drew up the infantry into new schiltroms; this has led one historian to argue that it was not until this point that the Scots adopted circular formations.[49] Some of the Scottish archers, now also driven to fighting hand-to-hand, were rallied by Sir John Stewart, but he was quickly killed and many of the archers were cut down by the English cavalry. The paradoxical career of Macduff of Fife also came to an end on the field at Falkirk.

The *Lanercost Chronicle* implies that the English cavalry did most of the fighting at Falkirk – attacking from all sides, as Wallace probably feared – although the narratives by Guisborough and Rishanger suggest that Edward's infantry also played a crucial role. It appears the cavalry drew off, but the static Scottish formations were now at the mercy of Edward's archers and crossbowmen, as well as others who hurled stones. Gaps then appeared, providing an opportunity for the cavalry to charge again, forcing a way between the ranks of the Scottish spearmen. There is evidence to suggest that Edward's infantry also fought hand-to-hand: the *millenar* William de Felton lost his horse at Falkirk, which might imply that he led his men into the fray and that they were consequently heavily engaged.[50]

The Scots were now assailed from all sides, and almost certainly were grievously outnumbered, but even the English *Lanercost Chronicle* makes it clear that those who remained 'stood their ground and fought manfully'.[51] Eventually, however, the Scots' losses took their toll, and the survivors broke and ran. Casualties in a rout were almost always heavy; we have already seen that noblemen, if they were fortunate, might be taken into captivity (honourable or otherwise), but the rank and file were often slaughtered without mercy. The Scottish fugitives were gleefully pursued by Edward's cavalry, as well as by his Welsh infantry (notwithstanding their truculent attitude before the battle). In the words of Rishanger, the Scots 'fell like blossoms in an orchard when the fruit has ripened'. But Edward's men did not quite have things all their own way. The Master of the Knights Templar in England, Brian de Jay, pursued some Scots into a bog; once he became caught in the mud, the Scots turned and killed him.

English sources, as we have seen, were inclined to emphasise the efforts of their own side, whereas Scottish medieval writers ascribed the Scots' defeat to treachery, highlighting the flight of their noble cavalry. The author of *Gesta Annalia* II tells us that the Scottish nobles were consumed with 'burning envy' towards William Wallace, whom they actively betrayed: thus he not only blamed the Comyns for leaving the field (although their presence at the battle is by no means certain), but he also gave a damning role to Robert (VII) Bruce, the future king: 'For, while the Scots stood invincible in their ranks, and could not be broken by either force or stratagem, this Robert Bruce went with one line, under Anthony Bek, by a long road round a hill, and attacked the Scots in the rear; and thus these, who had stood invincible and impenetrable in front, were craftily overcome in the rear.'[52]

The source of this extraordinary story is not known, but it is probably best interpreted as a literary or historical device; the chronicler was a supporter of Robert's son David II (who ruled from 1329 to 1371), a king who sought to rule with *raddure* (vigour, or dread), and he was always happy to incorporate material that highlighted the dangers of unchecked noble power (and therefore also the benefits of strong kingship).[53] Subsequent events demonstrate that if the youngest Robert Bruce was anywhere on the field at Falkirk, he was almost certainly on the side of the Scottish patriots. Nevertheless, this is a tale with a long tradition, and it has undoubtedly contributed to a sometimes ambivalent portrayal of Bruce, both in the historiography and in popular culture.

But what of Edward's most bitter enemy, William Wallace? Alongside the various stories of cowardice and treachery on the part of others, it must be said that William Wallace also saved himself by flight. Yet did this quintessential Scottish hero first fight hard alongside his men, only reluctantly leaving the field at the last possible moment, as many writers would have us believe?[54] A recent attempt to argue otherwise is not intended to denigrate the man or his achievements (which were undoubtedly profound); rather it seeks to make us remember that even the greatest historical figures were once not made of stone.[55]

*   *   *   *

Clearly the outcome at Falkirk can be explained in various ways, but Edward's military reputation is such that a number of historians have given him most of the credit for the English victory, notwithstanding the somewhat chaotic scenes in the English camp in the days and hours before the battle took place. For example, one modern writer has argued that, at a pivotal moment of the battle, 'Edward now took control, recalling the cavalry and advancing his archers and Gascon crossbowmen'.[56] He goes on to conclude that 'Edward's deployment of the various arms at his disposal was masterly – on the day he was the better general'. These are plausible conclusions, and many others have provided similar assessments, but is it really appropriate to give so much of the credit to Edward?

To question Edward's role is not to suggest that a general was unable to influence the outcome of engagements. Battle plans from the Middle Ages may be rare (presumably because they were not usually written down), but those that do survive make it clear that medieval commanders thought hard about tactical issues, and also that they learned from previous events.[57] Moreover, though combat was chaotic and confusing, there were often natural lulls in the fighting, sometimes mutually agreed by both sides,[58] and these could provide the opportunity for commanders to make tactical adjustments as the battle progressed. Orders could sometimes be conveyed by means of trumpets or horns. Fighting generals such as Richard the Lionheart (even though he avoided battles as much as possible) could also sometimes make a dramatic impact through well-timed personal interventions.

Evidence from the horse-lists suggests that all four battalions of cavalry were engaged at Falkirk, and this *may* suggest that Edward was personally involved in the fighting. Regrettably, however, beyond crediting the king with some suitably pious exclamations, the other sources tell us nothing whatsoever about his conduct once battle was joined. Moreover, even though it was surely possible to achieve a degree of cohesion within medieval armies – either by discipline or inspiration – it should never be forgotten that medieval battles were not only won and lost by great men; the outcomes were also determined by the actions of countless individuals, most of whose stories can never now be known. Think again, for example, of William de Felton: a man who was probably in command of a thousand others. The fact that even such a man is an obscure figure today provides a salutary reminder of how little we really know about the bloody reality of medieval combat.

Edward, nevertheless, had his victory and the shame of Stirling (as the English saw it) had been avenged, but Falkirk is not a battle that has left a deep impression in the collective memory of the British Isles. While it *was* celebrated in England, much like Dunbar before it,

1. A possible likeness of Edward I, from the sedilia at Westminster Abbey, dating from the early 1300s. Sedilia (from the Latin word for seat) are benches that were designed to be used by priests officiating at Mass. The sedilia at Westminster are made from oak, rather than the usual stone, and are intricately decorated.

2. Stirling Castle, which was besieged and captured by Edward I on two occasions, most notably in 1304. Stirling's strategic position made it a focal point during the Wars of Independence.

3. The projected site of the Battle of Falkirk. It is thought that Wallace took position on the ridge on the horizon, which is now occupied by a riding school, with Callendar Wood to his rear. The trees in the foreground obscure the view towards the bottom of the valley, through which flow the Glen and Westquarter Burns.

4. Caerlaverock Castle, which was besieged and taken by Edward I in 1300. It was described by the Caerlaverock poet as being 'like a shield'. Simon Ledingham's aerial photograph gives a good sense of the castle's unusual design.

5. The siege of Bothwell Castle, 1302. David Simon's imaginative reconstruction gives a prominent role to *le Berefrey* – the fearsome siege tower that was constructed on Edward I's orders – as well as several trebuchets.

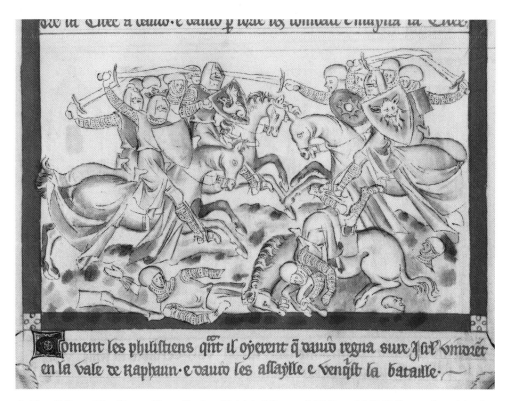

6. Detail from *The Queen Mary Psalter* (British Library MS Royal 2 B VII), produced in the early fourteenth century. This image depicts the army of the biblical King David fighting the Philistines, but the artist has included aspects of arms and armour that would have been familiar to Edward I (including *poleyns*). A variety of headgear is worn here, including closed helms and *bascinets*; the soldier at the top right is wearing a *chapel de fer*.

7. *Right:* A statue of William Wallace, in Aberdeen, created in the 1880s by William Grant Stevenson. There is no contemporary likeness of Wallace; this is an idealistic representation. Wallace is similarly commemorated in many places throughout Scotland.

IN HONOUR OF
WILLIAM WALLACE
GUARDIAN OF SCOTLAND

8. Dunfermline Abbey. Edward I spent the winter of 1303/4 here, with a large following. The abbey buildings were extended and fortified at this time, but much of the complex was destroyed when Edward left the site.

9. A depiction of a Welsh archer, dating from the late thirteenth century. Clerks of the English Exchequer used illustrations such as this one as pictograms; this enabled them to match copies of important documents, in this case related to Wales, to their originals (which would be kept in chests marked with similar images). This is one of several illustrations which portray Welshmen wearing a single shoe, although it is not clear why.

10. The Coronation Chair at Westminster Abbey, commissioned by Edward I to hold the Stone of Destiny. This photograph was taken before the Stone was returned to Scotland in 1996.

11. Lanercost Priory, near Carlisle. Edward I stayed here for several months during the last year of his life. Some of the priory buildings were modified in order to accommodate the king in greater comfort.

12. A statue of Robert Bruce, King of Scots, by Charles d'Orville Pilkington Jackson. The face is partly based on a cast of Bruce's skull, which was made when his skeleton was exhumed in the early nineteenth century. The statue was created in the 1960s and now stands near the Bannockburn Visitor Centre, Stirling.

the tone of the surviving evidence suggests that victory was only to be expected. In the contemporary *Song of the Scottish War*, for example, Edward is depicted as a righteous avenger whose anger is sanctioned on high. Wallace, by contrast, is characterised as a vain man who had received his just deserts.[59] His knightly status is mocked – it is as if 'a swan is made out of a raven' – and he is 'scarcely better than a mouse'. And there are some harsh words for the Scottish leader that any man in his position would surely have felt keenly: 'thy people now drink of the cup which thou hast prepared'.

In modern times, the cultural impact of the battle of Falkirk has also been somewhat limited north of the border. From a Scottish perspective, clearly the battle was no Bannockburn, but it also lacks the dark glamour of Flodden, where the king of Scots died fighting heroically amidst his men. James IV was famously criticised by one foreign visitor because he was always 'the first in danger' and took too many risks,[60] but the king patiently explained that he could not ask his subjects to do something he was not willing to do himself. Even if James did make mistakes in the lead-up to the battle – for which he paid dearly – a medieval king who showed solidarity with his people is easy to admire. The popular Scottish tradition of Falkirk, by contrast, is one of betrayal: a betrayal of ordinary Scotsmen by the members of an elite whose approach to warfare was (or so it would seem) the exact opposite of James IV's. In part this is a myth, but, like the majority of myths, it may contain a kernel of truth.

There are no reliable figures for the casualties on the Scottish side. Guisborough and Rishanger provide absurd numbers – 56,000 and 100,000, respectively – but we must surely assume that thousands were killed. On the English side the author of the *Lanercost Chronicle* was pleased to note that 'there were no noble men killed . . . except the Master of the Templars and five or six esquires',[61] but of course this does not account for fatalities among the infantry. Records show that more than three thousand of the infantry were suddenly removed from the pay roll. As one modern historian has put it, 'we are left to draw the inevitable conclusion that these men fell at Falkirk, the silent, but significant, casualties of an English victory'.[62] The battle of Falkirk should be remembered, on both sides of the border, as a tragic episode in medieval British history.

Chapter 6

The Days Were Long and Fine

Edward's campaign of 1298 had come close to disaster, but his victory at Falkirk restored the military reputation of the English and their king. In contrast, the Scots' defeat was a damaging blow to the credibility of 'William the Conqueror', and shortly afterwards Wallace resigned as Guardian of Scotland. Perhaps he was compelled to do so; from this point onwards the acknowledged leaders of the patriot cause – including members of the Bruce and Comyn families – would be drawn from Scotland's traditional elite. Yet Wallace remained a significant figure; he continued to play a role in more limited operations against the English, and subsequently took part in Scottish embassies overseas. What is more, Edward did not even come close to regaining full control of Scotland at this time, notwithstanding the horrific losses the Scots had suffered.

As we have seen, the English pay rolls suggest that Edward's own army had suffered heavy casualties at Falkirk, although it is likely that desertion shortly afterwards had also thinned the English ranks. Falkirk must also have sapped the energies of the king himself, given the injuries he had suffered before the battle, and he needed time to recover. A two-week siege of Stirling was necessary to recapture the castle, but this also provided an opportunity for Edward to recuperate. When the king pressed on with the campaign, English forces traversed the country, as in 1296, presumably attempting to overawe the populace (and their leaders) through a further show of force. St Andrews was spared – apparently as a mark of respect to the local saint – but Perth was sacked.

Edward himself moved westwards, towards Ayr. It is generally assumed that he was in pursuit of Robert (VII) Bruce, giving the lie to the notion that the younger Bruce fought for the English at Falkirk.

Edward met with little further resistance, although Bruce would prove to be an elusive quarry – as would many others. It had already become clear that the battle of Falkirk would not prove to be as decisive as Edward had hoped. The English king was now in command of a smaller, more mobile force, but the victualling of his army continued to pose problems. At Ayr Edward found the castle empty and in ruins (it was burned on Bruce's orders), and the Irish supply ships he was expecting never arrived. By this time, too, the sense of unity that Edward had established with his barons was starting to fracture.

Most of Edward's greatest subjects did not generally fight for pay, but they did expect to be rewarded for their service, and one way for him to do this was to grant them lands that had been forfeited by his enemies. It has been suggested that there was some lingering resentment over the way Edward had divided up the spoils of war in the wake of his Welsh conquest (particularly on the part of Norfolk and Hereford, who had received nothing at all), and the king had agreed that he would not grant lands in Scotland without the advice of his nobles.[1] With that being the case, there was understandable disquiet at Edward's arbitrary decision to grant the Isle of Arran to Sir Thomas Bisset (an Irish nobleman who had recently captured the island from the Scots). Norfolk and Hereford also began to gripe about monies they believed were due to them in their capacities as marshal and constable.

With supplies and morale now running low, it was considered prudent to retire towards England. Nevertheless, Edward was able to capture a number of other Scottish castles which had been held by the patriots. He also took possession of the important Bruce fortress of Lochmaben. In part this might be seen as a swipe against the younger Robert Bruce, even though Lochmaben was still technically owned by Bruce's father (who remained consistently loyal to Edward, and ultimately died in England). Lochmaben became the site of the first of Edward's *peles* in Scotland; the word 'pele' is derived from the old French word *pel*, meaning a wooden stake, and the peles were essentially fortified encampments that covered a large area of ground.[2] Edward remained in arms as late as October, when he took Jedburgh Castle; this consolidated the English control of south-eastern Scotland.

By this time, though, Norfolk and Hereford had long since left the army, pleading that their men were now exhausted; many others had followed their lead. As the winter drew in, Edward based himself at Newcastle, where preparations were made for the defence of the English position in southern Scotland: it was obvious that further campaigns would surely be necessary, although Edward was determined to hold on to his most recent gains.[3] Garrisons were placed in important castles, in addition to a more sizeable force, more than a thousand strong, which was based at Berwick. There was also concern for the defence of northern England, where a series of military appointments were made. The most significant landowners in the northern counties (those men whose lands were worth more than £30 per year) were persuaded to provide a mobile force of cavalry.

Given its crucial strategic position, there was a particular emphasis on the defence of Stirling. By early December the castle was already threatened by the Scots, and a force of several hundred men was organised to relieve the castle. Edward took a close personal interest in these activities; Sir Alexander Convers, an important royal clerk who was involved in the logistical aspects of the operation, was informed by the king that he expected the 'expedition to be done as hastily as you can but in such a good way and surely'.[4] The English relief force does appear to have successfully completed its mission – at least temporarily – and at the same time supplies were collected at Berwick to be conveyed to Stirling in due course. The stockpile included sixty quarters of wheat, sixty quarters of barley and sixty quarters of oats: enough to provision the garrison for around eight months.

In 1296 Edward had envisaged that castles would perform a dual role in Scotland – as administrative centres as well as military bases – but in the coming years their military function would be paramount. Many of the garrisons were relatively small: in 1298, for example, the garrison at Stirling numbered sixty-three. However, there were somewhat larger garrisons at a number of other Scottish castles, such as Roxburgh, where the soldiers were also expected to maintain order throughout a wider area; Lochmaben, now securely under royal control, was particularly important in this respect. Overall, it has been calculated that the garrisons equated to a small standing army, and naturally this made for an expensive commitment; the keepers of the castles were employed under contract, and their men were paid from the monies allocated to the commanders.

Victualling estimates for the garrisons were extremely generous, including large quantities of alcohol. A complex administrative and logistical network was put in place, and Edward's officials (such as John Droxford and John de Weston, as well as the aforementioned Convers) deserve great credit for this. In some areas, moreover, there is evidence to suggest that the English were able to purchase provisions from local Scottish people. At Stirling, for example, a woman called Eva was later imprisoned by the patriots and exiled from Scotland because she had collaborated with the English garrison there.[5] But English efforts were also dependent on a regular flow of money and supplies from the south, and this would prove more difficult to achieve.

*   *   *   *

When Edward himself turned southwards, at the end of the year 1298, he was already making plans for a further expedition to Scotland. For most of the next year, however, he would find himself distracted by other issues. In part this was due to renewed discontent on the part of his English subjects. Whilst the unity that had made the Falkirk campaign possible had undoubtedly owed a great deal to a genuine sense of outrage at the defeat at Stirling, and a renewed sense of purpose against a common foe, it had also been important that Edward had granted concessions to his critics. Now there was a growing feeling that the king had failed to deliver on his promises.

The key issue concerned the Royal Forest, which at this time encompassed large swathes of the English countryside (including unwooded areas under cultivation). During his time in Flanders Edward had agreed to reissue the famous Forest Charter, which was originally enacted in 1217, but as yet there was little indication that he was willing to act on the implications of this. The first clause of the charter committed the king to a 'perambulation', or inspection, of the Forest boundaries. This had, indeed, been carried out in 1225, but Henry III, Edward's father, had repudiated the agreed changes two years later; it was therefore anticipated that Edward would order a new perambulation. From Edward's point of view this was unpalatable because it was certain that the assessors would recommend a reduction in the Forest bounds. This was desirable in many local communities because the Forest was governed by different (and often more arbitrary) laws.

The question of the Royal Forest, among other matters, was discussed at two parliaments in the first half of 1299. The earl of Hereford had died and been succeeded by his son and heir, who appears to have been a less rebarbative character (and later married one of Edward's daughters), but the earl of Norfolk remained an outspoken critic of the king. Eventually, despite some uncharacteristically hamfisted attempts at prevarication, Edward was prevailed upon to confirm that a perambulation would once again take place. Whilst it may not seem immediately obvious how this issue is relevant to Scottish affairs, it has already become apparent that Edward's domestic troubles could have a great impact on his ability to wage war effectively elsewhere.

As was so often the case, Edward was also preoccupied with relations with France. In the previous year the kings of England and France – accepting a point of stalemate – had submitted their dispute over Gascony to the arbitration of Pope Boniface. Curiously, however, it was agreed that Boniface would act in a private capacity, not as the head of the Church. The Pope decided that Edward should be restored to all of his French lands, but in the event Philip the Fair retained control of much of Gascony (at least for now). Nevertheless, the idea of an Anglo-French marriage was revived. Here, then, was a symbol of progress, and Edward was now keen to marry again. A future marriage was planned between Edward's son, Edward of Caernarfon, and Philip's daughter Isabella. At this time Isabella was still too young to marry, but in June 1299 it was concluded that Edward I would marry Philip's sister Margaret as soon as was practically possible.

The Scottish patriots still maintained hopes of active French support, so these developments caused anxiety north of the border. However, the latest round of diplomacy did have one promising outcome for the Scots. By this time the Scots were also lobbying at the papal court (though French influence was also significant), and Edward subsequently agreed to surrender John Balliol into the neutral hands of the Pope: this was probably interpreted in Scotland as the first step towards a process of arbitration (although he did retain Balliol's son in captivity). At first sight, then, this was a puzzling decision on Edward's part, although the *Lanercost Chronicle* suggests that the king felt obliged to act 'out of obedience to the Holy Curia'. Perhaps John Balliol's release might also be viewed as a calculated gamble on Edward's part, helping to prepare the ground for the achievement of larger objectives. In fact, this concession cost Edward little in the short term (although it did have implications later).

On 18 July 1299 John Balliol was escorted across the Channel and delivered into the custody of the Pope's representative, the bishop of Vicenza. Thereafter he lived for some time in various places, including the abbot of Cluny's residence at Gevrey-Chambertin. As Balliol was leaving England, however, his baggage was impounded and opened. It included money and plate, some of which was returned to him. In a small, though perhaps not insignificant, act of defiance, Balliol had also somehow managed to conceal the Scottish royal seal and a golden coronet. It will come as no surprise to learn that both of these items were confiscated.

By the end of August all the preparations had been made for Edward's marriage. On 10 September he rode into Canterbury to meet his new bride, who was accompanied to England by the dukes of Burgundy and Brittany, as well as a large number of other French nobles. In view of the continued tensions between England and France, one might imagine the atmosphere was somewhat strained. However, the marriage itself, which was solemnised the following day, would prove to be more successful than might have been expected, despite the great age gap between the bride and groom: Edward was now sixty years old, whereas Margaret was probably twenty. Reading between the lines of the conventional reports of her accomplishments and beauty, it was surely important that Margaret appears to have been a sensitive and tactful woman; in particular, she established effective relationships with Edward's children, notably Edward of Caernarfon.[6]

Edward spent the rest of the autumn surrounded by his family and friends, and it is tempting to imagine he found a measure of peace in the company of his young bride. But as the weeks progressed it became clear that the king was impatient to return to Scotland. His commanders there had maintained a regular dispatch of news over the course of the year, and much of it was alarming. The patriots were growing in strength and confidence, and Edward's garrisons were increasingly beleaguered.

* * * *

The Scottish political community remained divided, although many Scottish noblemen were committed to the patriot cause at this time. Two new Guardians were chosen to replace Wallace: Robert (VII) Bruce, earl of Carrick, and John Comyn the younger, the heir to the lordship of Badenoch. (The last time we encountered Comyn he was with Edward in Flanders, but he absconded from Edward's army and made his way back to Scotland.) At this time Bruce had laid aside any pretensions towards the kingship, at least outwardly, because both of the Guardians exercised authority of behalf of the exiled John Balliol. Even so, Bruce and Comyn found it difficult to work together; these two young men, as yet still relatively inexperienced, appear to have developed a mutual antagonism that went beyond their families' long-standing rivalry.

At a meeting held at Peebles on 19 August 1299, the activities of William Wallace were a particular point of contention. By this time Wallace had left for the continent, where he subsequently spent time at the French court, but one of Comyn's followers asserted that he had left Scotland without permission; presumably he had travelled to France with Bruce's blessing, but not Comyn's. There was a heated argument, and Bruce and Comyn came to blows. According to the report of an English spy who had infiltrated the gathering, 'John Comyn leaped at the earl of Carrick and seized him by the throat'.[7]

The unseemly fracas at Peebles led to the appointment of a third Guardian, William Lamberton, bishop of St Andrews, who apparently assumed seniority and was expected to provide a calming influence. But Lamberton's promotion was almost certainly not to the Comyns' liking, because the other John Comyn, the earl of Buchan, had accused the bishop of indulging in treacherous schemes. Evidently Lamberton's loyalty to John Balliol was being called into question here, although the precise implications are unclear.

One might imagine that the divisions between the patriots' leaders would have severely damaged their cause, but they nevertheless appear to have established an effective administration in many parts of Scotland. This was particularly true north of the Forth, especially in the north-east, where the two branches of the Comyn family had reasserted their traditional dominance of the area. Here, control of the port of Aberdeen was vital, because it helped to facilitate continued trade and communication with the continent. South of the Forth, Selkirk Forest once again proved to be a troublesome area for the English, and of course Robert Bruce's earldom of Carrick was also an important centre of resistance to Edward.

The rugged country of south-western Scotland emerged as a key battleground. There was a murderous rivalry here between the English garrison of Lochmaben and the patriot garrison at Caerlaverock. Moreover, even though they are better known as a northern family, it should also be noted that the Comyns exerted considerable influence in this area: the Comyns of Badenoch held Dalswinton Castle, for example, to the north of Dumfries, while the earl of Buchan owned the spectacular clifftop castle of Cruggleton, known as 'the black rock of Cree', near the Isle of Whithorn. Both sides were keen to gain support in Galloway, whose people had long been famous (notorious?) for their warlike qualities and independence of spirit.

As the summer of 1299 progressed, and no substantial English campaign was forthcoming, the patriots became keen to increase the pressure on the English. In the wake of the meeting at Peebles, for example, after a fragile peace had been restored, a substantial force was assembled under the command of Sir Ingram de Umfraville and Sir Robert Keith (who would later become famous for his exploits at the battle of Bannockburn). Their troops were apparently drawn from the retinues of the great Scottish lords who had been present at Peebles; this menacing development was a cause of particular concern to Sir John Hastangs, the English sheriff of Roxburgh. By this time, however, the English administration was already taking steps to respond to the patriot resurgence. On 19 August (the same day as the Peebles meeting) orders were sent north from York by the Treasurer of England, Walter Langton, commanding English officials on both sides of the border to bring in any crops that had not yet been harvested, because he had received intelligence that these would be targets for mobile Scottish forces.[8]

Stirling Castle was a more conventional target for the patriots. We have seen that an initial threat to the English garrison had been repulsed; now the patriots intensified their efforts. Their forces were successively commanded by Sir Herbert Morham and Sir Gilbert Malherbe. Neither appears to have attempted a direct assault on the castle: presumably they lacked the manpower and equipment that would have made such an attack possible. Their main aim was to cut the supply lines from the south, in an effort to starve the garrison into submission.

* * * *

In November 1299 Edward took leave of his wife and travelled north. Disregarding the advice of his council, he attempted to launch another expedition to Scotland, specifically intended to relieve Stirling. Regrettably for Edward, the campaign degenerated into a fiasco. For once the provision of supplies was not an issue, as stockpiles had been built up at Berwick and Carlisle over the course of the year. Indeed, the receiver at Carlisle, Richard Abingdon, found it difficult to find sufficient storage space, notwithstanding the construction of new stores in Carlisle Castle. In fact, Edward's main problem was recruitment. Orders were sent out that 16,500 infantry should assemble at Berwick in mid-December, but only 2,500 men appeared – and most of these quickly deserted.[9]

On this occasion the response from the knightly classes was also disappointing. Along with war-weariness, there were other factors that might deter participation, perhaps above all the cost of campaigning; this was only rarely outweighed in Edward's Scottish wars by the rewards gained through pay, land grants or plunder. Another issue may have been fear of crime. There is some evidence to suggest that criminal elements (especially poachers) exploited the absence of lords, as well as of less exalted figures, to raid the lands of those who had joined the king on campaign. The earl of Surrey appears to have been a notable victim, though it has been noted that he was probably better placed to bear any losses than some other members of the gentry.[10] It was also significant that the promised perambulation of the Royal Forest (which had been scheduled to take place in the autumn) had still not occurred. For some, it has been argued, concern about the boundaries of the Royal Forest was hardening into a point of principle.[11]

The greatest magnates did send substantial retinues to join Edward in the north (including Norfolk, though he was too ill to serve in person), but this should not necessarily be taken as an indication of enthusiasm. According to Rishanger, an English earl (unfortunately unnamed) pointed out the obvious difficulties of waging a major winter campaign in Scotland, arguing strongly that Edward should delay any further operations until the following summer.[12] Ultimately Edward had little option but to acquiesce, providing another reminder that even the most forceful of medieval kings could achieve little in war without the support of the wider community. This disappointment must have come as a bitter blow to Edward, because he had evidently begun to appreciate the limitations of his strategy thus far: spectacular summer campaigns would ultimately prove to be futile without effective consolidation.

The failure of Edward's expedition sealed Stirling's fate. The siege was a long and increasingly grim business – Edward's commander at Stirling, John Sampson, had already held out for more than a year with barely sixty men – but the castle was now completely isolated and provisions were running low. In November there had been an attempt to replenish the castle's supplies: John FitzWalter, the master of the *Godale* of Beverley, was hired to convey provisions from Newcastle and run the blockade. But the mission was unsuccessful. Towards the end of the siege Sampson and his men were compelled to eat their valuable horses; this is known because Sampson later claimed compensation for their loss.[13] The garrison at Stirling was forced to surrender early in 1300; by this time the great castle of Bothwell had also fallen to the patriots. The victors at Stirling permitted their prisoners to return to England, escorting the men as far as Berwick, but this did nothing to alleviate Edward's sense of anger and frustration.[14]

* * * *

In order to be successful in Scotland, it was obviously necessary to secure a consistent supply of money and men, leaving aside more detailed strategic considerations, and Edward grudgingly accepted that this would be extremely difficult without the willing cooperation of his subjects in England. In March 1300, therefore, a new parliament was held, although Edward became increasingly irascible as matters proceeded. Concessions were demanded from the king in return for a tax, and the atmosphere grew tense. There was more pressure concerning the Royal Forest: 'When we have secure possession of *our* woods [my italics], we will willingly grant a twentieth, so that the folly of the Scots may be dealt with.'[15]

Ultimately Edward decided to do without the tax, and to press on regardless with a new Scottish campaign, although he must have realised that his financial position was precarious. The great Italian banking houses were an obvious source of funding that was often exploited by the medieval English kings; during the rest of his reign Edward was sometimes able to secure loans from various Italian families, especially the Frescobaldi. However, there was a limit to the support they were prepared to provide, and these loans did not completely offset the growing shortfall in Edward's finances. Presumably the Italians were mindful of the fate of the Riccardi of Lucca, who were ultimately bankrupted as a result of their earlier relationship with Edward.[16]

There had also been protests in parliament over renewed attempts to link military obligation to landed wealth. Now Edward wisely decided to let this matter drop, although it would appear there was also some reluctance to offer more traditional feudal service. A famous case concerns Hugh fitz Heyr, a minor landowner from Shropshire, who was technically obliged to serve the king 'with bow and arrow'.[17] When Hugh first spied the enemy, as noted by one of Edward's officials, he shot his single arrow and then went home.

Doubtless Hugh's rather literal interpretation of the terms of his tenure was regarded with some amusement at the time – though Edward would probably have preferred him to pay a fine, supplementing the royal coffers, rather than appearing in person. Edward's heavy cavalry would, of course, have received a much warmer welcome. Taking into account the various components of the cavalry, it has been calculated that at least 1,700 mustered in northern England: a good showing, then, but substantially smaller than the mounted force that rode with Edward in 1298.[18]

On this occasion, for the first time in Edward's Scottish wars, royal officials were not instructed to recruit Welsh infantry. Edward explained that 'we have given them leave to remain at home, because of the great work which they have done in our service in the past'.[19] This is often interpreted as an example of the king's sarcastic wit: a veiled reference to the Welsh mutiny before Falkirk.[20] It is more likely, though, that Edward's decision here was motivated by financial considerations: he did not need the consent of parliament in order to levy taxes from the royal lands in Wales, so this time he demanded Welsh money instead of Welsh men. The subsidy that was raised (£2,400, according to one estimate) was intended to pay the wages of an infantry force recruited in northern England; this consisted of some nine thousand men (although Edward had originally hoped for sixteen thousand).[21]

Even though Edward's expectations for the size of the host had been somewhat disappointed, the organisation of provisions remained a substantial operation. Orders for purveyance, in order to replenish the stockpiles in the north, had been set in train as early as 17 January 1300. As always, Edward demanded contributions from various parts of his realm. The sheriffs were given a deadline of 24 June to ensure the delivery of everything requested. By May, however, Edward and his officials had anticipated there was likely to be a shortfall (as witnessed by the pressure on the sheriff of Cambridge and Huntingdon, who was exhorted to make greater efforts). Nevertheless, vast quantities of foodstuffs were purveyed, though it would appear that the northern English counties were more willing to make contributions than their southern counterparts.

As we have seen, ships played a vital role in the conveyance of supplies and equipment, although by this time coastal communities were also chafing at Edward's demands. Relations between Edward and the Cinque Ports, a wealthy confederation of southern seaports, were particularly problematic; the ports believed they were owed money for service given in Edward's Gascon war.[22] Like many of Edward's other subjects, the men of the Cinque Ports were bound to provide the king with wartime service if he issued a feudal summons, but on this occasion Edward accepted that they could provide half of the specified number of ships. (In the event they provided thirty, as opposed to fifty-seven.) After fifteen days of unpaid service (which was clearly insufficient for Edward's needs) their crews would receive wages.[23] However, ships from other places also took part in this campaign; these included eight ships from ports in Ireland, which played an important role in transporting supplies.

* * * *

Edward's army was instructed to muster at Carlisle; obviously this marked a shift in strategy from his previous expeditions. This was a clear acknowledgement that south-western Scotland had become a major theatre of war in the two years since Edward's last effective intervention, and the king was determined to bring this unruly part of the country firmly under English control.

An important source for the ensuing campaign is an anonymous poem entitled *The Song of Caerlaverock*, which describes the early part of Edward's expedition. The poet, who was probably also a herald,[24] took pains to record the names of the leading members of Edward's forces, along with their arms, and his work is therefore a useful source for the composition of the army. The poem also includes brief pen-portraits of some of Edward's commanders, such as Nicholas Segrave, whom 'nature had adorned in body and enriched in heart'.[25] Special praise is reserved for Robert Clifford: 'If I were a young maiden, I would give him my heart and person [body], so great is his fame.'[26] The poem also refers to the love between Ralph de Monthermer and the king's daughter Joan, which led to a secret marriage.[27] Edward's followers are presented here as if they were the heroes of a chivalric romance. That is not to say, however, that the author could not also be a keen observer of military events.

Edward himself arrived at Carlisle on 25 June, and the army marched north in the first week of July. Here is a translation of the Caerlaverock poet's description of the scene, as the campaign now began in earnest:

> There were many rich caparisons embroidered on silks and satins; many a beautiful pennon fixed to a lance; and many a banner displayed. And afar off was the noise heard of the neighing of horses: mountains and valleys were everywhere covered with sumpter horses and wagons with provisions, and sacks of tents and pavilions. And the days were long and fine.[28]

Edward and his army advanced into Scotland via Annandale, stopping off at the royal pele of Lochmaben. At length, on 9 July, the English forces bore down upon the patriot stronghold of Caerlaverock, to the south-east of Dumfries, where Edward laid siege.

Tents and huts were put up for the soldiers, enhanced by 'leaves, herbs and flowers gathered in the woods, which were strewed within'.[29] As usual, the Caerlaverock poem conveys an impression of splendour: 'and one saw gold and silver, and of all rich colours the noblest and the best, entirely illuminating the valley'.[30] One might well imagine there is more than a pinch of poetic licence here, although other sources do suggest that a military encampment could be an impressive sight – at least before the mud and perhaps rain had quenched some of its glamour. The tents of elite warriors could be spectacular, embellished with beautiful embroidery and distinctive features such as cloth towers. They could also be extremely expensive. In the preparations for his first campaign, in 1307, Edward's grandson Gilbert de Clare spent £39 on five tents: these included a hall (which was forty feet long); a wardrobe chamber; a combined pantry and buttery; and two stables.[31]

Servants worked hard to ensure their masters were well catered for: we also know that Gilbert de Clare travelled with a wide range of cooking utensils, including bronze pots, a gridiron and two enormous cooking pans. Of course, though, despite the provision of certain comforts and welcome flashes of colour, life on campaign for the elite was still a long way removed from the lifestyle they enjoyed in times of peace. Only traces remain today, for example, of Edward I's palace at Westminster, yet this spectacular complex – which was beautified by his father and further developed by Edward himself – was surely one of the wonders of the European medieval world. The centrepiece was the remarkable 'Painted Chamber' (which was sadly destroyed by fire in the nineteenth century, although some drawings of its wonderful frescoes are fortunately still available).

In 1300 Caerlaverock Castle was still a recent addition to the local landscape. It had been constructed in the 1270s, when the lords of Caerlaverock, the Maxwells, had abandoned a smaller site nearby that was prone to flooding. The new castle was unusually shaped – as our poet described Caerlaverock, it was a fortress in the shape of a shield – and it incorporated some of the latest facets of design. There were round towers at two points of the triangle, which enabled *enfilade* shooting along the length of the wall, but these were dwarfed by Caerlaverock's most significant feature: its formidable twin-towered gatehouse (which also housed the lord's apartments). A powerful gatehouse of this type was also a feature of Kildrummy Castle, which may later have been strengthened on Edward's orders, as well as in Edward's great castles in Wales.

Caerlaverock, it must be stressed, was not one of Scotland's largest castles. The castle might even be seen primarily as a status symbol, bearing witness to the rise of the Maxwells: it still presents an elegant aspect today. The castle was also well sited for defence, however. The Caerlaverock poem explains that it could only be approached from the east, because on the other sides it was protected by the sea, woods and marshes. Drawing attention to the 'good walls' and deep moat, the poet tells us it was a 'strong castle, which did not fear a siege'.[32] The defences at Caerlaverock appear to have been further strengthened by a *brattice*, or hoarding; this was a wooden shed-like structure, providing additional protection and shooting opportunities for the defenders, which was attached to the top of the walls and projected outwards.

The beginning of a medieval siege often took on a formal, almost ritualised, tone, somewhat at odds with the misery and savagery that so often ensued. As was common, a parley took place. None of the men of the Maxwell family were present at the siege (the current lord was at that time in captivity in England), and the constable, Walter Benechafe, was willing to seek terms. The defenders offered to give up the castle if they were permitted to depart unharmed with their goods (including their arms and horses). But Rishanger, with his usual predilection for a colourful simile, tells us that Edward reacted to this suggestion 'like a lioness whose cubs have been taken from her'.[33] The king was infuriated by what he saw as Benechafe's effrontery in the face of overwhelming odds, and no agreement for surrender could be reached. Thereafter the English onslaught began.

*   *   *   *

Edward did not risk his own person under the walls of Caerlaverock, but his men-at-arms were keen to prove their valour: whilst a frontal assault might seem foolhardy, a successful *escalade* could bring great honour to the men who effected an entrance to the castle. English exploits were diligently recorded by the Caerlaverock poet, as the garrison provided a stubborn defence. We learn, for example, of the fortitude of Ralph de Gorges, 'a newly dubbed knight', who was knocked to the ground several times by stones hurled from the walls, but 'would not deign to retire'.[34]

Gorges, of course, was not acting alone. Many others, we are told, braved arrows or bolts from crossbows. As the poem depicts the English attack, there seems to have been a strongly competitive element; the author took great pains, again, to record the arms or banners of the knights and nobles involved. From a more practical perspective, his work appears to suggest that Edward's men focused most of their efforts on the gatehouse, although it is not clear what methods they employed. This is perhaps due to the poet's emphasis on the deeds of great men: a common feature of narrative accounts from this period. (There is no mention, for instance, of Englishmen using crossbows or longbows, although these must surely have been in evidence.)

We do learn that the castle was also subjected to a bombardment from Edward's siege machines. The engineering corps was under the direction of 'Brother Robert', who was perhaps a Dominican friar. (Taking holy orders did not always preclude military experience, as the activities of Hugh Cressingham and the bishop of Durham have shown.) Brother Robert is described in the records as 'Frater Roberto de Ulmo', and his name is sometimes given in modern accounts as 'Robert of Ulm', which might imply he was from the continent.[35] This is one possibility, although it might also be noted that the Latin word *ulmo* means 'elm', and the name 'de Ulmo' appears quite frequently in medieval English sources.[36] Whatever his origins, Brother Robert evidently knew his business, and he was employed by Edward for several months.

Brother Robert's efforts began with a machine called 'the Robinet', which hurled stones against the castle, although at the same time he was also supervising the fabrication of three much larger weapons.[37] The parts for these engines were landed at Caerlaverock's small harbour (the sea has now retreated almost a kilometre from the castle), along with a welcome replenishment of supplies. These weapons were almost certainly *trebuchets*: the most formidable machines that could be deployed by a besieging army before the introduction of cannon.

Essentially a trebuchet was a giant catapult. Its central component was a long timber beam, with a leather sling at one end and a counterweight at the other. (The counterweight was a large wooden box, filled with heavy material such as stones or sand.) The beam was attached to a pivot rod, which enabled it to rotate within a sturdy wooden frame. The 'throwing arm' of the trebuchet was winched downwards, thereby raising the counterweight, and the machine was 'cocked' by means of a trigger mechanism. When the trigger was released, the counterweight would fall rapidly, the beam would rotate, and a projectile (usually a large round stone) would be unleashed from the sling. It is thought that trebuchets had a range of up to 300 metres.[38] The value of trebuchets continued to be recognised into the early fifteenth century, at which time they were sometimes employed alongside gunpowder weapons.

Brother Robert's siege engines wreaked havoc on the castle's defences. The wear and tear on the mechanism ensured that it was not possible to maintain a continuous rate of shot – medieval sources suggest that trebuchets might launch between ten and twelve missiles over the course of a day – and few trebuchets possessed the capability to smash their way through strongly built walls. Nevertheless, a well-directed trebuchet missile could make short work of wooden hoardings or other additional structures, and the key role played by such machines was to undermine the effectiveness of the defences as 'fighting platforms', making the castle more vulnerable to *escalade*.[39] It is also very likely that the majority of missiles were sent over the walls, rather than against them directly; apparently Brother Robert's most significant achievement was to bring down the roof of the gatehouse. According to the poet, the beleaguered garrison saw this as a decisive moment.

After a day and a half of gruelling punishment, the defenders considered their position untenable, and they could take no more. The sixty-strong garrison put themselves completely at Edward's mercy, and their surrender was now accepted. The Caerlaverock poem implies the defenders had won Edward's respect: not only were the garrison granted 'life and limb', they also each received a 'new robe'.[40] For the author of the poem, with his clear emphasis on chivalric *mores*, Edward's generosity provided a fitting end to the siege. Unfortunately, however, modern historians have been unable to find any evidence of Edward's *largesse* in the administrative records.

Several sources, in contrast, imply that the men of the Caerlaverock garrison were harshly treated. The constable and twenty-one others were imprisoned in northern England; the *Lanercost Chronicle* tells us specifically that 'many' of the defenders were hanged – although its reliability in this instance has been questioned.[41] Moreover, whilst the Caerlaverock poet presented the siege as a marvellous spectacle, Peter Langtoft was rather less impressed: his account provides a rather less heroic impression of the campaign and the siege. He tells us that heavy rain caused flooding, which caused Edward to go a different way from the one planned. It was thus he came to Caerlaverock, which Langtoft describes as a 'poor little castle'. In Langtoft's work the stalwart defenders of the Caerlaverock poem become 'ribalds', who were 'vanquished at the entrance'.[42]

In truth, Caerlaverock Castle was no match for the English royal army, yet Langtoft surely underestimated the importance of Edward's victory: today Caerlaverock is something of a backwater, easily bypassed via the modern A75, but in the Middle Ages the sea-lanes were far more important and the castle's coastal location was significant. We have also seen that the Scottish garrison at Caerlaverock had hindered the consolidation of English control of Annandale. It is therefore very likely that Caerlaverock was a key target, although of course Edward hoped to achieve much more.

* * * *

With Caerlaverock now securely under English control, Edward pressed on into Galloway. Upon reaching the Bridge of Dee on 18 July, he moved south to Kirkcudbright, where the patriot commanders suggested a truce; they offered a cessation of hostilities in exchange for the return of John Balliol as king, together with the restoration of their confiscated lands in England. Unsurprisingly these terms were not acceptable to Edward, and the campaign continued, although the Scots were wary of meeting the English army in battle. Nevertheless, Edward's progress was slow and cautious; probably there were times when the king was kept waiting for seaborne supplies, although the bad weather alluded to by Langtoft might also have been a hindrance. Edward spent twelve days at Kirkcudbright, and then about a week at Twynholm. His next base was at Girthon, near the later settlement of Gatehouse-of-Fleet; a mysterious earthwork at Girthon, known as 'Palace Yard', may provide evidence that Edward had fortified his camp.[43]

Edward's aims do not always seem clear during this campaign. There were at least two occasions, however, when the two sides encountered each other in arms. The first of these took place when an English foraging party was ambushed by the patriots. Initially, quite understandably, the advantage lay with the Scots, but the English responded fiercely and their attackers were driven off. Sir Robert Keith[44] was captured, and was subsequently imprisoned in England for several years. The other episode, which took place at some point during the second week of August,[45] was more significant. Edward and his army reached the River Cree, where they found the patriots arrayed on the opposite bank. By this time Robert Bruce had resigned (or had been removed) as a Guardian, and he held himself aloof from this campaign. However, his replacement, the able Ingram de Umfraville, was present, alongside the Comyns; their presence seems to suggest that the patriots had gathered in considerable strength.

The precise location of this encounter is uncertain, but it can be assumed to have taken place somewhere between modern Creetown and Newton Stewart (then known as Lislas). Rishanger provides an account of the subsequent events.[46] Some of Edward's archers took advantage of the low tide to cross the estuary and harass the Scots, prompting the Scottish leaders to form their army up for battle. Edward sent the earl of Hereford to order the archers to withdraw, but as they believed he was bringing reinforcements they redoubled their efforts.

There were disturbing parallels with Stirling Bridge, when the English army had been similarly divided, but Edward himself now rescued the situation, acting with speed and decisiveness. He spurred his own horse forward and ordered a general assault. At this, the Scots scattered 'like hares before greyhounds', melting away into the rough terrain to the north. It is said that Edward now cursed the fact that he had brought no Welsh troops on this campaign, because the Welsh would surely have relished the pursuit of the Scots in the woods and hills.

On 16 August Edward was at Wigtown, where he appears to have taken stock. By this time his forces were sorely depleted. Presumably he was also running short of cash, because men were leaving the infantry in droves; measures taken to prevent or punish desertion had little effect. Doubtless Edward's nobles also had little appetite for what must have seemed increasingly like aimless wandering, and the king was advised to withdraw. There is documentary evidence to suggest that he had planned to strike northwards towards Ayr,[47] but the campaign now came to a desultory end.

* * * *

On his way back to England Edward spent some time at the beautiful Sweetheart Abbey, where John Balliol's mother was laid to rest alongside his father's heart. Here, Edward received a most unwelcome guest: Archbishop Winchelsey of Canterbury, with whom he had already clashed earlier in his reign. The problem now, though, concerned the message the archbishop conveyed from Rome. By this time, or so it would appear, Pope Boniface had been convinced of the merits of the Scottish case against Edward. Upon pain of suspension from his office, Winchelsey was compelled to travel north (suffering various hardships on the way), and obliged to present a broadside from Boniface. The document in question is known as *Scimus, Fili*: 'We know, my son'.[48]

The Pope's words must have been galling for Edward; they rehearsed many of the arguments that the Scots would themselves have put forward, castigating Edward for his policies against the Scots and for exploiting their weakened state. Edward permitted Winchelsey to read to the end of the document (first in Latin, and then in French), but then followed the predictable outburst: 'By God's blood! For Zion's sake I will not be silent, and for Jerusalem's sake I will not rest, but with all my strength I will defend my right [in Scotland] that is known to all the world.'[49]

In time, however, the Pope would receive a more measured response. This would follow in the next year, when the Pope was sent a detailed rebuttal of his claims, presenting arguments drawn both from recent precedent and antique myth.

In early September Edward returned to Cumbria. He spent some time at Rose Castle, a residence of the bishop of Carlisle, and also at Holm Cultram Priory. He was joined by his wife, who had recently given birth to their first son, Thomas of Brotherton (the eldest of three children). Nevertheless, Edward was also determined to maintain some impetus in Scotland. The true hero of the siege of Caerlaverock, Brother Robert the Engineer, was still employed in Edward's service. In mid-September Robert and a team of carpenters were busy in the royal Forest of Inglewood, to the south of Carlisle, selecting and gathering wood for use in the construction of a new pele at Dumfries.[50] Presumably the timber was shipped across the Solway Firth. We next find Brother Robert at Dumfries itself, in October, where Edward also appeared (in order to encourage the workmen, who received a small bonus). Edward was still at Dumfries when he agreed to a new meeting with representatives of the patriot leaders.

Once again the Scots proposed a truce, but Edward was

contemptuous of the terms they offered. Affecting astonishment at their presumption, the king laughed in their faces: 'Every one of you has done homage to me as chief lord of Scotland. Now you set aside your allegiance and make a fool of me as though I were a weakling.'

Conscious of the dignity of his office, one of the envoys refused to be cowed: 'You should not laugh: we offer peace in all seriousness. Exert your strength and see if might will triumph over right or right over might.'

At this, Edward's mood darkened. He warned the Scottish envoy that he would punish any further insolence by wasting Scotland from sea to sea.[51]

In truth it is likely that both sides would have welcomed a period of respite, and the ongoing Anglo-French negotiations provided Edward with a useful pretext. On 31 October Edward announced that he had accepted a personal request from Philip the Fair to agree to a truce in Scotland, and this would last until Whit Sunday (21 May) 1301. Edward did stress, in the writ sent out to all his officers, that Philip had intervened as a friend, rather than as an ally of the Scots: this was an important distinction to Edward, of course, because any formal acknowledgement of the 'Auld Alliance' would have implied his acceptance of Scotland's status as a sovereign power.

Work at Dumfries continued throughout the winter, but Edward himself turned south. His most recent Scottish campaign had started well, with the capture of Caerlaverock, but thereafter he had achieved very little. A few more Scottish prisoners would face years of captivity in England, but most of the patriot army had escaped unscathed. Once again Langtoft compared Edward to King Arthur, although this time unfavourably: Langtoft's work implies that Edward had lost some of his former vigour, because he slept too long in the mornings.[52] Perhaps Edward understood that he would need to conserve his energy for the further struggles to come? He had now invaded Scotland at the head of three great English armies, yet a final victory remained as elusive as ever.

Chapter 7

To Annoy His Enemies

The building work ordered at Dumfries in late 1300 was intended to be supported by other activity. After the removal of the English royal army from south-western Scotland it now fell upon Edward's lieutenant in the area, Sir John de St John, 'to bring to a good end his [Edward's] business in these parts'.[1] St John had been captured in Edward's service in Gascony, as we have seen, and spent almost a year as a prisoner of the French. He was not left to rot, however, because he was a man whom Edward greatly valued. After struggling to raise sufficient funds, Edward eventually paid a large ransom to obtain St John's release. St John returned to England in time to take part in the Falkirk campaign, and in January 1300 he was appointed Warden of the Western March. His remit included responsibility for military affairs in three English counties (Cumberland, Westmorland and Lancashire), as well as in much of south-western Scotland (at least in theory).

St John followed in the footsteps of several others – including Robert Clifford, over whom the Caerlaverock poet swooned – but all had so far proved unequal to the task. Indeed, Clifford had specifically asked to be relieved of his office – probably due to financial difficulties – but he continued to take an active role in Scotland. He agreed to serve under St John for pay, as well as certain other privileges, though it was firmly stipulated that he should not take action on his own initiative. Clifford, it would seem, was widely admired as a dynamic soldier, whereas John de St John was a man who could take a broader view. St John was a proven administrator, as well as an experienced warrior, and Walter of Guisborough believed that his governance of Gascony had been popular with local people.[2]

Towards the end of 1300 Edward hoped that St John would be able to bring Scotsmen 'to the king's peace', thus avoiding the need to crush them into submission.

That is not to say, of course, that Edward had abandoned his more extensive military ambitions in Scotland, but his financial difficulties were now acute. A new parliament took place at Lincoln early in 1301. Edward (speaking through Roger Brabazon, the chief justice of the King's Bench) bluntly stated his need for funds. But the king had already anticipated that in some areas he would need to give ground in his negotiations with parliament, because he expected more in return. On this occasion he requested a tax of a fifteenth from the laity, rather than the twentieth that had been demanded the previous year. The concessions sought from the king were outlined in a bill put forward by a Lancashire knight, Henry de Keighley. For Edward, the content of this bill must have seemed depressingly familiar, not least because the reform of the Royal Forest was yet again the main item on his critics' agenda.

By this time the perambulation of the Forest had, finally, been carried out. As expected, the findings – in some cases admittedly drawing upon a rather dubious store of local memories – suggested that the Forest bounds should be drastically reduced. Edward eventually agreed to accept the 'advice' of a committee appointed to rule on the matter, and the members endorsed the results of the perambulation. Yet they also received an ominous reminder that Edward's subjects had sworn oaths to uphold the rights of the crown – as had Edward himself, at the time of his coronation – and understandably this led to fears that the king would later seek vengeance against 'traitors'.

Edward did indeed refuse to forget (or forgive) this setback,[3] because he saw it as an assault on the royal dignity, and the acceptance of the committee's judgement was the major point conceded at Lincoln. However, Edward also confirmed another concession that had been discussed in the previous parliament. This had direct implications for the war effort in Scotland, because it was agreed that the use of prise – a royal right that was originally intended to provide for the king's household, and not for entire armies – would be severely curtailed.

Edward had accepted a (temporary) political defeat in return for the grant of the tax, but it is important to remember that his concessions were restricted to specific issues and were clearly defined. Ultimately the Lincoln Parliament would prove to be the last great domestic challenge of Edward's reign. Outside England, of course, his troubles continued – not least because the king of France continued to be a thorn in his side. A return to open warfare between England and France had been averted, but Philip the Fair was now arguing that he was unable to consent to a *lasting* peace (and therefore the full restoration of Gascony) unless his allies, the Scots, were also included. More positively, in the wake of receiving Pope Boniface's letter at Sweetheart Abbey, Edward had dispatched the earl of Lincoln to the papal court, accompanied by a high-powered embassy, and his ambassadors had received a surprisingly warm welcome.

Pope Boniface was a man who collected quarrels; at this time he was seeking to launch a 'crusade' against the kingdom of Sicily, having excommunicated King Frederick III, and as a result he needed funds. A deal was struck whereby the Pope would levy a tax of 10 per cent on the English church for three years, but Edward would be entitled to half of the profits. This neatly undermined the position of Archbishop Winchelsey of Canterbury, who had continued to oppose Edward's requests for financial assistance on the basis that papal approval was necessary. Less positively, the increasing respect accorded to John Balliol in papal circles was a more disturbing development, and John himself appears to have taken a renewed interest in the affairs of Scotland at this time. By the spring of 1301 a new sole Guardian, Sir John Soules, who had spent time in France, emerged as the leader of the patriots in Scotland; it is generally accepted that he was personally appointed by the exiled king.

* * * *

The impending tax revenues in England meant that Edward's financial position was stronger, at least potentially, than it had been for several years. Of course, the fifteenth and the 'crusading' tax monies would not appear in the king's treasury immediately, but Edward now felt able to make plans with confidence for a renewed offensive in Scotland. The next campaign also had personal significance for Edward because he expected it to mark the emergence of his eldest son as a warrior to be respected and feared (even though the boy was still only seventeen). By this time the younger Edward had already gained military experience – he had taken part in the most recent campaign in Scotland, albeit under the watchful eye of the trusted John de St John – but on this occasion he would receive his first independent command. As Edward explained in one of his letters, he wished Edward of Caernarfon to have 'the chief honour of taming the pride of the Scots'.[4]

Edward's relationship with his eldest son was complex. Edward of Caernarfon was the only surviving boy from the king's marriage to the late Queen Eleanor, and his father heaped upon the boy's shoulders expectations that would have weighed heavily on any man. The younger Edward did have some personal qualities. He was tall and strong, like his father, and well suited to martial pursuits. Moreover, whilst he was later characterised as 'luckless and chicken-hearted in war',[5] in truth he was no coward. There were aspects of his personality, however, that would prove him to be ill-suited to kingship and military command. Most significantly, he relied too heavily on his favourites, notably the handsome Gascon Piers Gaveston (although whether his relationship with Gaveston was homosexual in nature, as is often supposed, remains an open question). But of course most of Edward of Caernarfon's failures still lay far in the future, and at this time Edward I still had high hopes for his son.

At the age of sixty-two, Edward I must surely have been acutely aware of his own mortality. In accordance with his new status as king-in-waiting, Edward of Caernarfon received a substantial endowment of lands, the core of which was provided by the royal holdings in Wales. Following his birth at Caernarfon, the young Edward had had no further connection with the Welsh, but now he was given the formal title prince of Wales (starting a tradition that has continued to the present day). In April Edward of Caernarfon travelled to his new principality, where he received the homage of his leading Welsh subjects, as well as the fealty of the powerful Marcher lords. In May the two Edwards spent time together at Kenilworth – then one of England's greatest castles, with its distinctive red sandstone walls enveloped by a vast expanse of water – where they were also joined by the queen. In early June father and son set out for the north, seemingly united in the pursuit of a common goal.

In some respects the plans for the ensuing campaign were the most ambitious of the entire war. Along the way Edward and his son parted company, because it had been decided that the invasion forces would consist of not one but two armies: the first army, under Edward himself, would muster at Berwick and strike from the east; the other, under the prince (assisted by the earl of Lincoln), would gather in the west at Carlisle. Edward's strategy in this campaign, then, was more akin to a vice than a hammer; any resistance to the English in southern Scotland would be crushed into submission by the weight of the combined onslaught. Ultimately, it is possible that Edward hoped to push on into northern Scotland, but the primary objective was surely to consolidate English control of Scotland below the rivers Forth and Clyde.

Both the English armies were substantial. More than a thousand English landowners were individually called upon to provide cavalry service for Edward's army – another innovation that was never repeated – but unfortunately it is not clear how many appeared. However, the records show that, in addition to the cavalry, Edward gathered 7,500 infantry.[6] The prince's army, naturally enough, was mostly recruited in Wales, and may have been somewhat larger than his father's. The prince was also later joined in Scotland by forces from Ireland. The king was disappointed that Richard de Burgh, the powerful earl of Ulster, did not join the host, but the justiciar of the lordship, John Wogan, brought over two thousand troops to swell the prince's numbers. Wogan's forces included more than three hundred *hobelars*; these lightly armoured mounted infantry, riding small, tough horses, would play an increasingly important role in Anglo-Scottish warfare.

In the coming campaign it was ordained that supplies should be landed on Arran (which was still held by Thomas Bisset of Antrim), as well as being conveyed by sea to the more usual destinations of Berwick and Skinburness, which would suggest that the routes of the armies were well planned. However, the recent agreements concerning the use of prise meant that Edward had to tread carefully when he requested provisions. On this occasion the crown entered negotiations with representatives from the counties to determine the amounts that would be supplied, rather than imposing arbitrary quotas (as had been the case in the past). The sheriffs were not instructed to gather resources until agreements were reached, and the counties of Derby and Nottingham were even permitted to appoint their own collectors. The purveyance of foodstuffs was specifically described as a loan, and payment was to be made from the proceeds of the fifteenth.

In fairness to Edward and his advisers, we have seen that they had recognised for some time that purveyance was a considerable burden; as early as 1296 concern had been expressed about the effects on the poorest.[7] Payment for purveyance remained sluggish and uncertain, however, and Edward's demands continued to cause resentment for the rest of his reign. Two years later feelings were running particularly high in Yorkshire, whose people had made a particularly telling contribution to Edward's war effort in Scotland over the years.[8] There were allegations of corruption through false accounting: there were complaints that if the collectors took five quarters of wheat, the official record would state that only four had been received. In Sleford one of the collectors, William of Wetwang, was pursued by a local man carrying a drawn sword.

The system of purveyance was never perfected, and Edward's commissioners encountered increasing reluctance in some areas when they sought to recruit infantry. Nevertheless, it has been well observed that in 1301 men and resources were gathered 'from every obedient corner of Edward's "British" empire', so that the one 'rebel province', Scotland, would be finally brought to heel.[9] It should also be remembered, however, that many Scotsmen remained in Edward's allegiance at this time. One such was Sir Simon Fraser, the hereditary keeper of Selkirk Forest. Fraser had been captured during the Dunbar campaign, but had earned his freedom through service in Flanders. Thereafter he had been trusted to take on his family's traditional role – an extremely sensitive office, given the recent history of resistance in the Forest – and he had remained in post for nearly three years.

The English constable of Edinburgh Castle, John Kingston, had serious doubts about Fraser's loyalty to Edward, and in the summer of 1299 he accused Fraser of writing letters intended to lure him away from Edinburgh, which was subsequently attacked by the patriots. Fraser's integrity appeared to be proven when he was taken prisoner by the patriots and endured a brief period in captivity, and he was rewarded for his efforts in Scotland by becoming a member of Edward's household. Now, though, in the summer of 1301, with Edward's armies once again bearing down upon Scotland, Fraser resolved to change sides. Kingston's suspicions were finally confirmed when Fraser left Wark under cover of darkness, stealing the horse and armour of one of his colleagues, before riding hard across the border. Fraser's career in Edward's service was perhaps echoed by later Scots in English allegiance: 'But all or most of the Scots who were with the English were with them insincerely or to save their lands in England; for their hearts if not their bodies were always with their own people.'[10]

*   *   *   *

As Edward's forces marched into Scotland once more, in the summer of 1301, it might be suggested that Simon Fraser had chosen an inopportune moment to let his heart rule his head. It is possible, though, that the patriots expected great things from the diplomatic negotiations going on overseas. Certainly there were important developments in progress on the continent (which will be discussed in more detail below), but as the campaign progressed the English did enjoy some successes in the field. In July the prince of Wales penetrated deeply into south-western Scotland, bypassing much of Galloway and striking across country to Ayr. Here he met with the Irish, as well as having the opportunity to replenish his supply train. By the end of the month Prince Edward had taken the castle at Ayr – which had been left in peace for almost three years – and thereafter his forces moved southwards, along the coast.

Robert Bruce's own movements remain obscure in this period, but there is some evidence to suggest the younger Edward's army encountered some resistance from the patriots in Ayrshire.[11] The prince appears to have spent around another month in this area, during which time he also captured Turnberry Castle: this was Bruce's most cherished possession and the *caput* of his earldom of Carrick. English garrisons were established at Ayr and Turnberry to ensure that both of Prince Edward's prizes would be retained. Ayr became an important supply depot and centre of administration.

In the meantime, King Edward himself had been making laborious progress through the heart of southern Scotland, advancing cautiously through the wild country of Selkirk Forest, travelling via Selkirk, Traquair and Peebles. He was at Coldstream on 20 July, but it took a further month for him to reach Glasgow, where he received the pleasing news of his son's successes to the west. The king also set plans in motion for the siege of Bothwell Castle. As far as the Scots were concerned, by this time Bothwell had been inherited by the three-year-old son of the late Andrew Murray (although the boy himself was growing up in the safety of the north). Edward, on the other hand, declared the castle and lordship of Bothwell to be forfeit (the latter was thought to be worth around £1,000), and both were granted to Aymer de Valence. But first, of course, Edward would need to take the castle, and its patriot garrison showed a willingness to fight.

Bothwell, at this time, was another modern Scottish castle. Whilst the extravagant plans of William Murray *le riche* had never been completed, even in its unfinished state Bothwell was substantially more formidable than Caerlaverock. The castle's most significant feature was its massive round keep, or *donjon*, which is thought to have been modelled on similar examples in northern France (most notably at Coucy). In order to overcome the castle's defences Edward ordered the fabrication of a giant wooden siege tower, *le Berefrey* [Belfry]. As was the case with most siege engines, Berefrey was moved in parts before being assembled at the scene. It took two days and thirty carts to convey the beast from Glasgow, a journey of about ten miles, and a new bridge was hastily constructed across the Clyde.[12] The Scottish earl of March, who remained in Edward's allegiance, provided three *ballistae* (which resembled giant crossbows), and the besieging forces also included a party of miners from the Forest of Dean.

Unfortunately there are no good narrative accounts of the siege of Bothwell, so it is not known precisely how Berefrey was employed, although historians have a clear sense more generally of how siege towers might be used.[13] Siege towers were often mounted on wheels, and could be as much as eighty or ninety feet tall. Usually several storeys high, their sides were covered with wetted ox-hides (because siege towers were otherwise vulnerable to incendiary assaults). A drawbridge near the top of the tower would allow the men inside to access the ramparts of the castle, and many siege towers incorporated a battering ram near the base. However, the key role played by siege towers was to provide a fighting platform for archers and crossbowmen; this was vital in order to counter missiles from the defenders, as well as offering covering fire for an escalade or an attempt to undermine the castle's walls.

Naturally the defenders would not sit idly by while a siege tower was wheeled into position. It would sometimes be necessary for the besiegers to fill in ditches, or perhaps even to construct a corduroy road, made from carefully placed logs, to enable passage over rough ground; all this time the defenders would have maintained a constant stream of missiles. *Mantlets* (wooden or wicker screens) would provide some protection for the labourers, but this was difficult and dangerous work. Ultimately, though, it does seem that Berefrey played a significant role at the siege, because a siege tower known as 'Bothwell' was present at Edward's siege of Stirling three years later: this might well have been the same machine.[14] Even so, the defenders at Bothwell seem to have offered resistance for at least two weeks, although it is certain that the castle must have fallen by 22 September, at which point Edward moved on.

* * * *

What was the response of Sir John de Soules as Edward's armies advanced through Scotland? The Guardian continued the strategy of the previous campaign, and both Edward and his son found the Scots to be elusive. The *Lanercost Chronicle* tells us that the patriots 'would not fight with either army, but fled as they had done the previous year. Howbeit they took some fine spoil from the English and did much other mischief.'[15] Clearly Soules was reluctant to offer battle, although his caution does not imply cowardice or indolence. Soules did not owe his promotion as Guardian to his military talents (he was a skilled politician, as well as a stalwart patriot), but he was determined to limit the impact of Edward's latest invasion. What is more, he became more confident and aggressive as the campaign progressed, manoeuvring his forces with considerable flair.

In early September Edward received word from Sir Robert Tilliol, based at Lochmaben, informing him that the patriots (now including Sir Simon Fraser) had gathered in strength in central Ayrshire, controlling the road between the two English armies.[16] Soules and the bellicose earl of Buchan were based at Loudoun Hill, another volcanic relic (like the Abbey Craig), which dominates the landscape for miles around. From here, though, Soules wrongfooted the English by suddenly moving south towards Lochmaben, where his forces assaulted the pele. The English position in the south-west was somewhat weaker than usual, because some members of the garrisons had joined the royal armies on campaign – as had John de St John. Tilliol reported to Edward (although he was almost certainly exaggerating) that the attacking forces numbered over seven thousand.[17]

The patriots were repulsed after two days of savage fighting – and with two English armies operating in Scotland the Guardian could not afford to commit to a long siege – but the Scottish forces then went on to pillage the surrounding area (despite the fact that the immediate victims were ordinary Scottish people). Thus a pattern was set for this and subsequent campaigns: the struggle for Scotland would become a war of attrition. No single army or fortress in Scotland could hope to stand against an English royal army, but as Edward's forces made ponderous progress to the north, the patriots repeatedly sought to undermine his previous gains.

A flurry of communications from Edward's commanders in southern Scotland indicates that Soules was causing panic in the region closest to the border. Tilliol, the man with the best recent knowledge, was convinced that Soules would strike next against the English marches, but slightly later reports, gathered from spies in the patriot camp, suggested that the Scots had withdrawn into the forests of Galloway. Edward was anxious for more certain news, and pressed his men for further information.

Ralph Manton, an important administrator, received word from Sir Alexander Balliol, a Scot in Edward's allegiance, that 'whenever the enemy issues from Galloway, he will know two days before and will warn the king by two or three messengers what road they take'.[18] Balliol, as might be expected, was a kinsman of King John, but in his case there are no serious grounds to doubt his intentions (even though his reasons for supporting Edward are uncertain). Nevertheless, in early October Soules was able to out-manoeuvre the English again, appearing suddenly at Turnberry. The castle was retained, although the garrison endured a brief siege.

One might imagine that the prince of Wales should have been in a position to intercept Soules, although by this time he was based much further south. There are reports, for example, of a pilgrimage to Whithorn; it is not clear whether Prince Edward's movements were still part of any pre-conceived plan. A small mounted force under the earl of Lincoln was dispatched to reinforce Lochmaben, but it is generally assumed that most of the prince's army had now dispersed or had been dismissed. King Edward, however, remained more active to the north. Plans to invest Inverkip were abandoned (much to the chagrin of the earl of Lincoln, who had been 'granted' the castle), because he now had his eyes on a much greater prize: Stirling.

On 11 October Edward was at Dunipace, just eight miles from Stirling, although by this point the usual problem that bedevilled Edward's campaigns in Scotland – desertion by the infantry, due to a lack of ready cash to pay wages – was beginning to take its toll. Back in England the collection of taxes was now in progress, but it was unrealistic – or perhaps even disingenuous – of Edward to suggest that the Exchequer should already be 'sufficiently supplied'. Edward nevertheless dispatched a series of writs, urging greater efforts from his administration, because 'each time some [money] has come, the amount has been far too small'.[19] Anticipating stalling tactics from the Exchequer, Edward stated that he would 'not accept the excuse that it is dangerous to transport large quantities of coin' (even though this was obviously a reasonable concern).

In truth Edward's officials at York had stretched every sinew to ensure the king was adequately supplied – both with coin and provisions – and it might be remembered that some of the tax revenues had already been earmarked for other purposes (notably as payment for purveyance). Moreover, the king's demands that funds should be conveyed to him directly ensured that English garrisons in other parts of Scotland sometimes went without pay; as early as the end of August the garrison at Berwick was on the verge of mutiny and desertion. But still Edward wanted more: if only he had been able to cross the Forth, he claimed on 16 October, he 'would have done such exploit against his enemies that his business would have quickly reached a satisfactory conclusion'.

Dunipace marked the furthest extent of Edward's progress on this occasion, and thus another campaign came to a disappointing end. Yet Edward's primary objective for this campaign – to establish an effective English presence as far north as the Clyde–Forth line   had already been achieved. By this time, though, the king had received disturbing news from the continent: John Balliol had been set loose from papal custody, and was now at liberty in northern France. Was the exiled king about to attempt a comeback in Scotland, with a French army at his back?

* * * *

John Balliol was always treated with consideration during his time under the Pope's protection, although his freedom of movement was seriously restricted: in that sense, at least, the Pope had remained scrupulously neutral. It is often suggested that Balliol's release owed much to French pressure. It might also be remembered that William Wallace had spent time at the French court, pleading for further support, although the reception he received from Philip the Fair was characteristically ambiguous. But there had also been continued debate at the papal curia, where both Edward and the Scots had made further efforts to convince the Pope of the justice of their respective positions. Predictably, Edward's delegates made reference to the Brutus legend and the mythical exploits of King Arthur. More recent evidence was also cited to support Edward's assertion of superiority in Scotland (such as the Ragman Roll).

The Scottish delegation was led by Baldred Bisset, later described by the chronicler Andrew Wyntoun as a 'wise and cunning clerk'.[20] There is an appealing flash of dry wit in Bisset's dismissal of Edward's arguments: the king of England, it was said, 'refers to many things but proves few things'.[21] While Edward did not acknowledge the proceedings in Rome as a formal legal process, Bisset and his colleagues also constructed a more detailed submission.[22] Some modern historians have suggested that Boniface must have been convinced by Bisset's arguments,[23] therefore releasing John Balliol to pursue his rights. However, it is also possible that Balliol was removed by French agents, or absconded with their help, without Boniface's active consent. Either way, by late October Balliol was established on his ancestral estates in northern France, clearly under the protection and influence of Philip the Fair. Understandably, Edward was deeply concerned about the implications of these developments.

Edward's response to the renewed threat posed by John Balliol was twofold. First, he sent his treasurer, Walter Langton, by now well established as his most trusted minister, to enter negotiations with the French. Second, even though his army was now greatly depleted, Edward resolved to remain in Scotland over the winter. This was intended to 'annoy his enemies',[24] by whom Edward presumably meant both the Scottish patriots and Philip the Fair. An entry in the *Lanercost Chronicle* shows a good understanding of the significance of this decision: in the wake of earlier campaigns the patriots had been able to whittle away at the English position during the winter months.[25] Indeed, Edward now kept up his barrage of demands to the Exchequer, because he believed he 'was in danger of losing what he had previously won'.[26]

Towards the end of the year it did seem that Edward might have to give up some of his recent conquests, although in fact this owed nothing to the military efforts of the Scottish patriots. Langton was able to negotiate a long truce involving the English, French and Scots, and this would last until November 1302. However, it was also stipulated that all the castles and territory captured by Edward in the most recent campaign would be administered by *Frenchmen* for the duration of the peace.

Given that the French never arrived to take possession of any Scottish territory, modern writers have found it difficult to explain the meaning behind this extraordinary agreement. Philip the Fair's motives seem especially puzzling, because there is no real evidence of any French preparations for an intervention in Scotland. Having said that, a number of arguments have been put forward to try to make sense of Edward's thinking (or perhaps Langton's on his behalf). One possibility is that Edward might have considered using Scotland as a bargaining chip, pushing Philip the Fair towards the restoration of Gascony.[27] But it has also been suggested that Edward decided to 'call Philip's bluff' (in spite of the disturbing parallels with the agreement that had previously led to the loss of Gascony), thereby exposing the true weakness of Philip's commitment to the patriots.[28]

In any case, Edward conducted himself over the course of the winter as though he was unperturbed by his enemies' plans. He celebrated Christmas at Linlithgow, where a modest manor house was adapted for his use. He was joined here by the prince of Wales and Queen Margaret, who seems to have followed the late Queen Eleanor's example by joining her husband whenever possible. Edward also received the welcome news at Linlithgow that Robert Bruce, earl of Carrick, the former Guardian, had offered his submission (which Edward accepted once more). Naturally it has not escaped notice that Bruce's patriotism cooled at this point, when it seemed genuinely possible that John Balliol might return to Scotland. Yet Bruce's most pressing ambition was almost certainly to recover his position in western Scotland. Much of his earldom had now been lost, and Bruce had become an isolated figure in Scottish politics. His claim to the throne was still a distant dream.

Of course Bruce should also have been affected by the terms of the truce, as his lands and castles in Carrick had been captured during Edward's most recent campaign; the deadline set for the French to take possession of the disputed territory was 16 February. By the end of January, however, when Edward hosted a tournament, it must have obvious to everyone concerned that the French had no intention of coming to Scotland. On 19 February Edward recrossed the border into England, confident that his recent gains in Scotland would remain securely in his own hands.

* * * *

In practice, the passing of the February deadline made little difference to the wider diplomatic situation in 1302. Philip the Fair continued to profess friendship with the Scots, while exploiting the alliance for his own gain. But later in the year Philip encountered a major setback in Flanders, where he had established effective control after the failure of Edward I's expedition there. At the battle of Courtrai on 11 July a substantial French army, including the flower of French chivalry, was defeated by Flemish 'rebels'. It was an outcome that stunned the whole of Europe. The Flemish forces were mostly infantry armed with spears: the parallels with events in Scotland are inescapable. Philip was eventually able to reassert French dominance of Flanders, but this took a further three years.

Philip the Fair was also increasingly occupied by an escalating conflict with Pope Boniface. The trigger was a case involving a French bishop, whom Philip was thought to have mistreated. Much deeper and more long-standing issues were also at stake, though, as the great men of Europe sought to define the boundaries between spiritual and secular power. The dispute culminated in the shocking events of the following year, when Boniface himself was taken prisoner by a coalition of French forces and Philip's Italian allies. The Pope died shortly afterwards, almost certainly as a result of harsh treatment in captivity. But in 1302 Boniface was still in a position to seek powerful friends – such as Edward I – and his long-standing sympathy for the Scots evaporated.

All of these developments ensured that Philip the Fair was forced to reassess his own situation, approaching matters with his usual cold-eyed pragmatism. Philip quickly came to realise that he could not fight all of his enemies at once, and lasting peace with Edward I – who was similarly pursuing multiple objectives – now became an increasingly attractive option. This also meant, of course, that Philip began to reconsider the value of his alliance with the Scots. Evidently John de Soules discerned the change in the weather, and he was not naïve enough to trust in Philip's promises. In the autumn of 1302 Soules travelled to France in person, in the hope that he might retrieve the situation for the patriot cause. Yet towards the end of the year, when Edward and Philip agreed an extension of the truce, the Scots were pointedly excluded. Suddenly, therefore, the winds had shifted in Edward's favour.

Chapter 8

All This Scottish War

The renewal of the Anglo-French truce, in late 1302, provided a clear indication that Edward now wished to focus on the final defeat of the Scottish 'rebels'. The gradual shift in Edward's perspective is intriguing; it is difficult to believe that he had fully appreciated the challenges he might face in Scotland, and one might wonder if he privately regretted his decision to assert his claims there. And yet, having done so, he would undoubtedly have concluded that his honour was now at stake – making it impossible to withdraw without a catastrophic loss of face, in spite of the more tangible costs involved. Besides, the changes in the wider diplomatic situation had greatly simplified matters: with the prospect of outside interference receding, surely Edward's superior resources must eventually bring him victory?

For much of the year, the truce agreed in Scotland had been largely preserved, although both sides had taken the opportunity to consolidate their positions. Most notably, Edward ordered substantial building work at Linlithgow and Selkirk, where two new peles were to be established. Edward himself took a close personal interest in the proceedings, occasionally stipulating the specific features that should be included, but of course the more technical aspects were delegated to others. Plans for both schemes were begun in February 1302, before the king left Scotland to travel south.

At Linlithgow the work was supervised by Master James of St George, a Savoyard who provided Edward with valuable service for many years. Master James is best known for his role in the construction of Edward's spectacular castles in Wales, although it is now believed that he should be thought of as a skilled manager and organiser (as opposed to being regarded as a visionary architect, as was previously the case).[1] It was originally envisaged that the pele at Linlithgow should have a stone gatehouse and flanking towers. However, after Master James discussed the plans again with Edward in late April, it was decided that these should be replaced by timber structures. Even so, the pele covered an extensive area – the fortifications enclosed the whole of the promontory on which the later palace now stands – and a great deal of manpower was required. At one point in the summer there were also 140 women working alongside the male ditchers (although the women received a wage of 1½d, whereas the men received 2d).[2]

Some limited stonework was undertaken at Linlithgow, but there were greater opportunities for the masons at Selkirk, where the old motte-and-bailey castle was incorporated into the pele. By September both peles were close to completion. The work at Selkirk cost £1,400, while around £900 was spent at Linlithgow. Whilst both projects involved a considerable outlay of resources, these sums were dwarfed by the budget that had been made available for the castle programme in Wales; it is often suggested that his straitened financial circumstances prevented Edward from creating a similar legacy in Scotland.[3] Yet it should also be remembered that the peles were constructed in an area that was still technically a war-zone: speed and efficiency were therefore vital. A certain sense of urgency is conveyed by the fact that members of the hundred-strong garrison at Linlithgow were dragooned into working as labourers, 'because if they were not, the works could get seriously behind'.[4]

The truce was not perfectly maintained, since limited raiding appears to have continued. But there is also evidence to suggest that 'normal' life was sometimes able to resume, and that the English administration was gaining increasing acceptance south of the Forth. Legal records imply that English officials were not as dismissive of Scottish custom as they had been in 1296, and that Scots now felt able to make their petitions with some degree of confidence. It might also be significant that many of Edward's officials in Scotland, such as Sheriff Robert Hastangs of Roxburgh, had now been in post for several years. Perhaps by this time some of these men had won the trust and respect of local Scottish people, even if they had never gained their love?[5]

For many people in Scotland, on both sides of the Forth, the pause in the conflict must have come as a welcome relief. But in the autumn and winter of 1302/3, as the truce between Edward and the patriots neared its end, both sides began to prepare for a renewal of serious hostilities. From Edward's perspective, reorganisation was urgently necessary in south-west Scotland due to the recent death (from natural causes) of Sir John de St John, to whom the king still felt 'much bound'.[6] Military activities were also intensified in other parts of Scotland, where the garrisons were instructed to hold themselves in a state of high alert.

*   *   *   *

The truce expired formally at the beginning of November 1302, although the next major English campaign would be delayed until the following year. Plans for the new campaign were immediately set in progress, but Edward had already ordered Sir John Segrave, a veteran soldier who was then based at Berwick, to organise a more limited expedition. The main purpose of Segrave's mission was reconnaissance: '[. . .] and the foray being thus done, [to] send a special messenger to tell us the way in which it has been executed, together with the condition and news of [all] the parts of Scotland, with all possible haste'.[7]

Segrave was to be accompanied by Ralph Manton, who had played a key role in Edward's administration for several years. As 'Cofferer' of the Wardrobe, Manton effectively acted as paymaster-general for Edward's troops in Scotland, as well as serving in various other capacities.

By this time the patriots' efforts in Scotland were directed by John Comyn the younger, now lord of Badenoch following the death of his father. Comyn took on the role of Guardian (or 'Warden') in the absence of Soules, and in the New Year of 1303 he took the initiative. Edward's commanders appear to have expected another assault on Lochmaben, again suffering from faulty intelligence, but Comyn's fast-moving forces instead launched attacks on the new peles at Selkirk and Linlithgow. Linlithgow held out, but Selkirk fell to Comyn's men and the pele was virtually destroyed. Edward was furious. On 3 February he ordered the arrest of the keeper of Selkirk, Sir Alexander Balliol, who had emerged unscathed from the debacle. Eventually Balliol was able to convince Edward of his enduring loyalty (if not his competence), but his lands were confiscated and would not be restored until 1305.

Having abandoned the siege of Linlithgow, on 24 February Comyn fell upon Sir John Segrave at Roslin (to the south of Edinburgh). The Scots advanced under cover of darkness, and Segrave's forces appear to have become divided; thus Comyn achieved another victory. The Guardian's latest success was celebrated in *Gesta Annalia* II: '[. . .] there never was so desperate a struggle, or one in which the stoutness of knightly prowess shone forth so brightly'.[8] Segrave himself was badly wounded and captured, although he was freed shortly afterwards through the efforts of other English knights.

Ralph Manton, who was also taken prisoner at Roslin, was much less fortunate. Manton made a desperate appeal to Sir Simon Fraser, whom he almost certainly knew personally, offering a great sum of money if his life were spared. But Fraser's response was contemptuous: Manton was accused of corruption, and he was also upbraided because he had been captured, despite the fact he was a cleric, wearing a 'hauberk of iron'. 'You shall have judgement', concluded Fraser, 'according to your merit.' At this, as Peter Langtoft told the story, a 'ribald' seized Manton and put him to death: he first cut off Manton's hands, and then his head.[9] Manton's career has understandably been compared to that of Hugh Cressingham, who shared a similar fate.

The scale and significance of the battle of Roslin is often underestimated, although it is clear that Edward was deeply alarmed by the patriot resurgence. On 15 March he convened a council meeting in London, which eight of his commanders in Scotland were expected to attend, in order to determine the reasons behind recent failures.[10] Nevertheless, from Edward's point of view the setbacks in the north were offset by continuing developments on the continent. On 20 May 1303 a final peace was agreed between England and France, and the restoration of Gascony was finally achieved. In the following month a ceremony was held at St Emilion, formally confirming Edward's possession of his ancestral lands in southern

France – much as Philip had promised almost a decade before. Once again the terms agreed between Edward and Philip made no reference to Scotland, leaving Edward free to pursue his plans there.

By this time a powerful delegation of Scottish leaders – including James the Steward and Bishop Lamberton of St Andrews, as well as Sir John de Soules – had made their way to Paris, but they failed to divert Philip the Fair from his chosen course. It must have been clear to all that the Scottish patriots would receive no further support from France (in spite of Philip's promises to the contrary). A few days after the Anglo-French treaty was concluded, the Scots in Paris wrote to John Comyn, in whom their greatest hopes now rested, exhorting him to continue the struggle: 'For God's sake do not despair. If ever you have done brave deeds, do braver ones now. The swiftest runner who fails before the winning post has run in vain [cf Galations 2:2]. And it would gladden your hearts if you could know how much your honour has increased in every part of the world as the result of your recent battle with the English [at Roslin].'[11]

However, for the patriots in Scotland – now isolated in Europe and facing yet another onslaught from a determined enemy – the news from France must have been a bitter blow. What is more, the man in whose name they were fighting, John Balliol, had seemingly abandoned his own cause. Now burdened by extensive debts to the French crown, Balliol formally acknowledged that he was happy for Philip to pursue 'our said affairs, especially those which we have against the King of England, in the way which shall seem good to you'.[12] Thereafter Balliol lived quietly on his French estates, where he eventually died in 1314.

* * * *

Since 1298 none of Edward's campaigns had penetrated Scotland north of the Forth, where John Comyn of Badenoch and his allies had established effective control. But Comyn was not simply a warlord. Only limited evidence has survived, but there are indications that the writ of the Guardians – and technically, therefore, of King John Balliol – ran throughout much of northern Scotland. Comyn presided over courts, for instance, and arbitrated in disputes between

Scottish noblemen. Historians have also caught a glimpse of the other John Comyn, the earl of Buchan, who was similarly engaged; Buchan could be found 'holding pleas of his office near Aberdeen Castle', as Justiciar of Scotia.[13] Some of the men who might have found themselves on opposing sides in the squabbles of the 1280s and 1290s were now capable of working together. John, earl of Atholl, for example, whose family was associated with the Bruces, served under the Guardians as sheriff of Aberdeen.

In the forthcoming campaign Edward was particularly determined to take the fight to the patriots in their strongholds in north-eastern Scotland. In order to do this, of course, he and his army would need to cross the 'Scottish Sea' (i.e. the Forth): we have seen that the usual crossing point, at Stirling, provided an opportunity for the patriots to contest the passage. Moreover, while he was at Dunipace in 1301, Edward had referred specifically to his desire to *complete* a bridge across the Forth. This implies that the old bridge had not been adequately repaired after the patriots' victory at Stirling in 1297. In 1305 Edward ordered that the tolls from the ferry should be diverted towards the construction of a new bridge at Stirling,[14] but in the meantime he decided upon a more radical solution to the problem.

In January 1303 Edward ordered that three floating bridges should be fabricated in England, and then conveyed to Scotland by sea.[15] Thus a new temporary crossing of the Forth would be established, presumably at some point downstream from the traditional crossing-point at Stirling. Direction of the project was delegated to Master Richard of Chester, who was summoned to Windsor to discuss the plans with the king. Now probably in his sixties, Master Richard had worked alongside James of St George in Wales, and had similarly served Edward for many years. Indeed, Master Richard had been responsible for an earlier pontoon bridge that had been employed in the decisive campaign against Llywelyn of Gwynedd. Now Master Richard faced another challenging task, and the work was correspondingly expensive: around £940 was spent in total.

The construction of the bridges took place at the port of Lynn in Norfolk, where Master Richard supervised a large team of carpenters and blacksmiths. However, materials were also brought from further afield. Supplies of wood, used for beams, boards and joists, arrived from Yorkshire and Lincolnshire, as well as from closer by in Norfolk. The bridges were of different sizes: the largest, *maior pons*, was presumably wide enough for horses and wagons, whereas the smallest was suitable only for foot traffic. Thirty anchors were purchased to secure the pontoons in position. Records also show that the bridges were defensible: each incorporated a brattice and a drawbridge, and two of the brattices were equipped with *springalds* (a smaller version of the ballista).

For around three months the quayside at Lynn harbour was a hive of activity; at one point more than a hundred craftsmen were employed. Moreover, by this time Master Richard would have been well acquainted with Edward's exacting standards – he took great pains to keep the king informed of progress – although it is not clear whether the project was completed on schedule. Everything was certainly ready, however, by 24 May, when the various parts of the bridges were loaded on to a fleet of thirty ships (with the lead ship flying the flag of St George). Two pilot ships, the *Scarlet* of Grimsby and the *Godyere* of Grimsby, carried the thousands of iron bolts that would be necessary to assemble the bridges at their destination. A group of thirty carpenters accompanied the bridges on their journey to the Forth.

While Master Richard and his men were busy in Lynn, Edward and his advisers had been engaged in more conventional preparations for the forthcoming campaign. A feudal summons had been issued as early as the previous November, although the date of the muster had been brought forward after the defeat at Roslin. The nobles were encouraged 'to attend so powerfully accompanied that the contumacious resistance of the enemy may be overcome'.[16] As always, of course, Edward also needed supplies and money. On this occasion parliament was not expected to approve a grant of taxation, but a number of other sources were exploited to raise extra funds: debts to the Crown were called in (or commuted in exchange for service), and foreign merchants were given new rights in return for increased customs payments.

Fewer infantry appeared at the muster than in previous years – around 7,500 received pay in early June – but this was almost certainly a deliberate choice on the part of the king.[17] The emphasis this year was on *quality* rather than quantity: the commissioners were instructed to find men who were 'strong' and 'well-tried', as Edward anticipated this campaign would be long and gruelling.[18] But he also expected to gain reinforcements as he advanced into Scotland. Some 3,500 troops were raised in the lordship of Ireland (mainly due in this case to the efforts of the earl of Ulster, whose substantial debts to the Irish administration were written off in exchange), and an armada of 173 ships was gathered to transport them to Ayr.[19] Scots in Edward's allegiance were also expected to take on an increasingly prominent role: Robert (VII) Bruce was ordered to bring out the army of his earldom, together with as many cavalry as he was able to raise.[20]

By 16 May Edward had arrived at Roxburgh, where his latest army was instructed to assemble. On 30 May the king rode north, following the road towards Edinburgh via Lauder. As he travelled through the border regions, however, his men were harassed by the Scottish patriots. Rather than waiting to contest the crossing of the Forth, John Comyn of Badenoch had led his forces deep into southern Scotland, where they snapped at Edward's heels. At some point in early June a party of English knights, detached from the main army, sought billets at Melrose Abbey, where they were surprised and set upon by John Comyn himself. Sir Thomas Gray's father was caught up in the ensuing events, so the *Scalacronica* provides a vivid account. Again Comyn emerged out of the darkness, and after his men broke down the gates of the abbey the English were overwhelmed. The elder Thomas Gray was able to take refuge in a house outside the entrance, but when the Scots set fire to his shelter he was taken captive.[21]

Doubtless there were other similar incidents, although eventually, at some point in the second week of June, Edward was able to cross the Forth. Exactly where and how he did so is still a matter of debate. This might seem puzzling, given all the money and effort that had been expended on the construction and transportation of the pontoon bridges, yet Peter Langtoft, surely one of the best informed of the English chroniclers, tells us specifically that 'by chance there was no need of [them]'.[22] Records do confirm that the bridges arrived in the Forth as planned (they were subsequently transported to Berwick, and parts were later put to other uses), and most historians have disregarded Langtoft's testimony.[23] But it is also possible that Edward was able to use the ford at Stirling, following the more established road – especially if he had received certain intelligence that the crossing would not, after all, be contested.

Stirling Castle remained under the control of the patriots at this time, but the garrison would not have been large enough to hinder the progress of Edward's army. If Edward decided *not* to use the bridges, then this does suggest a more flexible outlook than is sometimes allowed – although in that case it would be interesting to know Master Richard of Chester's thoughts on the matter! At any rate, by 18 June Edward had reached the line of the River Tay at Perth, where he established a new base. He remained here for over a month, but later in the summer the king and his army would push further into northern Scotland, 'where never English king carried banner before'.[24]

* * * *

The halt at Perth was partly necessary to replenish Edward's supply train. Perth owed its prosperity during the Middle Ages to its strategic position at the highest navigable point of the River Tay, thereby allowing cargo to be brought quickly and efficiently to the heart of central Scotland. The town maintained important trading connections throughout Europe. Edward certainly recognised its importance, as in the following year he gave orders that it should be fortified (although the defences were later destroyed during the reign of his son). At high tide Perth was able to accommodate even the largest medieval vessels, and on this occasion a fleet of twenty-one ships brought provisions for Edward's army. This operation appears to have involved merchants from English ports in the north-east, but the king was also able to purchase supplies (including wine) more locally.[25] Business was always business, it would seem.

Another reason for the hiatus in the campaign was that Edward had received alarming news from south-western Scotland, and it was necessary to coordinate a response. Again, rather than confronting the English army directly, the patriots sought to undermine Edward's position in the south. Dumfries and Lochmaben were threatened by the patriot forces, with Sir Simon Fraser particularly prominent;

troops were also recruited in Galloway for a savage raid into north-west England. Again the situation was exacerbated because the English administration was under enormous pressure to divert every available source of money and supplies directly to the king. The receiver at Carlisle, James Delisle [Dalilegh], who was largely responsible for the support of the south-western garrisons, was placed in a desperately difficult position.

At one point there was a real possibility that both Dumfries and Lochmaben would fall, but the situation in the region was greatly improved after Edward detached a sizeable force from his own army to relieve the beleaguered garrisons. The prince of Wales was present on the campaign, and was involved in military operations in the north, but Edward chose to delegate this command to Aymer de Valence (who was appointed Edward's lieutenant in southern Scotland). Valence was accompanied, among others, by Robert Bruce. The arrival of the Irish was even more significant, and this time the famous earl of Ulster served in person. However, the patriots, including a force under John Comyn, remained active south of the Forth, raiding 'English' positions.

Towards the end of July 1303 Edward and his army moved north-east, marching to Montrose via Arbroath. It was probably at this point in the campaign that Edward enacted the devastating policy of fire and sword that is referred to in several chronicles, thereby demonstrating to the Scots north of the Forth that their 'Guardian' was unable to protect them. In the words of Langtoft:

Hamlets and towns, granges and barns,
Both full and empty, he burns everywhere.[26]

At Montrose Edward met with ships bringing siege engines from Edinburgh and other places. These were used at Brechin, around ten miles inland, where the patriots withstood a siege for five days.

The constable of Brechin, Sir Thomas Maule, was a flamboyant character. Each time a missile was launched against the castle, it was said, Maule emerged with a towel and mockingly wiped down the walls. But eventually Maule's luck ran out, and after he was killed the garrison quickly surrendered. The siege of Brechin is also notable because it provided the earliest recorded instance of the use of 'black powder' – i.e. gunpowder – at a medieval siege in Britain. The man responsible was certainly a Frenchman, Jean de Lamouilly, although unfortunately it is not clear how the explosive mixture was used.[27]

On 23 August Edward reached Aberdeen, where he expected the arrival of more ships, this time bringing coin so that he could pay his troops. Earlier in the campaign the infantry had received regular payments, but now their wages were badly in arrears. After five days of waiting Edward became impatient, and we can assume there was also much grumbling amongst the soldiers about the further delay. On 28 August Edward sent word to the long-suffering officials at the Exchequer. If he was not able to pay his men, he complained, 'they will go back to their own parts, as they are already doing from day to day'.[28]

Fortunately for Edward, the ships arrived later that day, although it must be stressed that desertion by the infantry was a lesser problem than it had been in the past. As late as November there were still 3,000 foot receiving wages, and the king was able to maintain a relatively large force of infantry and cavalry throughout the course of the winter.[29] As we have seen, there were hardened soldiers at every level, and perhaps on this occasion the quality of the infantry was genuinely of a higher standard. However, it was probably also significant that Edward was operating further north than in previous campaigns, as men who were considering leaving the army would not have relished the prospect of a long journey home through hostile territory. It would be interesting to know more about how the king maintained communications with the south (since messengers were clearly able to find their way through enemy lines). Walter of Guisborough believed that Edward deliberately left Stirling Castle in the hands of the patriots, in order to deter the less committed soldiers from deserting the host.[30]

From Aberdeen Edward and his army pushed deeper into what might be termed Comyn country, terrorising the inhabitants and extracting submissions from local leaders. They followed a broadly circular route, taking in Kinloss and Boat of Garten (among other places). Detachments appear to have ranged somewhat further afield, perhaps under the command of the prince of Wales, reasserting

English control of the castles at Urquhart and Cromarty.[31] Lochindorb Castle, the favourite residence of John Comyn's late father, was taken after a short siege.

*   *   *   *

As winter approached, Edward retired southwards, making his way through the bleak hills of the Mounth, but if the patriots expected him to return to England they would be sadly disappointed. Once again the king set out 'to annoy his enemies' by wintering in Scotland, establishing a fortified encampment at Dunfermline Abbey, on the north side of the Forth. In November the prince of Wales left his father to set up a separate base at Perth, where, apparently, he celebrated Christmas in lavish style.[32] In this fashion Edward and his son conveyed the clear message to the patriots that they were determined to see the matter through. Both of these locations also had symbolic resonance, as they had long been centres of Scottish royal power. While Scone (which is very close to Perth) was still bereft of its famous stone, Dunfermline was the mausoleum of the Scottish royal family (including Edward's late sister Margaret).

The patriots blinked first. William Wallace had now returned to Scotland, and had established a new military partnership with Sir Simon Fraser. However, in the New Year of 1304 the two men were put to flight in a skirmish at Happrew, where Sir John Segrave avenged his defeat at Roslin; by this time Wallace and Fraser were acting without the endorsement of the Guardian. By the end of the year 1303 John Comyn was already involved in preliminary negotiations for a general surrender.

Comyn had campaigned tirelessly in southern Scotland throughout the course of Edward's most recent campaign, though he had retired to the north of Scotland as the winter drew in. Thus it was from the region of Atholl, to the north of Perth, that Comyn made initial contact with the prince of Wales (as Edward perhaps had hoped). The subsequent discussions took some time. Whereas Robert Bruce (and others) had offered their submissions as individual magnates, Comyn believed he was speaking on behalf of the kingdom of Scotland. Most importantly, he asserted that the laws and customs of Scotland should be maintained as they were in the time of Alexander III.[33] No changes should be made unless the Scottish political community was consulted. This is a clear echo of the agreement at Birgham, from so many years before.[34]

Edward refused to offer any guarantees about the future direction of government in Scotland. It is often said that his own terms were surprisingly generous, although in truth they were not dramatically forgiving. He did promise that the lives of Comyn and his closest allies would be spared, and crucially there was no threat of disinheritance or imprisonment. However, the patriot leaders were forced to accept a period of exile from Scotland (although this was later commuted to a range of fines), so an element of punishment was clearly implied. On the other hand, Comyn was given private assurances that Edward would adopt a more conciliatory attitude once the Scots had acknowledged his lordship.[35]

It might conceivably be argued that John Comyn had earned Edward's grudging respect, yet there was surely an element of pragmatism behind any magnanimity on the king's part. Comyn was badly bruised, although by no means broken. While Edward's capture of Lochindorb was a blow to Comyn pride, the Guardian retained control of other castles in northern Scotland that were of much greater strategic importance. Thus he still possessed the capacity to offer further resistance had he chosen to do so. But on 9 February John Comyn rode to Strathord, north of Perth, where he formally offered his submission to Edward's representatives; on 16 February he knelt before Edward himself.

For reasons that will already be obvious to many readers, in the light of his fractious relationship with the most famous Robert Bruce, there has been a tendency to downplay Comyn's role in the struggle for Scottish independence. In the most recent historiography, however, John Comyn has been restored to his rightful place as one of the most able and tenacious of the Scottish leaders who offered resistance to Edward I. Moreover, Comyn did not finally submit to Edward, as some later traditions might suggest, because he was a French-speaking quisling who cared nothing for the Scottish people. In the wake of yet another ruthless English campaign, with no friends to help them, doubtless there were many Scots who agreed with

Comyn's conclusion that a negotiated settlement was now the best outcome available.

*   *   *   *

In March 1304 Edward held a parliament at St Andrews, which the greatest Scottish landholders were expected to attend. Of those who had opposed Edward in recent years, most now followed John Comyn's lead. On 14 or 15 March more than a hundred Scottish nobles offered, or in most cases renewed, their homage and fealty to Edward. Sentence of outlawry was passed on the few beleaguered diehards – including the patriot garrison of Stirling – who still refused to submit. Intriguingly this was done 'according to due process and the laws of Scotland'.[36] Edward was now keen to convey the impression that actions driven from above had the wider approval of the Scottish political community

Now Edward's focus turned to Stirling Castle. Militarily, he understood the *strategic* importance of Stirling, not least because it had been the site of two bitter defeats for the English in Scotland, but the reduction of the castle had also now become an issue of great *personal* significance. In a letter to Walter Langton, he referred to the forthcoming siege as a matter 'which we have so much at heart that we cannot have it more so, being that which will bring about the conclusion of all our business in these parts'.[37] Edward remained as determined as ever, but the complacency of 1296 was long gone. There is perhaps even a hint of weariness in an earlier message to the prince of Wales, dated 5 March, which makes a reference to 'all this Scottish war'.[38]

Planning for the operation against Stirling was extensive and protracted. The rest of Edward's letter to Langton was concerned with the effective provision of money and supplies, although the army also had more specific needs. Evidently Edward had been impressed by the efforts of Jean de Lamouilly: at the end of March he sent word to the Exchequer at York, requesting that his officials provide him with more of the materials necessary for Lamouilly's explosive black powder.[39] The key ingredients were saltpetre and sulphur; presumably the third component needed, charcoal, could be found more locally.

More conventional items were also in demand, of course, and Berwick, as was often the case, became the centre for the collection of provisions from the south. From Berwick some of the supplies were transported by sea to Blackness on the Forth (where a new supply depot had now been established), before they were moved on to Stirling.

The prince of Wales was instructed to find lead, which would be melted down and attached to the counterweights of trebuchets; this, of course, would allow for heavier counterweights, generating increased velocity within the mechanism and therefore greater power. It was suggested that, if necessary, the prince's men should remove the lead from church roofs, albeit making sure that 'the churches be not uncovered over the altars'.[40] That churches were indeed pillaged in some places is confirmed by later evidence: the following year the prior of St Andrews and the bishop of Brechin both received payments to compensate them for the loss of lead that had been seized in King Edward's name.

The siege of Stirling provided an opportunity for Edward to test the loyalty of the Scots who had entered his allegiance, and fresh troops were recruited in Scotland. A blockade was established to isolate the castle, with patrols dispatched to guard the fords; several Scottish magnates were involved in this activity. The Scottish nobles were also expected to contribute siege weapons to the growing arsenal that was assembled, although Robert Bruce found it difficult to find appropriate transport for the beam of one large engine. Upon receiving Bruce's letter to that effect, Edward sent men to help.[41] In the light of Bruce's later achievements, there is something almost comical about this episode: it is difficult to escape the conclusion that Bruce was somewhat lacking in enthusiasm for the task at hand.

An English clerk noted with satisfaction that Edward was greeted on the road to Stirling by seven Scottish women, who sang to the king, 'just as they used to do during the time of the late King Alexander'.[42] The patriots at the castle, though, had prepared a very different kind of welcome. Their commander, a young Scottish knight by the name of William Oliphant, was determined to defend his charge. As was the custom, before the siege began in earnest Oliphant was called upon to surrender. He requested leave to consult his lord, John de Soules (who was still in France), but Edward would brook no such delay.

Having failed to stall proceedings, Oliphant now scorned Edward's siege. Avoiding specific reference to John Balliol, or even to John de Soules, he proudly asserted that he held Stirling from 'the Lion' (presumably a reference to the heraldic symbol of the Scottish kings), and he invited Edward to do his worst.[43] Oliphant was an attractive figure, and some English chroniclers were impressed by his brave demeanour, but Edward's response was grim: 'If he thinks it will be better for him to defend the castle than yield it, he will see.'[44]

* * * *

Military operations intensified at Stirling on 22 April. The patriot garrison had no real hope of relief, and as each day passed their food supplies dwindled yet further. Several weeks earlier Edward had begun taking precautions to prevent local people from providing sustenance to the garrison; on 17 April, importantly, his forces had captured the garrison's boats, thereby cutting off another vital lifeline. But the king was not content simply to starve the patriots into submission, because he had decided upon an awesome display of military might. That there was an element of spectacle about the siege is confirmed by the fact that much of the royal court, including the queen, was present at Stirling. Indeed, Edward paid for an oriel window to be inserted into Queen Margaret's chambers in a house in the town so that the queen and her ladies could watch the proceedings in greater comfort.

By this time Edward's engineers had gathered an impressive array of siege equipment. As we have seen, siege engines were given picturesque names, and on this occasion the *Parson*, *Tout le Monde* and the aforementioned *Bothwell* were all present, along with many others. A large team of around a hundred carpenters and sawyers were on hand to build new engines, and quarriers were employed throughout the siege to ensure the trebuchets were kept well supplied with ammunition.[45] The scale and complexity of the operation are revealed by the fact that the stone was shaped several miles away, at Linlithgow, by masons working under the direction of Master Walter of Hereford.

The deployment of so much military hardware at Stirling must have offered a remarkable sight, especially if Lamouilly's pyrotechnics were at all effective, although there were various setbacks. The attempt to use a battering ram, which was poorly constructed, was particularly unsuccessful.

The *Scalacronica* suggests that the garrison offered fierce resistance. Sir Thomas Gray's work describes the alarming experience of his father, who had now been released from captivity and was present at Stirling: 'At this siege, Thomas de Gray, knight, was hit by a bolt from a springald through the head beneath the eyes; he was thrown to the ground as though dead [. . .] Thomas was carried away, and a troop was got ready to bury him – at which point he started to move and look about, and afterwards he recovered.'[46]

The elder Thomas Gray, it would seem, had an ability to cheat death that rivalled Edward's own, although the king himself was not to be outdone. In *Flores Historiarum* we are told that a missile from a springald pierced Edward's saddle, passing between his legs, although the king was miraculously unhurt. One version of this chronicle goes on to provide an increasingly elaborate interpretation of this episode, filled with Biblical allusions – the author was evidently keen to reinforce his image of Edward as the Lord's anointed.[47] Nevertheless, with the eyes of the court upon him, we might assume that the real Edward would not have flinched from danger. A variation of the *Flores* story appears in a somewhat later English chronicle, which was formerly attributed to William Rishanger.[48] It is said that Edward narrowly escaped death when a bolt from a crossbow lodged in his armour. But Edward, as presented here, was able to maintain his composure. He extracted the bolt, spat on it to show his contempt for the garrison, and threatened to hang the man who shot it.

Remarkably, the patriot garrison at Stirling held out for almost three months. They were assisted not only by the castle's imperious setting and its stone walls, but also by the deep cellars carved into the rock: as well as providing a safe store for provisions, these also offered an important refuge. Eventually starvation did prove to be the key factor, in spite of all Edward's efforts to take the castle by storm. With the situation now becoming desperate, Oliphant offered his surrender, but the king had not quite finished with Stirling Castle. By this time he had ordered the construction of a particularly fearsome new siege engine, and he was determined to see it in action. This machine became known as *Ludgar* or *Loup de Guerre*: Warwolf.

A letter written by an unknown correspondent, who was present at the siege, makes Edward's intentions clear: 'The king wills that none of his people enter [the castle] till it is struck with the Warwolf, and that those within defend themselves from the said wolf as best they can.'[49]

The sources do not explain exactly what Warwolf did – it is usually assumed to have been a giant trebuchet – but Edward did eventually have the satisfaction of witnessing it in operation. Langtoft, probably somewhat exaggerating, claimed it brought down an entire wall.[50]

Finally, on 20 July, Edward agreed to accept the garrison's submission. The account in *Flores* tells us that the patriots embraced their allotted role in the spectacle, emerging with ashes on their heads and halters round their necks, placing themselves utterly at Edward's mercy. This done, the king ultimately spared their lives – although Oliphant and his men were imprisoned.[51] Only fifty had survived from the initial 120; the number of casualties in Edward's army is unknown.[52] The victory was celebrated by a tournament.

The surrender of John Comyn, followed by the capture of Stirling Castle, restored Edward to the kind of position in Scotland he had enjoyed in 1296. Many Scots who were still on the continent, including James the Steward and Bishop Lamberton, would also return to seek Edward's grace. But not every Scotsman was willing to bend the knee to the king of England. John de Soules preferred a life in exile, and he later died in France.[53] William Wallace remained at large in Scotland itself, although by this time the former Guardian was sadly reduced in status; his energy and resourcefulness were still extremely evident, but he had returned to his earlier guise as a guerrilla chief, the leader of a band of desperate men. In order to bring Wallace to 'justice', Edward surmised, it was no longer necessary for him to raise vast armies: the king had determined this would become a matter for the Scots themselves. Edward's Scottish wars were over. Or so it must have seemed.

Chapter 9

Burn, Kill and Raise the Dragon

After the fall of Stirling Castle in July 1304, Edward spent a further month in Scotland. Towards the end of August he recrossed the border into England. He would never set foot in Scotland again. The rest of this year provided the opportunity for some leisure, and for the king to recover his strength. He stayed for almost two months at the royal manor of Burstwick in Yorkshire, and from there the royal court moved on to Lincoln, where Christmas was spent. Doubtless the king enjoyed the festivities, as the celebrations were unusually extravagant. The chronicles suggest that he was in a particularly generous mood, making lavish gifts to his followers. Dispensing his largesse as 'the king and lord of the monarchy of two realms', this was one of the high points of Edward's reign.[1]

In some respects this triumphant mood was maintained for much of the following year, but Edward was not content to rest on his laurels. For one thing, he became increasingly preoccupied with the question of crime in England, which had risen to disturbing levels during his absence in Scotland. There was a strong correlation between the level of disorder and Edward's wars, and a number of relevant incidents have been mentioned above. However, the most alarming development was the prevalence in several counties of armed gangs known as 'trailbastons' (from the French word for club, *bâton*), whose members engaged in violent robbery and extortion. Itinerant 'trailbaston commissions' were established, as a major new measure to target criminality. Their activities were controversial at the time, and modern historians have debated their effectiveness, but this initiative should undoubtedly be regarded as a serious attempt to address a genuine problem.[2]

Edward took a personal interest in the workings of the legal system, although of course he also turned his attention to other matters, including the settling of some personal scores. By this point he had reached an accommodation, of sorts, with the earl of Norfolk, but another old adversary, Archbishop Winchelsey of Canterbury, came under sustained attack. In early 1306 the new Pope, Clement V – a Gascon who was generally more amenable to Edward's wishes than Boniface VIII had been – was persuaded to suspend Winchelsey from office. At around the same time Clement absolved Edward of the oaths he had sworn to uphold various concessions he had made (concerning the Royal Forest and other matters), so the king's hostility to Winchelsey might be situated within a larger context.

There were also disputes with others, however, notably the bishop of Durham, Edward's former friend and companion-in-arms. Perhaps most significantly, there were a number of clashes between Edward and the prince of Wales. In the summer of 1305 Edward of Caernarfon became involved in a dispute with Walter Langton – apparently the prince had trespassed in one of Langton's parks – and this eventually led to a period of estrangement between father and son. King Edward was enraged when the prince insulted Langton in public, and banished his son from his presence.

Whilst Edward did not flinch from new conflicts, he also made renewed efforts to forge a lasting settlement in Scotland. In March 1305 a new parliament was summoned to Westminster. Towards the end of the session a mass took place at the abbey, in which Edward gave thanks for his victory over the Scottish patriots. This might appear rather insensitive, given that a number of leading Scots were present at the parliament, but Edward also took pains to consult them about the best way forward in Scotland. The three men chosen to give the king advice were Robert (VII) Bruce, John de Mowbray (an associate of John Comyn) and Robert Wishart, bishop of Glasgow.

Wishart, it might be recalled, had been a stalwart opponent of Edward's, and he had earlier been imprisoned in England. Released in 1300 on the understanding that he would act obediently to Edward in Scotland, he had continued to give tacit support to the patriot cause. Yet Edward had accepted Wishart's submission once again in 1304, and it is clear that the king now wished to reach an accommodation with leading figures of the Scottish establishment. It was agreed that the Scottish political community would be given time to consult amongst themselves, before further discussions would take place in the autumn.

* * * *

Even Simon Fraser was permitted to renew his fealty to Edward, but one of the patriot leaders was pointedly excluded from the growing spirit of reconciliation. This man, of course, was William Wallace, who was still at large in Scotland. As early as March 1304, in a letter to Alexander de Abernethy, Edward singled out Wallace for special treatment:

> And in reply to the matter wherein you have asked us to let you know whether it is our pleasure that you should hold out to William le Waleys [sic] any words of peace, know this, that it is not our pleasure by any means that either to him, or to any other of his company, you hold out any word of peace, unless they place themselves absolutely and in all things at our will, without any exception whatever.[3]

It is often suggested that Edward's attitude towards Wallace was clouded by personal animosity, and that he is diminished by his failure to recognise a worthy adversary.[4] Yet it might also be remembered that, unlike the Comyns and Bruces, as well as many others, Wallace's own status in Scotland was almost entirely derived from his implacable opposition to Edward's will: is it realistic to imagine that Edward could have found a place for such a man in the new Scotland he was trying to create? There is an intriguing passage in Langtoft's chronicle which suggests that Wallace did make a tentative offer of surrender, but that Edward refused to consider his terms.[5] Given that Wallace was ultimately not willing to submit 'absolutely', Edward was able to avoid the dilemma that his surrender might conceivably have posed.

Edward made the capture of Wallace another test of loyalty for Scots, such as Abernethy, who were now in English allegiance. In late

1304 John Comyn of Badenoch and Simon Fraser (among others) received orders to lend their support to the hunters, and it was noted that Edward would 'watch to see how each of them conducts himself'.[6] Robert Bruce had also been encouraged to pursue Wallace, somewhat earlier, after helping Segrave to best Wallace at Happrew: 'As the cloak has been well made, make the hood also.'[7] Yet eventually the dubious honour of taking Wallace fell to another Scot, Sir John Menteith. Wallace was captured near Glasgow in early August 1305, apparently while visiting a lover.[8] As is so often the case in such circumstances, there is a strong possibility that Wallace was betrayed by someone close to him.

On 22 August Wallace was brought into London, although Edward ostentatiously ignored him. On the following day he was tried at Westminster. He was accused of treason, as well as various other transgressions: these included the murder of the sheriff of Lanark; convening illegal parliaments; and encouraging the Scots to pursue the French alliance. Wallace spoke out only once, to deny the charge of treason; unlike most of the Scottish leaders, Wallace had never sworn an oath of allegiance to Edward, but his outburst was disregarded. Otherwise, as the account of his 'crimes' was read out to the court, Wallace made no further response. This is hardly surprising. It has been well observed that, in a different context, the list of charges might well have been given as a record of Wallace's achievements.[9]

The outcome, of course, was never in doubt. It was ordained that Wallace should be dragged through the streets of London to Smithfield, the place of execution, where he would be hanged, drawn and quartered. The gory details are well known and need no further elaboration here, although it is perhaps worth noting that, contrary to popular belief, this form of execution was not invented for Wallace.[10] Once sentence had been carried out, Sir John Segrave was given the task of escorting the 'quarters' northwards, where they were displayed, respectively, at Newcastle, Berwick, Stirling and Perth. Wallace's head remained in the capital, where it was exhibited for some time on London Bridge. Thus ended the remarkable life of Sir William Wallace; his legend has endured.

*   *   *   *

Edward himself was not present either at Wallace's trial or at his execution – instead he spent the day hunting – but he would soon need to return to Scottish affairs. It must be said, however, that Wallace's execution had little obvious impact – at least not in the short term. In September 1305 Edward welcomed a Scottish delegation to London as planned. Negotiations took place between the Scots and members of Edward's council, and eventually a broad outline for the future governance of Scotland was agreed. Not all of this could possibly have been to the Scots' liking, but the English also made a number of concessions.

Scotland was now to be regarded as a 'land' [*terre*] rather than a kingdom – a significant step – and it would be ruled in Edward's name by a lieutenant; this role was to be given to the king's nephew, John of Brittany.[11] However, the lieutenant was to be advised by a council that was made up almost entirely of Scotsmen, and four English justiciars would be matched by Scottish counterparts. The majority of sheriffs were to be Scots, in marked contrast to Edward's administration of 1296. Nevertheless, there were still a number of outstanding issues. Perhaps most significantly, as the pendulum had swung between Edward and the patriots, lands had been won and lost, and now there were competing claims of ownership. Yet some progress was made towards resolving this matter; generally it appears to have been anticipated that Scotsmen who had lost lands would be able to regain them, whereas the 'new' owners would receive cash compensation.

None of the above would have been possible without the king's assent, and Edward surely deserves a certain amount of credit for attempting to provide a more inclusive form of government in Scotland. Indeed, he was said to be delighted by the outcome of the process, but of course his efforts did not ultimately result in a permanent settlement. On 10 February 1306 Robert Bruce, earl of Carrick, met John Comyn, lord of Badenoch, in the church at Dumfries. Once again, there was an argument between them, and Bruce drew a weapon; shortly afterwards Comyn lay dead. Very soon all of Edward's plans for the peaceful governance of Scotland would lie in tatters.

It appears that Bruce's entourage also became involved in the fracas, and that Bruce was not the only man to strike a blow, although it is extremely uncertain exactly what happened and why.[12] It is usually assumed that the cause of the quarrel between the two men lay in Bruce's claim to the throne, and his inability to secure Comyn's support for a new insurrection against Edward's rule. Certainly there is circumstantial evidence to suggest that Bruce had never abandoned his personal ambitions – and is it significant that Bruce's father had passed away some time before, meaning that he was now free to pursue the family's claim in his own right?[13] It is also possible, however, that the meeting with Comyn was organised to address more routine local matters, before old memories and resentments flooded to the surface.[14]

At any rate, irrespective of his original intentions at Dumfries, Bruce was now in a dangerous position; he had put himself outside Edward's peace, and Comyn's friends and kinsmen would soon be clamouring for his death. He had also abused a sacred place by causing blood to be shed in a church, and he would later be excommunicated by the Pope. The time for caution was surely past, but Bruce appears to have hesitated before taking the next fateful step. Nevertheless, on 25 March 1306, at the traditional location in Scone, Robert Bruce was acclaimed king of Scots.

In truth Bruce was still the leader of a faction, but he did attract considerable support from the Scottish nobility. Obviously the Stone of Destiny was missing at his inauguration (by this time Edward had commissioned the famous Coronation Chair to hold it at Westminster), although Bishop Wishart provided vestments for the new king to wear. Wishart clearly set little store by his promises to Edward I, and he was even prepared to forgive sacrilege if it would advance the patriot cause; he had already absolved Bruce of the death of Comyn and urged him on. Sir Simon Fraser was another who eventually joined Bruce, as did the earl of Atholl. Intriguingly, Bruce also gained the support of Isabel, countess of Buchan, who abandoned her Comyn husband. At Scone she took on the traditional role of her young nephew, the earl of Fife, placing a crown on Bruce's head.

This was a dramatic moment, yet Bruce's wife was apparently unimpressed. His second wife, Elizabeth de Burgh was the daughter of the earl of Ulster; the marriage had been arranged at a time when Bruce appeared to stand high in Edward I's favour. Now, it is said, she mocked her husband as the 'King of Summer' (just as flowers soon lose their lustre).[15] Others were also unmoved. Some noblemen, like Earl Malise of Strathearn, now considered themselves honour-bound to hold true to their allegiance to Edward; when called upon to give support to Bruce, Strathearn famously contended that his oath was not 'fragile like glass'.[16] And, of course, the members of the powerful Comyn network, most of them former patriots, also ranged themselves against Bruce – and alongside Edward.

Bruce, then, was facing formidable odds, though from a military perspective he had already acted with speed and decision. In a more effective echo of his grandfather's attempted coup of 1286, Bruce launched a lightning campaign throughout south-western Scotland, taking the English and their Scottish allies by surprise. A number of key fortresses, including Ayr, Dalswinton and Inverkip, were taken by Bruce's men. Other castles, such as Lochmaben, Dunaverty on the Isle of Bute, and Loch Doon (a formidable Bruce stronghold on an island in a loch), were also garrisoned by the new King Robert's supporters. Bruce remained in contact with Edward's officials (although in this case it is unlikely that Edward would have shown any readiness to negotiate), but he adopted a confident and aggressive attitude. He was willing to defend himself, he said, with 'the longest stick that he had'.[17]

*   *   *   *

At first, Edward appears not to have understood the implications of the events at Dumfries, not least because he was not aware that Bruce was responsible. A letter written on 24 February expressed his concern that Comyn had been killed by *'some people'* [my italics] who were doing their best to 'trouble the peace and quiet' of Scotland.[18] At length, of course, Edward learned the truth. And when he heard that Bruce had claimed the throne of Scotland, we must imagine that his rage was terrible to behold. In the words of John Barbour, in his epic poem about the life of Robert Bruce, Edward 'went almost out of his mind'.[19]

Barbour was writing around seventy years later (albeit drawing upon more contemporary sources). Perhaps, then, it was no more than coincidence, yet the shock of Bruce's rebellion did coincide with a serious deterioration in Edward's health. For much of the spring the king did not stir from Winchester, and there can be no doubt that illness was the cause of his prolonged stay in the city. When he finally moved on, around the middle of May, he was transported in a litter. Later evidence records payments for special ointments, particularly for his legs, and he was also troubled by his neck (for which a kind of plaster was made).[20] This may perhaps indicate severe arthritis, although it is possible that the king was also suffering from various other ailments.

We have seen that Edward was already conscious of his age, but in spite of his growing infirmity he continued to *delegate* authority rather than abdicate responsibility. By this time he had outlived most of his contemporaries (the earl of Lincoln was a notable exception), which meant that younger men were now coming increasingly to the fore. Once again Edward's first thoughts turned to Aymer de Valence – the late Comyn's brother-in-law, as well as the king's own kinsman – who was then in his early thirties.[21] John of Brittany, who had shown little enthusiasm to take up his new role in Scotland, was temporarily sidelined. In the first week of April, as Edward's 'lieutenant and captain', Valence was dispatched north to confront Bruce.[22] Henry Percy, still also relatively young, though by this time a long-standing veteran of the Scottish wars, was given important military responsibilities in the west. By this time, too, a fragile reconciliation had been effected between Edward and his eldest son.

In April 1306 Edward of Caernarfon received confirmation that he had been fully restored to his father's favour: he was now to become lord of Gascony, emphasising his position as King Edward's undisputed heir. This was followed by the proclamation that a ceremony would take place at Whitsun, 22 May, at Westminster, where Edward would knight his eldest son. Others deemed worthy of the office of knighthood, including young men from England's noblest and wealthiest families, were also encouraged to attend.

Edward was entitled to raise a tax to help defray the costs of his son's elevation to knighthood, as his father had done before him, but this was surely of secondary importance. The sense of drama was heightened by the fact that Whitsun was thought to be the date chosen by King Arthur to host a similar occasion at Caerleon. Even if this allusion was lost on some of those who subsequently gathered at Westminster, they could not fail to be impressed by the scale and gravity of the proceedings.[23] The prince of Wales was dubbed by King Edward, as planned, in the chapel of Westminster Palace, before father and son moved on to the abbey. Here the focus remained on Prince Edward, as he knighted around 300 *tirones*, or 'tyros'. Then the entire company was made welcome at the palace, where Edward's deeper purpose would now become plain.

The palace was the setting for a lavish feast. At the high table, in front of the king, there were served two swans – though Edward had more than food on his mind.[24] We must imagine the king rising painfully to his feet, as the minstrels fell silent. Then, placing his hand over the birds, Edward swore a terrible oath of vengeance against Robert Bruce, before restating his desire to return to the Holy Land once Bruce had been defeated. It is unclear whether the prince of Wales had been forewarned of Edward's intentions, though for once he lived up to his father's expectations, swiftly repeating the same vows and adding for good measure that he would not rest for two nights in the same place until the latest Scottish insurrection had been quelled. Naturally, all the 'tyros' followed suit. This was an extraordinary moment: one that King Edward must surely have hoped would bind together a new generation of warriors in a common cause.

The events at the 'Feast of the Swans', as this occasion has become known, appealed strongly to contemporary *mores* – indeed, it started a trend for swearing vows on birds that swept throughout western Europe. But the ceremony also had more immediate implications. Two days later a message was dispatched to Aymer de Valence, informing him that he should expect the imminent arrival of the prince of Wales in Scotland.[25] It was said that King Edward himself would follow shortly afterwards, although he remained a sick man. Could the choice of swans at the Westminster feast be seen, therefore, as a tacit symbol of Edward's age and waning strength? Did the king intend his oath to be interpreted as his 'swan song'?[26]

* * * *

By this time Aymer de Valence had already set to work in Scotland, in command of around two thousand men. He quickly enhanced his growing reputation, and his successes continued throughout the summer of 1306. Edward exhorted Valence to take great pains to capture the bishops of Glasgow and St Andrews, and both were taken into custody in early June. Lamberton appears to have gone quietly, whereas Bishop Wishart, characteristically, had shown greater defiance. But on 8 June Wishart too was captured at Cupar in Fife, where he had been holding the castle 'as a man of war'.[27] Edward was delighted at this news, sending word that he was 'almost as pleased as if it had been the earl of Carrick'.[28] Shortly afterwards, Valence would come close to taking the most important quarry of all.

On 18 June Valence reached Perth. In the morning of the following day Bruce appeared outside the town, advancing from the west, in command of a sizeable force. Presumably his men now marched under the banner of the king of Scots. It was said, however, that Bruce and his men wore white shirts over their armour, in order to conceal their identities on the field. This suggests a less confident Robert Bruce than the inspirational (and conspicuous) figure that the English would later encounter at Bannockburn. Nevertheless, Bruce was eager to put the matter to the test. He sent a herald to Valence, inviting the English commander to meet him in battle.

Unwilling to face Bruce on his chosen ground, Valence declined Bruce's challenge[29] and remained ensconced behind Perth's new fortifications. Bruce was reluctant to assault the town and at around midday he drew off, retracing his steps to the west; he halted at Methven, roughly six miles away. As evening approached, his men dispersed to find provisions and quarters, and thus were taken completely unawares when Valence sallied out of Perth and launched a surprise attack. Bruce attempted to rally his men amidst the chaotic scenes, and Valence's own horse was killed, but eventually the 'English' gained the upper hand. John de Haliburton, a Scot in Edward's allegiance, halted one of the white-shirted knights by seizing the reins of his horse. Yet it soon became apparent that there were limits to his loyalty to Edward I: when Haliburton recognised the king of Scots, he decided to let him go.[30]

After this narrow escape, Bruce was able to extricate at least part of his army, although a good number of his supporters were captured or killed. Valence's men continued to pursue him in the coming days, first through Strathearn and then across the mountains into Strathtay. Bruce was finally brought to bay on the shores of Loch Tay, although he was again able to evade capture. Some of the pursuers, including Giles de Argentin, lost horses here.[31] This might suggest a fierce skirmish in which Bruce's men acquitted themselves well. By this time, however, the Bruce cause had suffered serious reverses in other parts of Scotland, enhancing the significance of the English victory at Methven. Edward of Caernarfon had taken Lochmaben, for example, and now began to reassert control in the south-west. His progress was temporarily halted by a breakdown in the supply chain, though by the end of July he had joined Valence at Perth.

Edward himself had set out from Westminster on 10 June, ostensibly on his way to join the war in person, but his progress north was slow and difficult. It took him ten days to reach Dunstable, which is barely thirty miles away. And Edward, it should be remembered, was not travelling amidst the hills and forests of Wales or Scotland, but rather on the well-trodden roads at the heart of his realm. On 28 May, shortly before the king left London, a new ordinance concerning the Royal Forest was issued; it included an unusually elaborate preamble, and it has been suggested that this may provide a reflection of Edward's condition, as well as his state of mind:

> While we behold the imperfection of human weakness, and weigh with attentive consideration the widespread burdens that lie upon our shoulders, we are indeed inwardly tormented [. . .] tossed about by the waves of diverse thoughts, and are frequently troubled, passing sleepless nights, dwelling in our inmost soul about what ought to be done.

Edward, it was said, was hopeful that God 'in the clemency of his goodness, will mercifully look upon and supply our deficiency'.[32]

Of course, there is a certain irony in these earnest references to 'mercy' and 'clemency', as the king was now fixated on vengeance against Bruce and his supporters. John Barbour tells us that Aymer de Valence was instructed to 'burn, kill and raise the dragon'.[33] (The unfurling of the dragon banner signified that no quarter would be given.) Other sources confirm that Edward encouraged his commanders to take a harsh approach in Scotland: he praised Valence, for example, for wasting Sir Simon Fraser's lands.[34] On 28 June Edward issued an order, apparently confirming an earlier command, that 'rebels' should be summarily executed (with the exception of Bruce, Fraser and Atholl, who should be held until the king's wishes were known).[35] Up to now, despite some instances of brutality, and threats to do even worse, the main purpose of Edward's Scottish wars had been to extract submission from the Scots, and a recognition of his 'rights'. The current campaign was explicitly envisaged as a war of punishment and terror.

Edward's attitude seems very clear, yet Valence was not a man to indulge in indiscriminate slaughter. He may also have been wary of interpreting Edward's commands too literally, as he had previously been given leave to take the 'middling' sort into 'the King's peace'.[36] Kinsmen and well-wishers were able to intercede on behalf of several of the noble captives who remained in custody north of the border. However, when Valence dispatched a number of his prisoners to England, Edward confirmed that he was no longer inclined to keep Scottish knights in English jails. On 4 August sixteen prominent Bruce supporters, including Alexander Scrymgeour, the hereditary standard-bearer of the king of Scots, were executed at Newcastle as traitors.

The men who died at Newcastle were spared most of the agonies of Wallace's execution, although the former Guardian's fate was no longer exceptional. Indeed, it is quite possible that the 'war of the earl of Carrick' touched Edward more deeply, at a personal level, than William Wallace had ever done. It has been argued that Edward's pursuit of Bruce and those closest to him – especially those who had been personally involved in his inauguration as king – can be seen as a *feud*, with all the dark connotations that word can imply.[37]

Edward stopped short of executing the high-ranking churchmen who had been captured, notably Bishops Lamberton and Wishart, but they were loaded down with chains and sent to prisons in southern England. Lamberton remained in captivity until the end of Edward's reign, and Wishart was not released until 1315, after the battle of Bannockburn. Edward also approached Pope Clement, seeking their deposition from office, and one might well wonder what their fate would have been if Edward had been successful in this endeavour.

By the beginning of August Edward had reached Northumberland, close to the Scottish border, but the long journey north had been a punishing ordeal. At Hexham Abbey, for example, one of the monks was paid a pound for administering medicines to the king, and other records suggest he needed constant care.[38] At the end of the month there is a strong possibility that the king was thought to be close to death, because he took steps to make landed provision for his younger children. As summer gave way to autumn he appears to have recovered some of his vitality – one of his followers observed that he was 'hearty and strong enough, considering his age' – yet it quickly became apparent that extensive travel was still beyond him.[39] In late September Edward and his entourage halted at Lanercost Priory, where he was to remain for almost six months.

* * * *

There must surely have been times when Edward was unable to cope with affairs of state, but he was determined to maintain his grip on the reins of power. It is generally assumed that he continued to assert his will, and that commands issued in his name truly reflected the wishes of the king himself. It is striking, certainly, that great pains were taken – on the whole – to ensure that he was kept adequately informed of events in Scotland. Records have been preserved which provide evidence of the expenses of messengers who travelled to and fro between Scotland and Northumberland.[40] Moreover, as the year 1306 progressed, Edward continued to receive encouraging news, and Bruce's position became increasingly precarious.

In early August Bruce suffered another defeat, this time at the hands of his own countrymen. At Dalry, at the head of Loch Tay, he encountered the forces of John Macdougall of Lorn, and it would appear that Bruce was fortunate to escape alive. The victorious commander, also known as John *Bacach* (the lame), was a close kinsman of the Comyns, and he would become one of Bruce's most tenacious enemies in the years to come.

Elsewhere in Scotland, Bruce's strongholds continued to fall. Sir Christopher Seton, Bruce's brother-in-law, was taken at Loch Doon. Seton, it might be noted, was an Englishman, but he was one of Bruce's closest friends; he was also thought to have been heavily involved in the murder of Comyn. Thus he was dispatched to Dumfries, the site of Comyn's death, where he met his own death on Edward's orders. Sir Simon Fraser was also taken in August, following a skirmish in the Forest. As a former knight of Edward's household who had broken his oath to Edward on more than one occasion, he could not have expected any further mercy. Edward commanded that Fraser should be taken in chains to London, where his death provided a gruesome spectacle to rival that of Wallace.

In the meantime Bruce had divided his dwindling forces, sending the earl of Atholl to Kildrummy, to the west of Aberdeen. Bruce's wife, together with a number of other noblewomen, had been sent here for safety, and Atholl was charged with the task of escorting them to safety abroad. Valence had already established control of the eastern seaports, however, and soon Kildrummy was besieged by a strong force under the prince of Wales. Led by Bruce's brother Neil, the castle's garrison offered fierce resistance, but eventually, in early September, Kildrummy fell to the prince's forces. Neil Bruce was captured. The earl of Atholl, together with the ladies, had managed to slip away, moving north towards the coast. Presumably he hoped to find a ship that would convey the women to safety in the Isles, or perhaps even to Norway. But their pursuers caught up with them at Tain, where all the members of the party were taken prisoner.

The fate of the men was predictable. Neil Bruce was tried by the prince of Wales in early October, after which he was drawn through the streets of Berwick and hanged. The prince had taken a leading role in the most recent campaign – showing a readiness to 'burn and kill' that would continue into his own reign as king – but his father remained the driving force behind the savage policy of retribution. Edward I received pleas from various people, including Queen Margaret, in her traditional role as intercessor, to spare Atholl's life. It was pointed out to Edward that Atholl was his kinsman, as the Scottish earl was descended from an illegitimate daughter of King John, but Edward was determined that Atholl must also die. Though the king remained in the north, this execution also took place in London. There was a grim reference to Atholl's rank, as he was hanged on a higher gallows than the other prisoners who died with him. Atholl's head joined a growing collection in the city, but the rest of his body, together with the gallows, was burned to ashes.[41]

The female captives included Bruce's wife Elizabeth and his sister Mary, his young daughter Marjory, and the countess of Buchan. The lives of the women were spared, but cruel and unusual punishments were devised for Mary Bruce and the countess of Buchan. Edward ordered that the two women should be confined in cages, at Roxburgh and Berwick Castles respectively. The countess of Buchan's cage was fashioned in the form of a crown, as a direct reference to her role in Bruce's inauguration as king of Scots. The cages were equipped with enclosed privies, but otherwise there was a deliberate intention of shameful display, so that all who cared to do so might watch the two women 'for spectacle'.[42]

According to *Flores Historiarum*, Edward ordained that the countess of Buchan should be kept in her cage for the rest of her life – and even after death.[43] In fact, she remained there until 1310, when she was transferred to custody in a convent, although her ultimate fate is unknown. Edward had originally ordered that Bruce's daughter should also be caged, at the Tower of London, but eventually he relented (perhaps because she was still only twelve years old), and she was moved to a Yorkshire nunnery. Curiously, Bruce's queen was treated with greater respect. As we have seen, there is a tradition that she had opposed her husband's decision to claim the Scottish throne, but it is probably more significant that Edward did not wish to antagonise her father, the earl of Ulster. Even so, Elizabeth was attended by women who were instructed to keep a sober countenance, and she, her step-daughter and Mary Bruce would all face years of captivity.

Robert Bruce himself remained elusive – and his exploits at this time have grown in the telling – but in September he was pinned down at Dunaverty Castle, at the tip of Kintyre. Yet when Edward's commanders fought their way into the castle, they discovered that Bruce had escaped again, vanishing into the Western Isles. During the winter of 1306/7 Bruce disappears from history, passing temporarily into legend. By this time, however, although the hunt for him continued, he was no longer seen as a serious threat. He was mocked in English rhymes, and also at the English court, as 'King Hobbe' (the crowned fool).[44] In spite of Edward's age and infirmity, it still appeared that Robert Bruce was no match for the Hammer of the Scots. His extraordinary comeback from this position, when his fortunes appeared to be at their lowest point, has been described as 'one of the great heroic enterprises of history'.[45]

* * * *

After the fall of Kildrummy and Dunaverty, a certain amount of complacency appears to have set in amongst the English in Scotland. A number of the younger knights, including Giles de Argentin and Piers Gaveston, deserted the army, leaving to take part in a tournament overseas. Edward was furious, ordering their immediate arrest as soon as they had returned, but on this occasion he was moved to clemency and forgiveness through the intervention of the queen. What troubled Edward most about this episode, perhaps, was that most of the men involved were close associates of the prince of Wales. The prince himself had not joined his companions in their recent adventures, as he was temporarily engaged on his father's business in southern England. But when he returned to the north, in February 1307, there was a furious row between King Edward and his son.

By this time King Edward was surely aware of the disturbing intimacy between Piers Gaveston and his son. When the prince informed him that he wished to grant lands in Gascony to Gaveston, there was an explosion of anger: 'You bastard son of a bitch! Now you want to give lands away – you who never gained any? As the Lord lives, were it not for the fear of breaking up the kingdom, you should never enjoy your inheritance!'[46]

The source of this story is Walter of Guisborough, and his account goes on to tell us that Edward – seemingly somewhat recovered from his recent infirmities – seized his son, beat him and tore out chunks of his hair. Orders were subsequently given that Gaveston should be exiled to the continent. The prince of Wales accompanied his friend to the south coast; his action ensured that Edward I would never see his eldest son again.

Edward's anger and impatience were also directed towards others, as by this time Robert Bruce had returned to the Scottish mainland. Seaborne efforts to find Bruce had led to nothing but frustration. Moreover, leaving aside the later tales of inspirational spiders and romantic liaisons, the king of Scots had gathered new resources. On his father's side he could be seen as an Anglo-Norman baron, but through his mother's family he possessed considerable links with the Gaelic world. Bruce found shelter somewhere in the Hebrides, or perhaps in Ireland, and the network he created in this period would provide him with the strength and confidence to make a new attempt to establish himself on the Scottish throne.

Bruce charged two of his younger brothers, Thomas and Alexander, to seek support in Galloway, but after landing they were quickly intercepted and defeated by a force of Galwegians loyal to Edward. The Galwegian commander, Dungal MacDowell, was later knighted as a reward for his efforts. Thomas and Alexander were both captured. The prisoners were dispatched south, initially to the prince of Wales, who was then still in northern England, along with the heads of several of Bruce's Gaelic allies. Alexander Bruce was a cleric in holy orders (he was, in fact, the Dean of Glasgow), yet on 17 February both brothers were executed in Carlisle.

Meanwhile, Robert Bruce had landed in Carrick, where Henry Percy had been installed as earl in his absence, but he met with a cool reception from the local population. It was during this campaign, however, that Bruce truly established his reputation for stealth and ruthless cunning. The king of Scots and his men created such havoc that Percy considered it prudent to abandon Turnberry Castle and leave the area. Bruce rendered his former home indefensible, as he now fully recognised that castles were more useful to the English than to the Scots.

At this time Edward was still at Lanercost, and evidently becoming increasingly frustrated. He sent a series of letters to his commanders in Scotland, expressing his 'great and not unnatural wonder' that he had not yet heard news of their success.[47] On 6 February Walter Langton was instructed to send a message to Valence, to inform him that Edward had received reports from elsewhere of his failures, and that he was aware that Valence was deliberately attempting to keep him in the dark.

Given that Bruce had not even landed on the Scottish mainland at this point, it is difficult to believe that Edward had genuinely heard any such news. Though the king evidently trusted and respected Valence, on this occasion he appears to have resorted to a rather mean-spirited device to encourage his lieutenant to increased efforts.

Under pressure from Edward to deliver results, it is easy to imagine Valence's own sense of frustration in the coming months. He was based at Ayr at the time of Bruce's landing, less than twenty miles from Turnberry, yet Bruce was able to slip away before Valence could respond. As winter turned to spring, Bruce maintained himself in the hills and forests to the south-east, establishing a base in the valley of Glentrool. In April Valence led a mounted foray into Glentrool, but when he encountered Bruce's forces he was forced to withdraw. In the following month Bruce appears to have gathered new recruits, and emerged from the wilds of Galloway. Valence suffered another reverse at Loudoun Hill, where Bruce had set up an ambush or road-block. Bruce's main target here was almost certainly Walter Langton, who was then engaged in a fact-finding mission in Scotland, together with the gold coin the treasurer had brought north.

Edward was furious that Valence had 'retreated before King Hobbe without doing any exploit', although these words would suggest that Valence was able to retire in good order from Loudoun Hill without sustaining heavy losses.[48] Whilst Bruce's recent successes must have been good for his morale, the strength of his position should not be exaggerated. Elsewhere in Scotland, however, there is circumstantial evidence to suggest that his cause was gathering momentum. On 15 May one of Edward's Scottish officials sent a letter south from Forfar:

> I hear that Bruce never had the goodwill of his own followers or of the people in general as much as now. It appears that God is with him, for he has destroyed King Edward's power both among the English and the Scots [. . .] May it please God to prolong King Edward's life, for men say openly that when he is gone the victory will go to Bruce.[49]

Bruce's new-found popularity owed much to the work of itinerant 'false preachers', who presented resistance to Edward as a Christian duty. In spite of the shocking events at Dumfries Kirk, and in defiance of the Pope, the bishop of Moray asserted that Bruce was engaged in a kind of crusade: a theme that was later taken up with enthusiasm by John Barbour. The king of Scots still had a long road ahead of him, but we are starting to see glimmers here of how Bruce's personal struggle would eventually become synonymous with a much larger cause.

Pro-Bruce propaganda also made reference to prophecy, which maintained a tremendous hold on the minds of medieval men. It had been foretold, apparently, that 'after the death of the covetous king [*le Roy Coveytous*]', the Scots would join together with the Welsh and live thereafter in peace. Of course Edward, whose death was imminently expected, might be characterised as the 'covetous king'; it is unsurprising that Scots were now able to relate their own experience to that of the Welsh. This prophecy, it might be added, was attributed to Merlin. English writers had attempted to appropriate the Arthurian legends for their own purposes, and Edward's association (and perhaps self-identification) with the fabled king might be seen as an important development in this process. Yet in the 'Celtic fringes' of Britain there was tenacious resistance to the idea that King Arthur should be regarded as an Englishman: tenacious resistance that continues to this day.

*   *   *   *

In March 1307 Edward finally left Lanercost, and based himself at Carlisle. Orders were sent out shortly afterwards for the organisation of yet another Scottish campaign; Edward had resolved to take matters back into his own hands. On 15 May it was reported that the king had witnessed a parade of four hundred men, all decked out with leaves to celebrate Whitsun: a sight which made him 'much pleased and merry'.[50] The writer added that Edward planned to go to Dumfries, though 'not until after Midsummer'. However, by the time of Edward's sixty-eighth birthday, on 17 June, by which time further troops had begun to assemble in the city, the king was nowhere to be seen. Understandably, there were fresh rumours that Edward was on the point of death – if he had not died already – and there was a serious possibility that his forces would disintegrate before the campaign had even begun.

Upon hearing these tidings, Edward stirred himself to another great effort. There was no more time to waste, and the army was ordered to prepare to march. Edward gave his litter as an offering at Carlisle Cathedral; from this point onwards he would ride at the head of his men, as he had done throughout his reign. It was a magnificent gesture. At moments like this one gains a sense of the awesome responsibility of medieval kingship: of the intensity of a life that was never chosen, and was lived out almost always amidst a sea of watchful eyes. Yet if the spirit was still willing, the flesh was weak. Walter of Guisborough believed that Edward was suffering from dysentery.[51] The king left Carlisle on 26 June, but ten days later he had covered barely six miles.[52]

Edward was now a dying man, and numerous stories about this time have found their way into later sources.[53] According to the *Brut* chronicle, Edward called his most faithful lieutenants to his side. Aymer de Valence was present, as were the earl of Lincoln and Robert Clifford. Edward charged his loyal followers to guide and support his eldest son, and also to obey his final commands. One of Edward's instructions, as recounted by the later chronicler Jean Froissart, was quite astonishing. The king wished that, after his death, his bones should be boiled and taken with the army each time the English went to war in Scotland. Edward 'believed most firmly', it was said, 'that as long as his bones should be carried against the Scots, those Scots would never be victorious'.

On 6 July Edward was at Burgh by Sands on the Solway Firth. This is a desolate place, which must have offered him little comfort. From here it was a short march to the Solway fords and the crossing into Scotland, yet Edward's travels had finally come to an end. His body ravaged by age and illness, his mind exhausted, the king of England was barely clinging to life. On the following day, when his attendants sought to rouse him and help him to eat, he gave up the struggle at last.

Epilogue

The outcomes of military affairs are not determined solely by individuals, but even so, with the benefit of hindsight, it is clear that the death of Edward I was a turning point in the Scottish Wars of Independence. The reactions of English contemporary writers would suggest they had witnessed the passing of a great man:

> Of England he was lord.
> and a king who knew much of war,
> In no book can we read
> of a king who sustained better his land.
> All the things which he would do,
> wisely he brought them to an end.
> Now his body lies in the earth;
> and the world is going to ruin.[1]

Some of the tributes paid to Edward were relatively conventional, although his death was also recognised as an event of international significance; it was said that the Pope, upon hearing the news, collapsed to the floor with shock and grief.[2]

Edward was laid to rest in an austere black marble tomb, now adorned only by its famous inscription. The first part of this, describing Edward as 'the Hammer of the Scots', is well known, but the second part, *Pactum Serva* ('Keep the vow'), has not entered the public consciousness to the same extent. The second part has led historian Marc Morris to suggest that 'the letters as they appear today were evidently painted in the sixteenth century, but the sentiments they express are almost certainly earlier'.[3] Thus the inscription might be seen as a reminder to his son, and others, of the oath the younger man had sworn to subdue the Scots. Yet was it ultimately Edward's final rebuke?

Edward I's successor, Edward of Caernarfon, now King Edward II of England, did have some personal qualities. However, he lacked his father's grim determination to achieve victory in Scotland, and he swiftly became distracted by other concerns. Robert Bruce is said to have commented that 'he feared the bones of the dead king more than he feared the live one, and that it was a greater feat of war to wrest six inches of territory from Edward I than to gain a whole kingdom from his son'.[4] Many rulers would have struggled to cope with Edward I's legacy of debt, war and building resentment against the crown's demands, but Edward II's problems were exacerbated by his poor management of the nobility. His reign would be defined by internal conflict, which ultimately led to his deposition and death. His continued infatuation with the recalled Piers Gaveston – whose arrogance inflamed the new king's noble opponents – did nothing to help his cause.

In 1307 Edward II ignored his dying father's wishes. Edward I's last campaign was hastily abandoned after a desultory incursion into southern Scotland, and the new king of England travelled south to be crowned. He would not return to Scotland until 1310, and in the next three years the English war effort lost any sense of momentum. Edward's supporters in Scotland received little tangible assistance, even though they clamoured for aid. English garrisons remained secure in the great castles of the Scottish lowlands, but Bruce was able to break out from the south-west. In other areas of the country the patriot cause made great strides. By the end of 1308 Bruce had comprehensively defeated the Comyn faction in Scotland; the Comyn earl of Buchan fled south to England, dying shortly afterwards. In 1309 Bruce held his first parliament at St Andrews.

In 1314, as is well known, the Scots inflicted a shattering defeat on the English at the battle of Bannockburn. Edward II was lucky to escape capture, but in the exchange of prisoners that followed Bruce's queen was returned to Scotland (as was Robert Wishart). In the succeeding years Bruce took the war to England (and Ireland), ravaging the northern counties. At one point Bruce's Scottish enemies had pursued him with dogs, but now Bruce was the hunter and his quarry was the king of England himself. In 1322 Edward II was almost captured in Yorkshire. After Edward II's deposition, the English agreed a peace treaty with Bruce, acknowledging his right to the Scottish throne. Edward I and his courtiers had mocked Robert Bruce as 'King Hobbe', while also planning that he should suffer an excruciating death on the gallows. Yet Bruce eventually died in his bed, safely back in the fold of the Church and secure in his position as king of Scots.

This, of course, was not the end of the matter. Edward III of England reopened the conflict, ironically supporting Edward Balliol in a bid for the Scottish crown, and it was perhaps fortunate for Scotland that he later became distracted by a new war with France. Nevertheless, the renewal of the 'Auld Alliance' helped to ensure that Anglo-Scottish relations remained fraught with tension for the rest of the Middle Ages. There were long periods of truce, in which there were opportunities for more constructive interactions,[5] but the two kingdoms remained officially at war for almost two hundred years.[6] In the Anglo-Scottish marches raiding, or *reiving*, became a way of life. Berwick-upon-Tweed, once a flourishing port and a centre of commerce, became a military base that passed back and forth between the two sides. Edward I had made grand plans for the re-founding of Berwick in the wake of the sack of 1296, but the town has never recovered its former status.

Various national stereotypes were already in existence by the end of the thirteenth century – for instance the notion that the English had tails – but as the years passed the boundaries between English and Scottish identities hardened. In the *Luttrell Psalter*, produced during the reign of Edward III for an English veteran of the Scottish wars, the Scots are depicted as painted savages slaughtering defenceless English people; these images make an interesting complement to the evidence of English chronicles.[7] But the Scots responded in kind; Blind Harry's *Wallace* is perhaps the most obvious retort, although the same sentiments can be found elsewhere. Opposition to, and defiance of, the English became an important component of Scottish culture, even during periods when bloodshed was largely avoided.

It is often suggested that the Wars of Independence helped to *create* a stronger sense of Scottish identity. Perhaps, however, in some cases the conflict obliged people to find new ways to articulate feelings that were already deeply held. For several years the Scottish patriots continued to justify their resistance on the basis of their allegiance to John Balliol – even if he were a distinctly uninspiring figure in person – but what are we to make of Oliphant's claim that he held Stirling 'of the Lion'? And then there are the following words, adapted from the work of Sallust during the reign of Robert Bruce, which have taken on a life of their own: 'It is in truth not for glory, nor riches, nor honours, that we are fighting, but for freedom – for that alone, which no honest man gives up but with life itself.'[8]

The so-called *Declaration of Arbroath* had a specific purpose – it was essentially another attempt to curry favour with the Pope – but historical documents can always be interpreted in many different ways.

*   *   *   *

England would remain the dominant kingdom in the British Isles, but Edward's failure to subjugate Scotland heralded the waning of English influence. Wales would remain under English rule – despite the heroic efforts of Owain Glyndŵr – but there was a resurgence of native power in Ireland. Edward's 'British project' would not be pursued seriously again, in any meaningful sense, until the era of the Tudors. Why, though, was Edward I not able to achieve a lasting military victory over the Scots? A final assessment of Edward's Scottish wars must take into account various factors – naturally including the efforts of the Scots – but of course we must also give serious consideration to the role of the king himself.

By 1296, when Edward's Scottish wars began, the dashing young man who had led the charge at Lewes was already long gone. Even so, albeit perhaps with some adjustments, Edward was able to cope with the rigours of campaign life until he was well into his sixties. He did indeed 'know much of war', yet in truth he has a mixed record as a military leader. Michael Prestwich has observed that Edward does not emerge from his Scottish wars as a particularly imaginative or inspired commander, but also that the English appear to have performed more effectively when the king campaigned in person.[9] Both points are well made.

In some respects, warfare brought Edward's attributes to the fore.

His courage at the siege of Stirling in 1304, where he scorned the missiles from the walls, helped to sustain the impression that God had preserved him for great things. At the River Cree in 1300, when others might have hesitated, his decisive action prevented the possibility of a serious reverse. Moreover, whilst he did endure a difficult relationship with some of his nobles, there were many others – such as Valence, Lincoln and Surrey – in whom he inspired consistent loyalty (if not always entirely effective service). And one quality that Edward certainly possessed – perhaps to a greater extent than any other man who wore the English crown – was force of will: a determination to assert and defend what he saw as his rights against any and all comers. The story that Edward wished his bones to be boiled down and left unburied so that he could lead his armies posthumously against Scotland may be apocryphal, but there is surely at least a trace of the real man in this.

At Falkirk in 1298 it is surprisingly difficult to account for Edward's personal role. It is intriguing that none of the chroniclers chose to exalt his martial exploits, although his determination and leadership in the days before the battle were surely significant. As far as military tactics are concerned, more generally, there is little evidence of the speed and flair of his youth. It was the Scots' decision to turn the conflict into a war of attrition, but Edward appears to have embraced this; after all, he might have concluded, he had already defeated the Welsh in similar circumstances. Throughout the whole of Edward's Scottish wars there was a constant refrain: one more push, one more concentration of massive force, and Edward's power would eventually prevail. These methods did bring results in Scotland – most notably the submission of John Comyn in 1304 – but the costs were enormous.

By medieval standards the logistical effort involved in Edward's Scottish wars was phenomenal – Edward clearly had an eye for talent in this area – but the supply chain was always precarious. Even if the people of England, Wales and Ireland could be persuaded (or compelled) to provide sufficient supplies, this did not guarantee that they would arrive when and where they were needed. In part this was due to the vagaries of the Scottish landscape, and the weather, which the Scots could also turn to their advantage in the field; whereas for the Welsh of Gwynedd their mountains ultimately became a prison, and Prince Llywelyn was killed when he tried to break out to the south, the Scots were much harder to pin down. Moreover, Edward experienced a range of financial difficulties in his later years as king; the problems involved in maintaining a regular supply of coin ensured that his vast infantry forces were dangerously prone to desertion. Scotland posed a much larger challenge than Wales had done – in every sense.

There were some notable English successes, and Edward must be given a share of the credit for these, but he must also take responsibility for some of the failures. Above all, even though he does seem to have respected certain individual Scots (such as John Comyn the Younger), he was too slow to appreciate the powerful feelings that his actions had unleashed north of the border, and because of this he consistently underestimated the strength of Scottish resistance. Whilst we have seen that Edward could be more subtle and flexible than is often supposed, and that he could be open to compromise (at least temporarily), he did not always work hard enough to understand other men. The complacency and arrogance he displayed in 1296, having seemingly won a crushing victory, would prove disastrous for his cause in Scotland.

By 1305 it appeared that Edward had learned some important lessons; not every Scotsman shared Wallace's and Wishart's uncompromising principles, and it must have appeared that there was a real opportunity, at last, for an enduring settlement. However the English response to Bruce's insurrection – at which time Edward's powers were clearly waning – was badly miscalculated. True, Edward's commanders did come close to taking Bruce – who might conceivably have become a mere footnote in British history. But the savage treatment of Scottish prisoners – both male and female – was entirely counter-productive. As more Scotsmen died, we are told, more joined the new king – 'notwithstanding the terrible vengeance inflicted on the Scots who adhered to the party of the aforesaid Robert'.[10]

In March 1307, by which point he had resolved to take matters fully back into his own hands, Edward did express concern about the direction of Scottish affairs. He was particularly perturbed, apparently, that 'some people' – meaning the prince of Wales? – had interpreted his recent orders in a fashion that was 'too harsh and rigorous'.[11] Edward now ordained that all those who had been 'compelled' to join Bruce should be pardoned. By this time, however, doubtless many Scotsmen had concluded that Edward's actions spoke much louder than his words.

Modern historians should attempt to avoid anachronistic judgements of medieval personalities, yet it will come as no surprise to learn that medieval Scottish writers offered sterner assessments of Edward than their English peers. Walter Bower took comfort from his belief that Edward would be punished after his death for his sins in life. On the night of Edward's passing, according to Bower, an English knight saw a vision in which the king was accosted by demons. As they carried Edward's spirit away, lashing him with whips and flails, the demons laughed and mocked him:

Behold King Edward, raging like a leopard!
At one time, while he was alive, he evilly struck down the Lord's people.
You will go, dear friend, as our companion on such a journey
to the place where you are condemned to associate with devils.

At the last moment, it is said, the old king repented of his folly: 'Alas, why have I sinned? [. . .] at great cost I have brought torments upon myself.'[12]

On this earth, of course, the ambitions of great men invariably have larger consequences for others. Edward's decision to pursue war in Scotland ultimately caused suffering for thousands, on both sides of the border. Whilst it is not easy to recapture the experiences of 'ordinary' people, the story of Edward's Scottish wars must be their story too.

The real Edward might well have responded to his critics that he could not have acted otherwise; even if he had fully appreciated the scale of the challenge facing him in Scotland, he would surely have contended that his honour was in jeopardy – thereby making withdrawal impossible. And yet, even though this was a king who set such store by the defence of his 'rights', would Edward really have taken much pride in his famous soubriquet? The 'Hammer of the Scots' would almost certainly have preferred to be known today as the Hammer of the French, or (even better) the Hammer of the Muslims. Edward saw the crusade as the highest calling available to secular men, and his ambition to 'recover' the Holy Land should be taken seriously. We might imagine that Edward saw the intransigence of the Scots, alongside the machinations of Philip the Fair, as the greatest barrier preventing him from fulfilling this goal.

Edward was never the most sanguine of men, but frustration at the thwarting of his wider ambitions surely accounts, at least in part, for his terrifying anger when Robert Bruce rebelled. The ageing king was raging against the dying of the light, against the death of his dreams. In that respect, it could be argued that Edward's famous epitaph – *Scottorum Malleus*: the Hammer of the Scots – is not really a tribute to the man encased in that sombre tomb. Paradoxically, it might also be seen as a tribute to his Scottish enemies – men such as Bruce, Comyn, Murray and Wallace – who opposed Edward with such great vigour, and at such great cost.

Abbreviations

Barbour, *The Bruce*	John Barbour, *The Bruce*, ed. A.A.M. Duncan (Edinburgh, 1997).
Barrow, *Robert Bruce*	G.W.S. Barrow, *Robert Bruce and the Community of the Realm of Scotland* (4th edition, Edinburgh, 2005).
Bower	Walter Bower, *Scotichronicon*, ed. D.E.R. Watt et al (Aberdeen and Edinburgh, 1987–98), 9 vols, vi.
CCR	*Calendar of Close Rolls* (HMSO, 1892–).
CDS	*Calendar of Documents Relating to Scotland*, ed. J. Bain *et al* (Edinburgh, 1881–1988), 5 vols.
Chronicle of Bury St Edmunds	*The Chronicle of Bury St Edmunds, 1212–1301*, ed. Antonia Gransden (London, 1964).
England and Scotland at War	Andy King and David Simpkin (eds), *England and Scotland at War, c.1296–c.1513* (Leiden, 2012).
Fisher, Wallace	Andrew Fisher, *William Wallace* (2nd edition, Edinburgh, 2007, first published 2002).
Flores	*Flores Historiarum*, ed. Henry Luard (Rolls Series, 1890), 3 vols, iii.
Guisborough	*The Chronicle of Walter of Guisborough*, ed. Harry Rothwell (Camden Society, lxxxix, 1957).
History of the King's Works	R. Allen Brown, H.M. Colvin and A.J. Taylor, *The History of the King's Works: Volume 1: The Middle Ages* (HMSO, 1963).
HMSO	Her Majesty's Stationery Office.
Impact of the Edwardian Castles	Diane M. Williams and John R. Kenyon (eds), *The Impact of the Edwardian Castles in Wales* (Oxford, 2010).
'John of Fordun'	*John of Fordun's Chronicle of the Scottish Nation*, ed. William F. Skene (Edinburgh, 1873).
Lanercost Chronicle	*The Chronicle of Lanercost, 1272–1346*, tr. Sir Herbert Maxwell (Glasgow, 1913).
Langtoft	*The Chronicle of Pierre de Langtoft*, ed. Thomas Wright (Rolls Series, 1868), ii.
A Military History of Scotland	Edward M. Spiers, Jeremy Crang and Matthew Strickland (eds), *A Military History of Scotland* (Edinburgh, 2012).

Morris, *Great and*　　Marc Morris, *A Great and Terrible King:*
Terrible King　　　　*Edward I and the Forging of Britain* (London, 2009,
　　　　　　　　　　　first published 2008).
Palgrave, *Documents*　*Documents and Records Illustrating the History of*
　　　　　　　　　　　Scotland, ed. Sir Francis Palgrave (HMSO, 1837).
Prestwich, *War,*　　　Michael Prestwich, *War, Politics and Finance under*
Politics and Finance　*Edward I* (London, 1972).
Prestwich, *Edward I*　Michael Prestwich, *Edward I* (revised edition,
　　　　　　　　　　　London, 1997).
Prestwich, *Armies and*　Michael Prestwich, *Armies and Warfare in the*
Warfare　　　　　　　*Middle Ages: The English Experience* (Yale, 1999,
　　　　　　　　　　　first published 1996).
PRO　　　　　　　　　Public Record Office, London.
Rishanger　　　　　　*Willelmi Rishanger, Chronica et Annales*, ed. Henry
　　　　　　　　　　　T. Riley (Rolls Series, 1865).
Scalacronica　　　　*Sir Thomas Gray's Scalacronica, 1272–1363*, ed.
　　　　　　　　　　　Andy King (Surtees Society, ccix, 2005).
Soldier Experience　Adrian R. Bell, Anne Curry et al (eds), *The Soldier*
　　　　　　　　　　　Experience in the Fourteenth Century (Woodbridge,
　　　　　　　　　　　2011).
Stevenson, *Documents*　*Documents Illustrative of the History of Scotland*, ed.
　　　　　　　　　　　J. Stevenson, (Edinburgh, 1870), 2 vols, ii.
Stones, *Anglo-Scottish*　*Anglo-Scottish Relations, 1174–1328: Some Selected*
Relations　　　　　　*Documents*, ed. E.L.G. Stones (Oxford, 1965).
TNA　　　　　　　　The National Archives.
Traquair, *Freedom's*　Peter Traquair, *Freedom's Sword: Scotland's War of*
Sword　　　　　　　*Independence* (London, 1998).
Watson, *Under the*　Fiona J. Watson, *Under the Hammer: Edward I and*
Hammer　　　　　　*Scotland* (Edinburgh, 2005, first published 1998).
Wallace Book　　　Edward J. Cowan (ed.), *The Wallace Book*
　　　　　　　　　　　(Edinburgh, 2007).

Notes

References, unless abbreviated (see pp. 195–6), are given in full on the first occasion in which they appear in each chapter but in shortened form thereafter.

Chapter 1. Setting the Scene

1. *Matthew Paris's English History from the Year 1235 to 1272*, tr. J.A. Giles (London, 1854) vol. III, pp. 30–1.
2. See Nigel Saul, *For Honour and Fame: Chivalry in England, 1066–1500* (London, 2011), p. 76.
3. Matthew Paris included a famous story in which a blameless young man, whom Edward encountered on the road, was ordered to be mutilated by Edward's followers. Marc Morris interprets this account as 'exaggerated gossip', because the details are so vague, although he also notes that record sources provide other evidence of delinquent behaviour on the part of Edward's household. Morris, *Great and Terrible King*, p. 28.
4. Maurice Keen, *Chivalry* (London, 1984), p. 16.
5. See Richard W. Kaeuper, *Chivalry and Violence in Medieval Europe* (Oxford, 1999), pp. 121–8 and *passim*.
6. *The Metrical Chronicle of Robert of Gloucester*, ed. William Wright (Rolls Series, 1887), 2 vols, ii, p. 765.
7. *English Historical Documents, 1189–1327*, ed. Harry Rothwell (London, 1975), pp. 904–5.
8. See Morris, *Great and Terrible King*, p. 207.
9. Caroline Burt, *Edward I and the Governance of England* (Cambridge, 2013).
10. The most obvious evidence is perhaps provided by the work of the 'Trailbaston' commissions, which is briefly discussed below (p. 167).
11. Andrew M. Spencer, *Nobility and Kingship in Medieval England: The Earls and Edward I, 1272–1307* (Cambridge, 2014), quote at p. 259.
12. One issue concerned the building of castles. Llywelyn objected

to English lords building castles on land to which he had a claim; he also argued that the English government had no right to prevent him from building a castle and borough at Dolforwyn, on his own land, as it sought to do. Prestwich, *Edward I*, pp. 173–4.

13. Quoted in Prestwich, *Edward I*, p. 205.

14. See Prestwich, *Edward I*, p. 111.

15. Morris, *Great and Terrible King*, p. 145.

16. Quoted, in translation, in E.L.G. Stones, *Edward I* (Oxford, 1968), p. 2. For an alternative translation, which differs in some respects, see Antonia Gransden, *Historical Writing in England, c. 550 to c. 1307* (London, 1974), p. 506.

17. T.F. Tout, 'Margaret (1240–1275)', rev. Norman H. Reid, *Oxford Dictionary of National Biography* (Oxford, 2004) [http://www.oxforddnb.com/view/article/18045].

18. For this episode, see Morris, *Great and Terrible King*, p. 129.

19. For a good discussion see G.W.S. Barrow, 'The Anglo-Norman Impact, c. 1100 to c. 1286', in *Scotland: The Making and Unmaking of the Nation, c. 1100–1707*, ed. Bob Harris and Alan R. MacDonald (Dundee, 2006), pp. 17–31.

20. Is it significant, as argued by A.A.M. Duncan, that even Scottish supporters of Edward I tended to send letters to him in Latin, given that Edward would almost certainly have preferred to receive letters written in French? (Latin, unlike Scots or Gaelic, would of course have been understood by educated men on both sides of the border.) See A.A.M. Duncan, *The Kingship of the Scots, 842–1292* (Edinburgh, 2004), pp. 173–4. However, Geoffrey Barrow cites some more circumstantial evidence of the use of French in Scotland, and is therefore inclined to take a more cautious view: G.W.S. Barrow, 'French after the Style of Petithachengon', in *Church, Chronicle and Learning in Medieval and Early Renaissance Scotland*, ed. Barbara Crawford (Edinburgh, 1999), pp. 187–94.

21. Geoffrey of Monmouth, *The History of the Kings of Britain*, tr. Lewis Thorpe (London, 1966), esp. pp. 54–75.

22. Stones, *Anglo-Scottish Relations*, p. 40.

23. For the English alternative, which omits Alexander's defiant words and has Robert Bruce 'the Noble' swear fealty on his behalf, see Stones, *Anglo-Scottish Relations*, pp. 38–40.

24. See Jessica Nelson, 'Yolande (d. in or after 1324)', *Oxford Dictionary of National Biography* (Oxford, 2008) [http://www.oxforddnb.com/view/article/96816].

Chapter 2. To Reduce the King and Kingdom of Scotland to His Rule

1. For a discussion of this oath, see A.A.M. Duncan, 'The Community of the Realm of Scotland and Robert Bruce', *Scottish Historical Review*, 45 (1966), pp. 186–7.

2. Dauvit Broun has recently demonstrated there were indeed seven Guardians (as opposed to six, as was previously thought), though Bishop William of Dunkeld may have died shortly after his appointment. See Dauvit Broun, 'New Information on the Guardians' Appointment in 1286 and on Wallace's Rising in 1297' (2011). Available online via http://www.breakingofbritain.ac.uk/feature-of-the-month/.

3. 'Institutions' being defined here in the sense of a well-established collection of customs, traditions and laws.

4. Alan Young, *Robert the Bruce's Rivals: The Comyns, 1212–1314* (East Linton, 1997), p. 151.

5. See, for example, Michael Brown, *The Wars of Scotland: 1214–1371* (Edinburgh, 2004), p. 159.

6. Michael Brown, 'Aristocratic Politics and the Crisis of Scottish Kingship, 1286–96', *Scottish Historical Review*, 229 (2011), pp. 1–26, especially pp. 5–10.

7. Bower, p. 8; see also Brown, *Wars of Scotland*, p. 158.

8. Prestwich, 'Edward I and the Maid of Norway', *Scottish Historical Review*, 188 (1990), p. 164.

9. The term is derived from the southern French word *bastir*, meaning 'to build'.

10. See Morris, *Great and Terrible King*, p. 217.

11. *Lanercost Chronicle*, p. 59.

12. Abernethy received no further punishment, but he was still in prison in 1291 and appears to have died in custody. His motive for the murder of Earl Duncan remains uncertain.

13. The terms of the Birgham agreement are printed and translated in G.W.S. Barrow, 'A Kingdom in Crisis: Scotland and the Maid of

Norway', *Scottish Historical Review*, 188 (1990), pp. 137–41.

14. Quoted in Fiona Watson, 'The Wars of Independence', in *Scotland: The Making and Unmaking of the Nation, c. 1100–1707*, ed. Bob Harris and Alan R. Macdonald (Dundee, 2006), p. 33.

15. *Scottish Historical Documents*, ed. Gordon Donaldson (Edinburgh, 1970), pp. 41–3, quotation at p. 43.

16. A.A.M. Duncan, *The Kingship of the Scots, 842–1292* (Edinburgh, 2002), pp. 199, 208, quoting the 'Bamburgh memorandum' of 1321.

17. Quoted in Morris, *Great and Terrible King*, p. 231.

18. Quoted in Morris, *Great and Terrible King*, p. 240.

19. For the most important modern account of the Great Cause, which provides a detailed discussion of all the available evidence, see Duncan, *Kingship of the Scots*, especially chapters 12 and 13. For a clear summary of the key issues, see, *inter alia*, A.D.M. Barrell, *Medieval Scotland* (Cambridge, 2000), pp. 96–103.

20. Duncan, *Kingship of the Scots*, p. 316; Brown, *Wars of Scotland*, p. 167.

21. The King of Norway's claim was based on the right of his late daughter, although his action was perhaps intended as a lever to obtain the last of the money that was owed for his late wife's dowry. Edward possessed a distant claim to the Scottish throne through his descent from Matilda of Scotland, the queen of Henry I of England. However, it is more likely that he briefly considered asserting his right on the basis that Scotland should 'revert' to him, now that he was recognised as overlord, in the absence of a direct heir.

22. It is sometimes suggested that Count Florence was encouraged to put forward a spurious claim by Edward, as the delay would enable the latter to consolidate his grip on Scotland. This point is discussed, for example, in Barrell, *Medieval Scotland*, pp. 101–2.

23. Stones, *Anglo-Scottish Relations*, pp. 63–4.

24. Intriguingly, a treatise was produced early in John's reign that was presumably intended to provide guidance for the new king. Now known as 'The Scottish King's Household', it was written in French and provides information about various aspects of royal administration in Scotland. See Amanda Beam, *The Balliol Dynasty, 1210–1364* (Edinburgh, 2008), pp. 125–6.

25. Stones, *Anglo-Scottish Relations*, p. 65.

26. Stones, *Anglo-Scottish Relations*, p. 66.
27. Morris, *Great and Terrible King*, p. 269, quoting the Evesham Chronicle.
28. Edward eventually felt compelled to swear an oath that his actions had *not* been motivated by lust!
29. Edward had received 100,000 marks three years earlier, when he was permitted to take control of a papal tax, which was intended to be used as funds for a crusade. This was held on Edward's behalf by the Riccardi, with whom he had a longstanding relationship. However, the Riccardi had also been taken by surprise by the turn in political events: they had invested the money elsewhere, Philip of France confiscated some of their assets, and they now lacked the liquidity to meet Edward's demands.

Chapter 3. The Bodies Fell Like Autumn Leaves
1. Stevenson, *Documents*, pp. 20–1.
2. See Prestwich, *War, Politics and Finance*, pp. 93–4.
3. It has been estimated that between a quarter and a third of the cavalry were usually knights. See Prestwich, *Armies and Warfare*, p. 51.
4. Prestwich, *Armies and Warfare*, p. 34.
5. Only a man's most expensive horse would be listed, although the value enrolled would be the result of negotiation with a royal clerk. In some cases the valuation may have reflected the social status of the owner, as opposed to the true market value of his horse.
6. Prestwich, *Armies and Warfare*, p. 35, citing the work of Andrew Ayton.
7. For a more detailed discussion of the armour worn in the period covered by this book, see Christopher Gravett, *English Medieval Knight 1200–1300* (Oxford, 2002) and Idem, *English Medieval Knight 1300–1400* (Oxford, 2002). See also Frédérique Lachaud, 'Armour and Military Dress in Thirteenth- and Early Fourteenth-Century England', *Armies, Chivalry and Warfare in Medieval Britain and France*, ed. Matthew Strickland (Stamford, 1998).
8. Lachaud, 'Armour and Military Dress', p. 357.
9. See Plate 6.
10. Prestwich, *War, Politics and Finance*, p. 47.
11. Prestwich, *War, Politics and Finance*, p. 52.

12. See, for example, Nigel Saul, *For Honour and Shame: Chivalry in England, 1066–1500* (London, 2011), p. 26.

13. Andrew M. Spencer, *Nobility and Kingship in Medieval England: The Earls and Edward I, 1272–1307* (Cambridge, 2014), p. 82.

14. See David Simpkin, *The English Aristocracy at War: From the Welsh Wars of Edward I to the Battle of Bannockburn* (Woodbridge, 2008), especially pp. 183–5. Simpkin's work offers a very detailed account of the mechanics of recruitment.

15. Cited in Prestwich, *War, Politics and Finance*, p. 101.

16. Gerald of Wales, *The Journey Through Wales and The Description of Wales*, tr. Lewis Thorpe (London, 1978), pp. 112–13.

17. Adam Chapman, 'Welshmen in the Armies of Edward I', *Impact of the Edwardian Castles*, pp. 179–80, quoting the work of Lodewyk van Veltham.

18. For a preliminary study, see David Bachrach, 'Edward I's Centurians: Professional Soldiers in an Era of Militia Armies', *Soldier Experience*, pp. 109–28.

19. Lachaud, 'Armour and Military Dress', pp. 347–8.

20. For the figures in this paragraph see A.Z. Freeman, 'Wall-Breakers and River-Bridgers: Military Engineers in the Scottish Wars of Edward I', *Journal of British Studies*, 10:2 (1971), p. 2.

21. See, for example, G.W.S. Barrow, 'The Army of Alexander III's Scotland', *Scotland in the Reign of Alexander III*, ed. Norman Reid (Edinburgh, 1990), pp. 132–47; and the chapters by Michael Prestwich and Matthew Strickland in *A Military History of Scotland*.

22. Matthew Strickland, 'The Kings of Scots at War, c. 1093–1286', in *A Military History of Scotland*, pp. 118–19.

23. Watson, *Under the Hammer*, pp. 23–4.

24. Barrow, 'The Army of Alexander III's Scotland', pp. 141–2.

25. Barrow, 'The Army of Alexander III's Scotland', p. 139, citing Hakon's Saga.

26. For this story, see Guisborough, pp. 271–2; and *Scalacronica*, p. 37.

27. Guisborough, p. 273.

28. *Lanercost Chronicle*, p. 134; Rishanger, p. 373.

29. For more information about medieval English chronicles, see Antonia Gransden, *Historical Writing in England I, c. 550 to c. 1307* (London, 1974), and Idem, *Historical Writing in England II, c. 1307*

to the Early Sixteenth Century (London, 1982). For the broader context see Chris Given-Wilson, *Chronicles: The Writing of History in Medieval England* (London, 2004). For a discussion of *Gesta Annalia* II, see Dauvit Broun, 'A New Look at Gesta Annalia attributed to John of Fordun', in *Church, Chronicle and Learning in Medieval and Early Renaissance Scotland*, ed. Barbara Crawford (Edinburgh, 1999).

30. Guisborough, p. 274.
31. Rishanger, p. 373.
32. See Traquair, *Freedom's Sword*, p. 47; Matthew Strickland, 'A Law of Arms or a Law of Treason? Conduct of War in Edward I's Campaigns in Scotland, 1296–1307', in *Violence in Medieval Society*, ed. Richard Kaeuper (Woodbridge, 2000), p. 66.
33. Rishanger, p. 374.
34. Strickland, 'Law of Arms', p. 67.
35. A point forcefully made by Sean McGlynn, for example in the context of his discussion of similar events at Limoges in 1370. See Sean McGlynn, *By Sword and Fire: Cruelty and Atrocity in Medieval Warfare* (London, 2008), especially pp. 182–5.
36. Cynthia Neville (ed.), 'A Plea Roll of Edward I's Army in Scotland, 1296', *Miscellany of the Scottish History Society*, vol. XI (1990). Available online at http://www.deremilitari.org/ RESOURCES/SOURCES/plearoll.htm. The original is preserved in the National Archives (E39/93/15).
37. For John's *diffidatio*, see Stones, *Anglo-Scottish Relations*, pp. 70–4.
38. *Lanercost Chronicle*, p. 136.
39. See Traquair, *Freedom's Sword*, p. 49.
40. For a discussion of this invasion and its significance, see McGlynn, *By Sword and Fire*, pp. 208–19.
41. Guisborough, p. 278.
42. For a more detailed account of the Battle of Dunbar, see, for example, Traquair, *Freedom's Sword*, pp. 50–1.
43. *Chronicle of Bury St Edmunds*, p. 131.
44. Quoted in Prestwich, *Edward I*. The translation quoted there is by E.L.G. Stones. See also Langtoft, p. 253, for a somewhat less engaging translation.

45. See Traquair, *Freedom's Sword*, p. 50; Prestwich, *Edward I*, p. 473. For an alternative interpretation, whose author is more inclined to take these figures seriously, see Alistair Macdonald, 'Courage, Fear and the Experience of the Later Medieval Scottish Soldier', *Scottish Historical Review*, 235 (2013), p. 203.

46. The earl of Mar appears to have died in custody in 1297. William, earl of Ross, remained in custody until 1303, when he agreed to swear fealty to Edward and was restored to his estates. In 1306 he was responsible for the capture of the earl of Atholl and Robert the Bruce's wife (see p. 180), for which he was later obliged to make reparation.

47. Langtoft, p. 251.

48. *Lanercost Chronicle*, p. 144.

49. These were the so-called Crown of Arthur and *Y Groes Nawdd*, a sacred relic that was believed to be a piece of the true cross.

50. Langtoft, pp. 265–7.

51. *Scalacronica*, p. 39.

Chapter 4. He Lifted Up His Head

1. See *Scalacronica*, p. 218, n. 16.

2. 'John of Fordun', p. 319.

3. For an excellent summary of Cressingham's career see Henry Summerson, 'Cressingham, Hugh of (d. 1297)', *Oxford Dictionary of National Biography* (Oxford, 2004; online edition, Jan. 2008) [http://www.oxforddnb.com/view/article/6671].

4. Barbour, *The Bruce*, pp. 54–6.

5. Stevenson, *Documents*, p. 198.

6. Michael Brown, *The Wars of Scotland: 1214–1371* (Edinburgh, 2004), p. 181.

7. Guisborough, p. 296. Quoted and translated in Barrow, *Robert Bruce*, p. 110.

8. Rishanger, p. 226, quoted and translated in Alexander Grant, 'Bravehearts and Coronets: Images of William Wallace and the Scottish Nobility', in *Wallace Book*, p. 102. Similar sentiments can be found in most English chronicles of this period.

9. Bower, p. 83.

10. 'John of Fordun', p. 321.

11. The best modern biography of Wallace is Fisher, *Wallace*, which discusses most of the relevant evidence; see pp. 5–26 for Wallace's early life. See also *Wallace Book*, especially the essays by A.A.M. Duncan and Alexander Grant.

12. For a discussion of this and other related matters, see A.A.M. Duncan, 'William, Son of Alan Wallace: The Documents', in *Wallace Book*, pp. 42–63, especially pp. 47–53.

13. It has been pointed out that both William and Malcolm Wallace were given the names of Scottish kings, which is perhaps suggestive of aspiration. See Grant, 'Bravehearts and Coronets', pp. 91–2. Grant is also inclined to believe that Malcolm's knighthood was long-standing: i.e. that he did not owe his knighthood to his association with William, after the latter had achieved power and influence in Scotland.

14. *CDS*, ii, no. 822, p. 191.

15. An argument cautiously suggested in Grant, 'Bravehearts and Coronets', pp. 102–3.

16. Blind Harry, *The Wallace*, ed. Anne McKim (Edinburgh, 2003), pp. 117–18.

17. For a good discussion, see Duncan, 'William, Son of Alan Wallace', pp. 58–9, and references there cited. See also *Scalacronica*, p. 41.

18. He was forced to leave valuables behind. Guisborough, p. 295.

19. As noted in a letter to Edward from Hugh Cressingham. Stevenson, *Documents*, pp. 202–3.

20. Dauvit Broun, 'New information on the Guardians in 1286 and on Wallace's rising in 1297' (2011). Available online via http://www.breakingofbritain.ac.uk/feature-of-the-month/.

21. *CDS*, ii, no. 887, p. 233.

22. *CDS*, ii, no. 900, p. 235.

23. Alternatively, of course, he might have been acutely conscious of his role in the events at Lanark, and therefore considered it prudent to make his own terms. As noted in Broun, 'New information on the Guardians'.

24. Stevenson, *Documents*, p. 212.

25. Stevenson, *Documents*, p. 202. It is often suggested that Cressingham had raised this force in Northumberland, but given the

numbers involved this seems unlikely. Since Welshmen are known to have fought with Cressingham at the Battle of Stirling in September, it seems probable that he was able to recruit on a much wider scale.

26. Stevenson, *Documents*, pp. 202–3.

27. Stevenson, *Documents*, p. 227.

28. Stevenson, *Documents*, p. 207.

29. Stevenson, *Documents*, pp. 223–4.

30. Stevenson, *Documents*, p. 226.

31. Prestwich, *War, Politics and Finance*, pp. 171–5.

32. Prestwich, *Edward I*, pp. 408–9; Idem, *Plantagenet England, 1225–1360* (Oxford, 2005), p. 168.

33. Pope Boniface's position was outlined in the bull *Clericis Laicos*, issued in 1296.

34. Guisborough, p. 290. Quoted and translated in Prestwich, *Edward I*, p. 416.

35. Guisborough, p. 291. Quoted and translated in Andrew M. Spencer, *Nobility and Kingship in Medieval England: The Earls and Edward I, 1272–1307* (Cambridge, 2014), p. 237.

36. Prestwich, *Edward I*, p. 421.

37. See Prestwich, *Edward I*, p. 392.

38. *Flores*, p. 296. Quoted and translated in Prestwich, *Edward I*, p. 422.

39. Prestwich, *Edward I*, p. 422. It was intended that the funds raised from the sale of the wool would be used to pay outstanding debts to Edward's allies on the continent.

40. Prestwich, *Edward I*, p. 422.

41. See Fisher, *Wallace*, pp. 97–8, 113.

42. See Morris, *Great and Terrible King*, pp. 303–4.

43. Guisborough, pp. 298–303. For a good modern account, including a more detailed analysis of the sources, see Michael Prestwich, 'The Battle of Stirling Bridge: An English Perspective', in *Wallace Book*, especially pp. 65–71. For a particularly detailed narrative, which follows Guisborough closely, see Pete Armstrong, *The Battles of Stirling Bridge and Falkirk: William Wallace's Rebellion* (Oxford, 2003), pp. 35–52.

44. Guisborough, p. 300. Quoted and translated in Barrow, *Robert Bruce*, p. 114.

45. *Lanercost Chronicle*, p. 164.

46. Sir Charles Oman, *A History of The Art of War in the Later Middle Ages: Volume II: 1278–1485* (London, 1991, first published 1924), p. 76.

47. Andrew M. Spencer, 'John de Warenne, Guardian of Scotland and the Battle of Stirling Bridge', *England and Scotland at War*, pp. 39–52.

48. See Scott L. Waugh, 'Warenne, John de, sixth earl of Surrey (1231–1304)', *Oxford Dictionary of National Biography* (Oxford, 2004) [http://www.oxforddnb.com/view/article/28734]. Waugh describes Surrey as 'hesitant and perhaps even pusillanimous on the battlefield and in politics'.

49. *Chronicle of Bury St Edmunds*, p. 144.

50. Prestwich, 'The Battle of Stirling Bridge', p. 74.

Chapter 5. The Road to Falkirk

1. Quoted in Morris, *Great and Terrible King*, p. 306.

2. These letters included a famous message to the burghers of Lubeck in Germany, encouraging the resumption of trade with Scotland; this letter is the original source of our knowledge about Wallace's seal, for which see above, p. 67, and the references there cited.

3. For a discussion, see Fisher, *Wallace*, pp. 113–14.

4. Guisborough, p. 304. Quoted and translated in Colm McNamee, 'William Wallace's Invasion of Northern England', *Northern History*, 26 (1990), p. 40.

5. 'John of Fordun', p. 322.

6. Guisborough, p. 304.

7. *Flores*, p. 321.

8. Guisborough, pp. 305–6.

9. For this paragraph see McNamee, 'William Wallace's Invasion of Northern England', pp. 49–52.

10. It should be noted that, unusually, the earls agreed to serve in return for pay – perhaps due to the increased difficulties involved in winter campaigning. See Prestwich, *Edward I*, pp. 478–9.

11. The Roll is printed in *Scotland in 1298. Documents relating to the campaign of King Edward the First in that year, and especially to the*

Battle of Falkirk, ed. Henry Gough (Paisley, 1888), pp. 131–57.

12. Prestwich, *Edward I*, p. 479. See also Prestwich, *War, Politics and Finance*, pp. 68–9.

13. David Simpkin, *The English Aristocracy at War: From the Welsh Wars of Edward I to the Battle of Bannockburn* (Woodbridge, 2008), pp. 79–91.

14. Simpkin, *English Aristocracy at War*, p. 93.

15. For this paragraph, see Watson, *Under the Hammer*, p. 61; Adam Chapman, 'Welshmen in the Armies of Edward I', in *Impact of the Edwardian Castles*, pp. 178–9.

16. *Chronicle of Bury St Edmunds*, p. 144.

17. See, for example, John Gillingham, *The Wars of the Roses* (London, 1981), p. 45.

18. Stevenson, *Documents*, p. 351.

19. David Bachrach, 'Military Logistics during the Reign of Edward I of England, 1272–1307', *War in History*, 13:4 (2006), pp. 423–40, especially p. 425, citing the work of J. Masschaele.

20. *Scotland in 1298*, p. 124.

21. Watson, *Under the Hammer*, p. 63.

22. Watson, *Under the Hammer*, p. 62, quoting PRO [now TNA] E101/552/2.

23. Quoted in Dauvit Broun, 'Rethinking Scottish origins' (Inaugural Lecture as Professor of Scottish History, 12 November 2013), available online at http://glasgow.academia.edu/DBroun, p. 24.

24. Fisher, *Wallace*, p. 137.

25. Bower, pp. 89–91.

26. Bower, p. 85.

27. See Fisher, *Wallace*, p. 94 (although Fisher is inclined to see a glimmer of truth in Bower's account).

28. Bower, p. 89.

29. *CDS*, ii, no. 1689, p. 456.

30. These included Geoffrey Mowbray, William Hay of Lochwarret (now Borthwick) and William Ramsay of Dalhousie. See Barrow, *Robert Bruce*, p. 134.

31. Guisborough, pp. 323–8. My own narrative has also been particularly influenced by the modern accounts in Pete Armstrong, *The Battles of Stirling Bridge and Falkirk: William Wallace's Rebellion*

(Oxford, 2003), pp. 62–79; Fisher, *Wallace*, pp. 139–57; and Watson, *Under the Hammer*, pp. 61–7.

32. See Watson, *Under the Hammer*, pp. 63–4.

33. Guisborough tells us specifically that Bek was sent from Kirkliston, after Edward had already been staying there for several days, although given the limited timescale available it seems possible that his chronology might be slightly flawed here.

34. Guisborough, p. 325. Quoted and translated in Barrow, *Robert Bruce*, p. 131.

35. *Scotland in 1298*, pp. 127–8. Quoted and translated in Watson, *Under the Hammer*, p. 66.

36. Guisborough, p. 326. Quoted and translated in Fisher, *Wallace*, p. 146.

37. Armstrong, *Stirling Bridge and Falkirk*, p. 64.

38. For the most important narrative accounts, see Guisborough, pp. 327–8; Rishanger, pp. 385–7; *Lanercost Chronicle*, p. 166; 'John of Fordun', p. 323. Relevant excerpts from these sources are also printed (in the original Latin), together with various others, in *Scotland in 1298*, pp. xv–xxxii.

39. An alternative site to the north of Falkirk has been favoured in the past, but in the absence of any new evidence I am inclined to accept the conclusions of the most recent historians of the battle – particularly in the case of Pete Armstrong, who has evidently made a careful study of the relevant terrain. (For a brief description of the battlefield and the surrounding area today, see Armstrong, *Stirling Bridge and Falkirk*, pp. 91–3.)

40. Guisborough, p. 327. Quoted and translated in Fisher, *Wallace*, p. 150.

41. See J.F. Verbruggen, *The Art of Warfare in Western Europe*, tr. S. Willard and R.W. Southern (2nd English edition, Woodbridge, 1997), pp. 184–5.

42. Rishanger, p. 385.

43. For a wide range of other examples, see Verbruggen, *Art of Warfare in Western Europe*, pp. 217–21, especially p. 219.

44. See, for example, Matthew Bennett, 'The Myth of the Military Supremacy of Knightly Chivalry', in *Armies, Chivalry and Warfare in Medieval Britain and France*, ed. Matthew Strickland (Stamford, 1998), pp. 304–16.

45. For an excellent recent example, see Alistair Macdonald, 'Courage, Fear and the Experience of the Later Medieval Scottish Soldier', *Scottish Historical Review*, 235 (2013), pp. 179–206.
46. Quoted and translated in *Society at War: The Experience of England and France during the Hundred Years War*, ed. Christopher Allmand (new edition, Woodbridge, 1998), p. 28.
47. Quoted and translated in Prestwich, *Armies and Warfare*, p. 220.
48. For a more detailed discussion, see Verbruggen, *Art of Warfare in Western Europe*, pp. 187–90.
49. A.A.M. Duncan, 'The Battle of Falkirk', in *The Oxford Encyclopedia of Medieval Warfare and Military Technology*, ed. Clifford J. Rogers (Oxford, 2010), vol. II, p. 34.
50. Felton is identified as a *millenar* in J.E. Morris, *The Welsh Wars of Edward I* (Stroud, 1998, first published 1901), p. 287.
51. *Lanercost Chronicle*, p. 166.
52. 'John of Fordun', p. 323.
53. See Alexander Grant, 'Bravehearts and Coronets: Images of William Wallace and the Scottish Nobility', in *Wallace Book*, p. 101.
54. See, for example, Fisher, *Wallace*, pp. 166–7.
55. Macdonald, 'Courage, Fear and the Experience of the Later Medieval Scottish Soldier', pp. 204–6.
56. John Sadler, *Border Fury: England and Scotland at War 1296–1568* (Harlow, 2006, first published 2005), pp. 75–6.
57. For some interesting examples of medieval battle plans, and further discussion, see Matthew Strickland and Robert Hardy, *The Great Warbow: From Hastings to the Mary Rose* (Stroud, 2005), pp. 319–25, 339–43.
58. This apparently occurred, for instance, at the Battle of Neville's Cross, fought in 1346 between the English and the Scots. See Strickland and Hardy, *The Great Warbow*, p. 453 n. 123.
59. *The Political Songs of England*, ed. Thomas Wright (Edinburgh, 1888), 4 vols, iii, pp. 15–27, especially pp. 24–5.
60. Norman Macdougall, *James IV* (East Linton, 1997), p. 286, quoting Pedro de Ayala.
61. *Lanercost Chronicle*, p. 166.
62. Watson, *Under the Hammer*, p. 67.

Chapter 6. The Days Were Long and Fine

1. Morris, *Great and Terrible King*, p. 314.
2. For Edward's peles, see Chris Tabraham, '*Scottorum Malleus*: Edward I and Scotland', in *Impact of the Edwardian Castles*, pp. 186–8.
3. For the figures in this and the next three paragraphs, see Watson, *Under the Hammer*, pp. 69–76.
4. Watson, *Under the Hammer*, p. 77, quoting PRO [now TNA] E101/7/9.
5. Discussed in Watson, *Under the Hammer*, p. 79.
6. See John Carmi Parsons, 'Margaret (1279?–1318)', *Oxford Dictionary of National Biography* (Oxford, 2004; online edition, Jan. 2008) [http://www.oxforddnb.com/view/article/18046].
7. Barrow, *Robert Bruce*, pp. 140–1, quoting PRO [now TNA] c.47/22/8.
8. Watson, *Under the Hammer*, p. 84.
9. Prestwich, *Edward I*, pp. 483–4.
10. During the years between 1297 and 1304 there were several investigations of trespasses into Surrey's private parks. Discussed in Andrew M. Spencer, 'A Warlike People? Gentry Enthusiasm for Edward I's Scottish Campaigns, 1296–1307', *Soldier Experience*, p. 107.
11. Marc Morris has argued, citing the contemporary opinion of Peter Langtoft as further evidence, that Edward faced a 'deliberate, political boycott' during this campaign. Morris, *Great and Terrible King*, p. 321.
12. Rishanger, pp. 402–3.
13. *CDS*, ii, no. 1949, p. 518.
14. Rishanger, p. 407.
15. Prestwich, *Edward I*, p. 525, quoting the Annals of Worcester.
16. See above, p. 36.
17. Palgrave, *Documents*, pp. 218–19.
18. Watson, *Under the Hammer*, p. 104.
19. Prestwich, *Edward I*, p. 486, quoting PRO [now TNA] E159/73 m.16.
20. See, for example, Traquair, *Freedom's Sword*, p. 94.
21. Morris, *Great and Terrible King*, p. 324. For the Welsh subsidy, see Rees Davies, *Age of Conquest: Wales 1063–1415* (Oxford, 2000, first published 1987), p. 386.

22. The ports claimed they were owed almost £2,500. Royal clerks subsequently argued that this claim was offset by other payments they had already made, although eventually the crown agreed to pay a lesser sum of £500. See Prestwich, *War, Politics and Finance*, p. 144.

23. See Prestwich, *War, Politics and Finance*, p. 143.

24. Maurice Keen, *Chivalry* (Yale, 1984), p. 139.

25. *The Roll of Caerlaverock*, ed. Thomas Wright (London, 1864), pp. 4–5.

26. *The Roll of Caerlaverock*, p. 14.

27. This was Joan's second marriage. Her first marriage was to Gilbert de Clare, earl of Gloucester (d. 1295), with whom she had several children.

28. *The Roll of Caerlaverock*, p. 1.

29. *The Roll of Caerlaverock*, p. 26.

30. *The Roll of Caerlaverock*, p. 26.

31. Clifford J. Rogers, *Soldiers' Lives Through History: The Middle Ages* (Westport, USA, 2007), p. 35. Clare succeeded to the earldom of Gloucester in 1308, and was killed at the Battle of Bannockburn.

32. *The Roll of Caerlaverock*, p. 25.

33. Rishanger, p. 440.

34. *The Roll of Caerlaverock*, p. 30.

35. *Liber Quotidianus Contrarotulatoris Garderobae, 1299–1300*, ed. J. Topham *et al* (London, 1787), p. 165. He is described as 'Robert of Ulm', for example, in Prestwich, *Armies and Warfare*, pp. 285–6. Ulm is in southern Germany.

36. See R.H. Richens, *Elm* (Cambridge, 2012, first published 1983), pp. 215, 221.

37. *The Roll of Caerlaverock*, p. 34.

38. Kelly DeVries and Robert Douglas Smith, *Medieval Military Technology* (second edition, Toronto, 2012), p. 126.

39. As noted in Rogers, *Soldiers' Lives Through History: The Middle Ages*, p. 123.

40. *The Roll of Caerlaverock*, p. 35.

41. *Lanercost Chronicle*, p. 175. For further discussion, see Matthew Strickland, 'A Law of Arms or a Law of Treason? Conduct of War in Edward I's Campaigns in Scotland, 1296–1307', in *Violence in*

Medieval Society, ed. Richard Kaeuper (Woodbridge, 2000), pp. 69–71.
42. Langtoft, pp. 247–8.
43. See Tabraham, 'Scottorum Malleus', p. 188.
44. Keith made his peace with Edward in 1303, and became an important official in Edward's Scottish administration of 1305. However, he later swore allegiance to Robert the Bruce, and went on to lead the Scottish cavalry at Bannockburn.
45. Rishanger dates the encounter to 8 August ('the [full] moon before the feast of St Lawrence [i.e. 10 August]'), whereas E.W. Safford's itinerary of Edward's movements, which is based on administrative evidence, does not place him at the Cree until 12 August. Rishanger, p. 441; *Itinerary of Edward I: Part II: 1291–1307*, ed. E.W. Safford (List and Index Society, 132, 1976), p. 160.
46. Rishanger, pp. 440–2.
47. Watson, *Under the Hammer*, p. 108.
48. *Scimus, Fili* is printed and translated in Stones, *Anglo-Scottish Relations*, pp. 81–7.
49. Rishanger, p. 447. Quoted, in translation, in Traquair, *Freedom's Sword*, p. 98.
50. See above, note 35. Discussed by H.M. Colvin in *History of the King's Works*, p. 411.
51. Rishanger, p. 447. Quoted and translated in Barrow, *Robert Bruce*, p. 149.
52. Langtoft, p. 327.

Chapter 7. To Annoy His Enemies
1. Stevenson, *Documents*, p. 296 (where the letter is misdated; see also Watson, *Under the Hammer*, p. 109).
2. Guisborough, p. 245.
3. Henry de Keighley was briefly imprisoned towards the end of Edward's reign.
4. *CDS*, ii, no. 1191, p. 305.
5. *Lanercost Chronicle*, p. 240.
6. For the figures in this paragraph, see Prestwich, *Edward I*, p. 493.
7. Prestwich, *War, Politics and Finance*, p. 128.
8. Prestwich, *War, Politics and Finance*, pp. 132–3.

9. Morris, *Great and Terrible King*, p. 332.

10. Barrow, *Robert Bruce*, p. 248, quoting the *Lanercost Chronicle*. (See also *Lanercost Chronicle*, p. 195, where a slightly different translation is offered.)

11. Barrow, *Robert Bruce*, p. 159.

12. *History of the King's Works*, p. 412.

13. See Clifford J. Rogers, *Soldiers' Lives Through History: The Middle Ages* (Westport, USA, 2007), pp. 124–5.

14. As noted in Chris Tabraham, *Scotland's Castles* (London, 2005), p. 49.

15. *Lanercost Chronicle*, p. 174.

16. Stevenson, *Documents*, p. 431.

17. Stevenson, *Documents*, p. 432.

18. *CDS*, ii, no. 1230, p. 314. Discussed in Watson, *Under the Hammer*, p. 128.

19. For these writs, see *CDS*, v, nos 260–3, pp. 168–9.

20. Quoted in Barrow, *Robert Bruce*, p. 154.

21. Quoted in Traquair, *Freedom's Sword*, p. 102.

22. Among many other arguments, the Scots put forward an alternative ancient history of the British Isles, in which an unbroken line of independent Scottish kings derived their descent from Scota, the daughter of an Egyptian pharaoh.

23. See, for example, Barrow, *Robert Bruce*, pp. 155–6.

24. Morris, *Great and Terrible King*, p. 335, quoting *Parliamentary Writs*, ed. Palgrave.

25. *Lanercost Chronicle*, p. 172.

26. *CDS*, v, no. 263, p. 169.

27. Traquair, *Freedom's Sword*, p. 108.

28. Morris, *Great and Terrible King*, pp. 335–6.

Chapter 8. All This Scottish War

1. See Nicola Coldstream, 'James of St George', in *Impact of the Edwardian Castles*, pp. 37–45.

2. For a good discussion of the works at Linlithgow and Selkirk, including all the figures in this and the next paragraph, see *History of the King's Works*, pp. 412–15.

3. See, for example, Morris, *Great and Terrible King*, p. 338.

4. *History of the King's Works*, p. 414, quoting PRO [now TNA] E101/9/30/(19).
5. For this paragraph see Watson, *Under the Hammer*, pp. 154–9.
6. *CDS*, v, no. 292, pp. 174–5.
7. Stevenson, *Documents*, p. 448.
8. For the account of Roslin, see 'John of Fordun', pp. 325–8, quote at p. 326.
9. Langtoft, pp. 345–7.
10. Watson, *Under the Hammer*, p. 171.
11. Barrow, *Robert Bruce*, p. 167, quoting *Acts of the Parliament of Scotland*, i, pp. 454–5.
12. Stevenson, *Documents*, pp. 449–50, quote at p. 449.
13. Alan Young, *Robert the Bruce's Rivals: The Comyns, 1212–1314* (East Linton, 1997), p. 174, quoting the cartulary of Arbroath Abbey.
14. *CCR, 1302–1307*, p. 299.
15. For the next three paragraphs, see *History of the King's Works*, pp. 416–17; Michael Haskell, 'Breaking the Stalemate: The Scottish Campaign of Edward I, 1303–4', in *Thirteenth-Century England VII*, ed. Michael Prestwich, Richard Britnell and Robin Frame (Woodbridge, 1999), p. 226.
16. Morris, *Great and Terrible King*, p. 339, quoting *Parliamentary Writs*, ed. Palgrave, pp. 366–7.
17. Prestwich, *War, Politics and Finance*, pp. 97–8.
18. See Haskell, 'Breaking the Stalemate', pp. 229–31.
19. Morris, *Great and Terrible King*, p. 339.
20. Watson, *Under the Hammer*, p. 174.
21. *Scalacronica*, pp. 45–7.
22. Langtoft, p. 349.
23. See, for example, Haskell, 'Breaking the Stalemate', p. 226.
24. Langtoft, p. 349.
25. Watson, *Under the Hammer*, pp. 174–5.
26. Langtoft, p. 349.
27. Prestwich, *Edward I*, p. 499. Prestwich (p. 501) suggests the mixture would have been put into earthenware pots, which would then be launched into the castle.
28. Watson, *Under the Hammer*, quoting PRO [now TNA] E159/76 m.21.

29. Haskell, 'Breaking the Stalemate', pp. 229–31.
30. Guisborough, p. 357.
31. Watson, *Under the Hammer*, p. 180.
32. 'John of Fordun', p. 328.
33. Palgrave, *Documents*, p. 287.
34. As noted in Barrow, *Robert Bruce*, p. 169.
35. Traquair, *Freedom's Sword*, p. 116.
36. See Watson, *Under the Hammer*, p. 188.
37. Stevenson, *Documents*, pp. 475–7, quote at p. 476.
38. Stevenson, *Documents*, pp. 472–3, quote at p. 473.
39. Stevenson, *Documents*, pp. 479–80.
40. Stevenson, *Documents*, p. 481.
41. Stevenson, *Documents*, pp. 482–3.
42. *CDS*, iv, p. 475.
43. *Scalacronica*, p. 47.
44. *Flores*, p. 118, quoted and translated in Barrow, *Robert Bruce*, p. 168.
45. Traquair, *Freedom's Sword*, pp. 119–20.
46. *Scalacronica*, p. 47.
47. *Flores*, p. 318. Discussed in Antonia Gransden, *Historical Writing in England, c. 550 to c. 1307* (London, 1974), pp. 462–3.
48. See Rishanger, pp. 222–3 (where this chronicle is printed alongside the other writings that can be more firmly attributed to William Rishanger).
49. *CDS*, ii, no. 1560, p. 405.
50. Langtoft, p. 357.
51. Oliphant later entered English allegiance. He was the commander at Perth when the town was taken by Robert the Bruce in 1313.
52. Haskell, 'Breaking the Stalemate', p. 233.
53. The date of Soules' death is uncertain, but he is thought to have died before 1310.

Chapter 9. Burn, Kill and Raise the Dragon

1. *Flores*, pp. 120–1.
2. For a more detailed discussion, see Caroline Burt, *Edward I and the Governance of England* (Cambridge, 2013), pp. 216–35.

3. Stevenson, *Documents*, p. 471.

4. See, for example, Barrow, *Robert Bruce*, pp. 170, 179.

5. Langtoft, p. 353.

6. Palgrave, *Documents*, p. 276. Quoted and translated in Fisher, *Wallace*, p. 222.

7. Barrow, *Robert Bruce*, p. 185; see also *CDS*, ii, no. 1465, p. 383.

8. Langtoft, p. 323.

9. Barrow, *Robert Bruce*, p. 178.

10. Dafydd ap Gruffydd endured a similar fate almost twenty years before, and other earlier examples might also be cited.

11. Stones, *Anglo-Scottish Relations*, pp. 121–2.

12. The various narrative sources that describe the incident are discussed and quoted extensively by A.A.M. Duncan in the notes of *The Bruce* (pp. 78–81).

13. In 1304, at the siege of Stirling, Bruce had sealed a pact of mutual assistance with Bishop Lamberton of St Andrews. Both men had submitted to Edward by this time, but as the pact did not except their allegiance to the English king, it is difficult to imagine this was not treasonable in some way (as Edward would have understood it). See Barrow, *Robert Bruce*, p. 171.

14. Michael Brown, *The Wars of Scotland, 1214–1371* (Edinburgh, 2004), p. 199.

15. *Flores*, p. 130.

16. Palgrave, *Documents*, p. 320.

17. Stones, *Anglo-Scottish Relations*, p. 133.

18. *CDS*, ii, no. 1747, p. 471.

19. Barbour, *The Bruce*, p. 90.

20. J.R.H. Moorman, 'Edward I at Lanercost Priory 1306–7', *English Historical Review*, 263 (1952), p. 173.

21. Valence's date of birth is uncertain, but is estimated to have been around 1275. See J.R.S. Phillips, 'Valence, Aymer de, eleventh earl of Pembroke (d. 1324)', *Oxford Dictionary of National Biography* (Oxford University Press, 2004; online edn, Jan. 2008) [http://www.oxforddnb.com/view/article/942].

22. *CDS*, ii, no. 1754, p. 473.

23. *Flores*, pp. 131–2.

24. Conceivably the 'swans' took the form of a *subtlety* or *entremet*,

an elaborate type of dish that was served between larger courses, often as a form of entertainment. In the later medieval period birds would sometimes be cooked, seasoned and then served in their plumage, although foodstuffs were also shaped to resemble other things (such as castles).

25. *CDS*, ii, no. 1773, pp. 476–7.
26. As suggested in Malcolm Vale, *The Princely Court: Medieval Courts and Culture in North-West Europe* (Oxford, 2001), pp. 218–19.
27. Palgrave, *Documents*, p. 349.
28. *CDS*, ii, no. 1786, pp. 479–80.
29. Guisborough claimed that Valence was initially unwilling to fight because it was a holy day – the Sunday after the feast of St John – but in fact it was a Tuesday. For a discussion, see *The Bruce*, pp. 94–5 (note).
30. *Scalacronica*, p. 53. In Barbour's narrative, Bruce's reins are seized by Sir Philip Mowbray, who is much keener to prevent the escape of the 'new-made king', but of course the outcome is the same. Barbour, *The Bruce*, p. 100.
31. *CDS*, v, no. 492, p. 213.
32. *The Statutes of the Realm*, ed. Alexander Luders *et al* (Record Commission, 1810), 11 vols in 12, i, p. 147. Translation adapted following Morris, *Great and Terrible King*, p. 356. The ordinance itself was particularly concerned with the problem of corrupt officials, who were apparently exploiting the resources of the Forest for their own benefit (and to 'the intolerable damage' of Edward and his heirs).
33. Barbour, *Bruce*, p. 90.
34. *CDS*, ii, no. 1782, pp. 478–9.
35. *CDS*, ii, no. 1790, pp. 480–1.
36. Letters Patent dated 7 April. See *CDS*, ii, no. 1755, p. 473.
37. Matthew Strickland, 'Treason, Feud and the Growth of State Violence: Edward I and the "War of the Earl of Carrick", 1306–7', in *War, Government and Aristocracy in the British Isles, c. 1150–1500*, ed. Chris Given-Wilson, Ann Kettle and Len Scales (Woodbridge, 2008), especially pp. 102–4.
38. Prestwich, *Edward I*, p. 507; above, n. 20.
39. *CDS*, ii, no. 1832, p. 491.

40. *CDS*, v, no. 492, pp. 216–17.
41. Matthew Strickland (see above, n. 37) interprets the execution of the earl of Atholl as a particularly significant moment. Atholl, a magnate with English royal blood in his veins, would have been seen – unlike noble Welshmen – as a member of a wider aristocratic world. No earl had been executed as a traitor in England since the reign of William the Conqueror. Strickland therefore argues that Atholl's death paved the way for the bloodletting of Edward II's reign (and later), which included the execution of Edward II's own uncle.
42. *Scalacronica*, p. 53.
43. *Flores*, p. 324.
44. *The Political Songs of England*, ed. Thomas Wright (Edinburgh, 1888), 4 vols, iii, p. 70.
45. Barrow, *Robert Bruce*, p. 213.
46. Guisborough, p. 382. Quoted and translated in Morris, *Great and Terrible King*, p. 359.
47. *CDS*, ii, nos 1895 and 1896, p. 504.
48. *CDS*, ii, no. 1979, p. 526.
49. Quoted in Barrow, *Robert Bruce*, pp. 222–3; see also *CDS*, ii, no. 1926, p. 513.
50. *CDS*, ii, no. 1979, p. 526.
51. Guisborough, p. 379.
52. For the date of Edward's departure from Carlisle, see Morris, *Great and Terrible King*, p. 418, n. 46.
53. For the references and quotations in this paragraph, see Prestwich, *Edward I*, p. 557.

Epilogue
1. *The Political Songs of England*, ed. Thomas Wright (Edinburgh, 1888), 4 vols, iv, p. 25. See also, for example, Langtoft, pp. 381–3; *Lanercost Chronicle*, p. 182.
2. See Morris, *Great and Terrible King*, p. 363.
3. Morris, *Great and Terrible King*, pp. 377–8.
4. Colm McNamee, *Robert Bruce: Our Most Valiant Prince, King and Lord* (Edinburgh, 2011, first published 2006), p. 138, quoting *Annales Paulini*.

5. David Ditchburn discusses a wide range of interesting evidence in *Scotland and Europe: The Medieval Kingdom and its Contacts with Christendom, 1214–1560* (East Linton, 2000).

6. The so-called 'Treaty of Perpetual Peace', signed in 1502, lasted barely ten years. There was further conflict as the sixteenth century progressed, some of which was just as savage and intensive as the more famous Wars of Independence.

7. See Michael Camille, *Mirror in Parchment: The Luttrell Psalter and the Making of Medieval England* (London, 1998), pp. 284–9.

8. *The Declaration of Arbroath* [http://www.nas.gov.uk/downloads/declarationArbroath.pdf].

9. Prestwich, *Edward I*, pp. 514–15.

10. *Lanercost Chronicle*, p. 182.

11. *CDS*, ii, no. 1909, p. 598.

12. Bower, pp. 331–3.

Bibliography

Allmand, Christopher (ed.), *Society at War: The Experience of England and France during the Hundred Years War* (new edition, Woodbridge, 1998)

Anglo-Scottish Relations, 1174-1328: Some Selected Documents, ed. E.L.G. Stones (Oxford, 1965)

Armstrong, Pete, *The Battles of Stirling Bridge and Falkirk: William Wallace's Rebellion* (Oxford, 2003)

Bachrach, David, 'Military Logistics during the Reign of Edward I of England, 1272-1307', *War in History*, 13:4 (2006)

Bachrach, David, 'Edward I's Centurians: Professional Soldiers in an Era of Militia Armies', in Adrian R. Bell, Anne Curry *et al* (eds), *The Soldier Experience in the Fourteenth Century* (Woodbridge, 2011)

Barbour, John, *The Bruce*, ed. A.A.M. Duncan (Edinburgh, 1997)

Barrell, A.D.M., *Medieval Scotland* (Cambridge, 2000)

Barrow, G.W.S., 'The Army of Alexander III's Scotland', in Norman Reid (ed.), *Scotland in the Reign of Alexander III* (Edinburgh, 1990)

Barrow, G.W.S., 'A Kingdom in Crisis: Scotland and the Maid of Norway', *Scottish Historical Review*, 188 (1990)

Barrow, G.W.S., 'French after the Style of Petithachengon', in Barbara Crawford (ed.), *Church, Chronicle and Learning in Medieval and Early Renaissance Scotland* (Edinburgh, 1999)

Barrow, G.W.S., *Robert Bruce and the Community of the Realm of Scotland* (4th edition, Edinburgh, 2005)

Barrow, G.W.S., 'The Anglo-Norman Impact, c. 1100 to c. 1286', in Bob Harris and Alan R. MacDonald (eds), *Scotland: The Making and Unmaking of the Nation, c. 1100-1707* (Dundee, 2006)

Beam, Amanda, *The Balliol Dynasty, 1210-1364* (Edinburgh, 2008)

Bell, Adrian R., Curry, Anne *et al* (eds), *The Soldier Experience in the Fourteenth Century* (Woodbridge, 2011)

Bennett, Matthew, 'The Myth of the Military Supremacy of Knightly Chivalry', in Matthew Strickland (ed.), *Armies, Chivalry and Warfare in Medieval Britain and France: Proceedings of the 1995 Harlaxton Symposium* (Stamford, 1998)

'Blind Harry', *The Wallace*, ed. Anne McKim (Edinburgh, 2003)

Bower, Walter, *Scotichronicon*, ed. D.E.R. Watt (Aberdeen and Edinburgh, 1987-1997), 9 vols, vi

Broun, Dauvit, 'A New Look at Gesta Annalia attributed to John of Fordun', in Barbara Crawford (ed.), *Church, Chronicle and Learning in Medieval and Early Renaissance Scotland* (Edinburgh, 1999)

Broun, Dauvit, 'New Information on the Guardians' Appointment in 1286 and on Wallace's Rising in 1297' (2011); available online via http://www.breakingofbritain.ac.uk/feature-of-the-month/

Broun, Dauvit, 'Rethinking Scottish origins' (Inaugural Lecture as Professor of Scottish History, 12 November 2013); available online at http://glasgow.academia.edu/DBroun

Brown, Michael, *The Wars of Scotland: 1214-1371* (Edinburgh, 2004)

Brown, Michael, 'Aristocratic Politics and the Crisis of Scottish Kingship, 1286-96', *Scottish Historical Review*, 229 (2011)

Brown, R. Allen, Colvin, H.M. and Taylor, A.J., *The History of the King's Works: Volume 1: The Middle Ages* (HMSO, 1963)

Burt, Caroline, *Edward I and the Governance of England* (Cambridge, 2013)

Calendar of Close Rolls (HMSO, 1892-)

Calendar of Documents Relating to Scotland, ed. J. Bain *et al* (Edinburgh, 1881-1988), 5 vols

Camille, Michael, *Mirror in Parchment: The Luttrell Psalter and the Making of Medieval England* (London, 1998)

Chapman, Adam, 'Welshmen in the Armies of Edward I', in Diane M. Williams and John R. Kenyon (eds), *The Impact of the Edwardian Castles in Wales* (Oxford, 2010)

The Chronicle of Bury St Edmunds, 1212-1301, ed. Antonia Gransden (London, 1964)

The Chronicle of Lanercost, 1272-1346, tr. Sir Herbert Maxwell (Glasgow, 1913)

The Chronicle of Pierre de Langtoft, ed. Thomas Wright (Rolls Series, 1868), ii

The Chronicle of Walter of Guisborough, ed. Harry Rothwell (Camden Society, lxxxix, 1957)

Coldstream, Nicola, 'James of St George', in Diane M. Williams and John R. Kenyon (eds), *The Impact of the Edwardian Castles in Wales* (Oxford, 2010)

Cowan, Edward J. (ed.), *The Wallace Book* (Edinburgh, 2007)

Crawford, Barbara (ed.), *Church, Chronicle and Learning in Medieval and Early Renaissance Scotland* (Edinburgh, 1999)

Davies, Rees, *Age of Conquest: Wales 1063-1415* (Oxford, 2000, first published 1987)

The Declaration of Arbroath [http://www.nas.gov.uk/downloads/declarationArbroath.pdf]

DeVries, Kelly and Smith, Robert Douglas, *Medieval Military Technology* (second edition, Toronto, 2012)

Ditchburn, David, *Scotland and Europe: The Medieval Kingdom and its Contacts with Christendom, 1214-1560* (East Linton, 2000)

Documents Illustrative of the History of Scotland, ed. J. Stevenson (Edinburgh, 1870), 2 vols, ii

Documents and Records Illustrating the History of Scotland, ed. Sir Francis Palgrave (HMSO, 1837)

Duncan, A.A.M., 'The Community of the Realm of Scotland and Robert Bruce', *Scottish Historical Review*, 45 (1966)

Duncan, A.A.M., *The Kingship of the Scots, 842-1292* (Edinburgh, 2004)

Duncan, A.A.M., 'William, Son of Alan Wallace: The Documents', in Edward J. Cowan (ed.), *The Wallace Book* (Edinburgh, 2007)

Duncan, A.A.M., 'The Battle of Falkirk', in Clifford J. Rogers (ed.), *The Oxford Encyclopedia of Medieval Warfare and Military Technology* (Oxford, 2010), vol. II

English Historical Documents, 1189-1327, ed. Harry Rothwell (London, 1975)

Fisher, Andrew, *William Wallace* (2nd edition, Edinburgh, 2007, first published 2002)

Flores Historiarum, ed. Henry Luard (Rolls Series, 1890), 3 vols, iii

Freeman, A.Z., 'Wall-Breakers and River-Bridgers: Military Engineers in the Scottish Wars of Edward I', *Journal of British Studies*, 10:2 (1971)

Geoffrey of Monmouth, *The History of the Kings of Britain*, tr. Lewis Thorpe (London, 1966)

Gerald of Wales, *The Journey Through Wales and The Description of Wales*, tr. Lewis Thorpe (London, 1978)

Gillingham, John, *The Wars of the Roses* (London, 1981)

Given-Wilson, Chris, *Chronicles: The Writing of History in Medieval England* (London, 2004)

Gransden, Antonia, *Historical Writing in England I, c. 550 to c. 1307* (London, 1974)

Gransden, Antonia, *Historical Writing in England II, c. 1307 to the Early Sixteenth Century* (London, 1982)

Grant, Alexander, 'Bravehearts and Coronets: Images of William Wallace and the Scottish Nobility', in Edward J. Cowan (ed.), *The Wallace Book* (Edinburgh, 2007)

Harris, Bob and MacDonald, Alan R. (eds), *Scotland: The Making and Unmaking of the Nation, c. 1100-1707* (Dundee, 2006)

Haskell, Michael, 'Breaking the Stalemate: The Scottish Campaign of Edward I, 1303-4', in Michael Prestwich, Richard Britnell and Robin Frame (eds), *Thirteenth Century England VII* (Woodbridge, 1999)

John of Fordun's Chronicle of the Scottish Nation, ed. William F. Skene (Edinburgh, 1873)

Kaeuper, Richard W., *Chivalry and Violence in Medieval Europe* (Oxford, 1999)

Keen, Maurice, *Chivalry* (London, 1984)

Lachaud, Frédérique, 'Armour and Military Dress in Thirteenth- and Early Fourteenth-Century England', in Matthew Strickland (ed.), *Armies, Chivalry and Warfare in Medieval Britain and France: Proceedings of the 1995 Harlaxton Symposium* (Stamford, 1998)

Liber Quotidianus Contrarotulatoris Garderobae, 1299-1300, ed. J. Topham *et al* (London, 1787)

Macdonald, Alistair, 'Courage, Fear and the Experience of the Later Medieval Scottish Soldier', *Scottish Historical Review*, 235 (2013)

Macdougall, Norman, *James IV* (East Linton, 1997)

McGlynn, Sean, *By Sword and Fire: Cruelty and Atrocity in Medieval Warfare* (London, 2008)

McNamee, Colm, 'William Wallace's Invasion of Northern England', *Northern History*, 26 (1990)

McNamee, Colm, *Robert Bruce: Our Most Valiant Prince, King and Lord* (Edinburgh, 2011, first published 2006)

Matthew Paris's English History from the Year 1235 to 1272, tr. J.A. Giles (London, 1854) vol. III

The Metrical Chronicle of Robert of Gloucester, ed. William Wright (Rolls Series, 1887), 2 vols, ii

Moorman, J.R.H., 'Edward I at Lanercost Priory 1306-7', *English Historical Review*, 263 (1952)

Morris, J.E., *The Welsh Wars of Edward I* (Stroud, 1998, first published 1901)

Morris, Marc, *A Great and Terrible King: Edward I and the Forging of Britain* (London, 2009, first published 2008)

Nelson, Jessica, 'Yolande (d. in or after 1324)', *Oxford Dictionary of National Biography* (Oxford, 2008) [http://www.oxforddnb.com/view/article/96816]

Neville, Cynthia (ed.), 'A Plea Roll of Edward I's Army in Scotland, 1296', *Miscellany of the Scottish History Society*, vol. XI, (1990); available online at http://www.deremilitari.org/RESOURCES /SOURCES/plearoll.htm

Oman, Sir Charles, *A History of The Art of War in the Later Middle Ages: Volume II: 1278-1485* (London, 1991, first published 1924)

Parsons, John Carmi, 'Margaret (1279?–1318)', *Oxford Dictionary of National Biography* (Oxford, 2004; online edition, Jan 2008) [http://www.oxforddnb.com/view/article/18046]

Phillips, J.R.S., 'Valence, Aymer de, eleventh earl of Pembroke (d. 1324)', *Oxford Dictionary of National Biography* (Oxford, 2004; online edition, Jan 2008) [http://www.oxforddnb.com/view/article/942]

The Political Songs of England, ed. Thomas Wright (Edinburgh, 1888), 4 vols

Prestwich, Michael, *War, Politics and Finance under Edward I* (London, 1972)

Prestwich, Michael, *Edward I* (revised edition, London, 1997)

Prestwich, Michael, *Armies and Warfare in the Middle Ages: The English Experience* (Yale, 1999, first published 1996)

Prestwich, Michael, *Plantagenet England, 1225-1360* (Oxford, 2005)

Prestwich, Michael, 'The Battle of Stirling Bridge: An English Perspective', in Edward J. Cowan (ed.), *The Wallace Book* (Edinburgh, 2007)

Prestwich, Michael, 'The Wars of Independence, 1296-1328', in Edward M. Spiers, Jeremy Crang and Matthew Strickland (eds), *A Military History of Scotland* (Edinburgh, 2012)

Richens, R.H., *Elm* (Cambridge, 2012, first published 1983)

Rogers, Clifford J., *Soldiers' Lives Through History: The Middle Ages* (Westport, USA, 2007)

The Roll of Caerlaverock, ed. Thomas Wright (London, 1864)

Sadler, John, *Border Fury: England and Scotland at War 1296-1568* (Harlow, 2006, first published 2005)

Safford, E.W. (ed.), *Itinerary of Edward I: Part II: 1291-1307* (List and Index Society, 132, 1976)

Saul, Nigel, *For Honour and Fame: Chivalry in England, 1066-1500* (London, 2011)

Scotland in 1298. Documents relating to the campaign of King Edward the First in that year, and especially to the Battle of Falkirk, ed. Henry Gough (Paisley, 1888)

Scottish Historical Documents, ed. Gordon Donaldson (Edinburgh, 1970)

Simpkin, David, *The English Aristocracy at War: From the Welsh Wars of Edward I to the Battle of Bannockburn* (Woodbridge, 2008)

Sir Thomas Gray's Scalacronica, 1272-1363, ed. Andy King (Surtees Society, ccix, 2005)

Spencer, Andrew M., 'A Warlike People? Gentry Enthusiasm for Edward I's Scottish Campaigns, 1296-1307', in Adrian R. Bell, Anne Curry *et al* (eds), *The Soldier Experience in the Fourteenth Century* (Woodbridge, 2011)

Spencer, Andrew M., 'John de Warenne, Guardian of Scotland and the Battle of Stirling Bridge', in Andy King and David Simpkin (eds), *England and Scotland at War, c.1296–c.1513* (Leiden, 2012)

Spencer, Andrew M., *Nobility and Kingship in Medieval England: The Earls and Edward I, 1272-1307* (Cambridge, 2014)

Spiers, Edward M., Crang, Jeremy and Strickland, Matthew (eds), *A Military History of Scotland* (Edinburgh, 2012)

The Statutes of the Realm, ed. Alexander Luders *et al* (Record Commission, 1810), 11 vols in 12, i

Stones, E.L.G., *Edward I* (Oxford, 1968)

Strickland, Matthew (ed.), *Armies, Chivalry and Warfare in Medieval Britain and France: Proceedings of the 1995 Harlaxton Symposium* (Stamford, 1998)

Strickland, Matthew, 'A Law of Arms or a Law of Treason? Conduct of War in Edward I's Campaigns in Scotland, 1296-1307', in Richard Kaeuper (ed.), *Violence in Medieval Society* (Woodbridge, 2000)

Strickland, Matthew, 'Treason, Feud and the Growth of State Violence: Edward I and the "War of the earl of Carrick", 1306-7', in Chris Given-Wilson, Ann Kettle and Len Scales (eds), *War, Government and Aristocracy in the British Isles, c. 1150-1500* (Woodbridge, 2008)

Strickland, Matthew, 'The Kings of Scots at War, c. 1093-1286', in Edward M. Spiers, Jeremy Crang and Matthew Strickland (eds), *A Military History of Scotland* (Edinburgh, 2012)

Strickland, Matthew, and Hardy, Robert, *The Great Warbow: From Hastings to the Mary Rose* (Stroud, 2005)

Summerson, Henry, 'Cressingham, Hugh of (d. 1297)', *Oxford Dictionary of National Biography* (Oxford, 2004; online edition, Jan 2008) [http://www.oxforddnb.com/view/article/6671]

Tabraham, Chris, *Scotland's Castles* (London, 2005)

Tabraham, Chris, '*Scottorum Malleus*: Edward I and Scotland', in Diane M. Williams and John R. Kenyon (eds), *The Impact of the Edwardian Castles in Wales* (Oxford, 2010)

Tout, T.F., 'Margaret (1240–1275)', rev. Norman H. Reid, *Oxford Dictionary of National Biography* (Oxford, 2004) [http://www.oxforddnb.com/view/article/18045]

Vale, Malcolm, *The Princely Court: Medieval Courts and Culture in North-West Europe* (Oxford, 2001)

Verbruggen, J.F., *The Art of Warfare in Western Europe*, tr. S. Willard and R.W. Southern (2nd English edition, Woodbridge, 1997)

Watson, Fiona J., *Under the Hammer: Edward I and Scotland* (Edinburgh, 2005, first published 1998)

Watson, Fiona J., 'The Wars of Independence', in Bob Harris and

Alan R. MacDonald (eds), *Scotland: The Making and Unmaking of the Nation, c. 1100–1707* (Dundee, 2006)

Waugh, Scott L., 'Warenne, John de, sixth earl of Surrey (1231–1304)', *Oxford Dictionary of National Biography* (Oxford, 2004) [http://www.oxforddnb.com/view/article/28734]

Willelmi Rishanger, Chronica et Annales, ed. Henry T. Riley (Rolls Series, 1865)

Williams, Diane M. and Kenyon, John R. (eds), *The Impact of the Edwardian Castles in Wales* (Oxford, 2010)

Young, Alan, *Robert the Bruce's Rivals: The Comyns, 1212–1314* (East Linton, 1997)

Index

Comyn, John, earl of Buchan, 69–71,
117–18, 130, 154, 172, 188
Comyn, John, lord of Badenoch (d.
1302), 21–2, 69–71, 160
Comyn, John, lord of Badenoch (d.
1306), vi, 71, 117, 130, 151–4, 156,
158, 160–2, 166, 170–4, 180, 191–2,
194
Comyn, William, bishop of Brechin, 24
Condom (France), 28
Confirmation of the Charters, 83
Constantine II, king of Alba (Scotland),
91
Convers, Alexander, 113–14
Conwy, 36
Corbridge, 57
Cotton, Bartholomew, 46
Coucy, 140
Courtrai, battle of, 147
Cree, river, skirmish at, 129–30, 191
Creetown, 130
Cressingham, Hugh, treasurer of
Scotland, 62–3, 69, 71–3, 77, 79–80,
82, 84, 127, 152, 205
Cromarty, 160
Cruggleton, 118
Cupar, 176
Cuthbert, Saint, 86, 92

Dafydd ap Gruffydd, prince of Wales,
11–12, 217
Dalry, 179
Dalswinton, 118, 173
David I, king of Scots, 15–18, 22, 32,
57
David II, king of Scots, 107
David, son of Alexander III, 19
Delisle, James, 158
Dirleton, 96
Dolforwyn, 198
Douglas, William, lord of, 52, 55,
69–70
Draycote, Peter, sheriff of Lincoln,
95
Droxford, John, 114

Dumfries, 23, 118, 131–3, 157–8,
171–3, 180, 185
Dunaverty, 173, 181–2
Dunbar, battle of, 57–9, 61, 65, 80, 108
Dundee, 77–8, 84
Dunfermline Abbey, 160
Dunipace, 143–4, 154
Dunkeld, William, bishop of, 21, 27,
199
Dunstable, 177
Durham, 86
bishop of, *see* Bek, Anthony

Eden, river, 90
Edinburgh, 56, 59, 78, 84, 95, 97, 139,
152, 156
Edmund, earl of Lancaster, Edward I's
brother, 35
Edward I, king of England
anger, hot temper and pursuit of
vengeance, 13–14, 55, 92, 126, 131,
134, 151–2, 173, 177–8, 182–4, 194
appearance, 13–14, 102
arrogance and complacency, 6, 60–1,
81, 192
attitude towards William Wallace, 92,
166, 169–70
buys horses and military equipment,
40–1
commitment to chivalry and the
crusade, 4–5, 7–8, 24–6, 35–6, 55,
193–4
courage and martial prowess, 6, 8,
14, 82, 165, 190–1
determination and obstinacy, 14,
24–5, 33–4, 51, 76–7, 98–9, 149,
162, 186, 188, 192
illness and effects of age, 132, 136,
173–5, 177, 179, 185–6, 190, 192
military strategy and tactics, 6, 11,
54, 57, 60, 73–4, 86–8, 95–9, 101–2,
107–8, 111–14, 119–20, 123–4,
126, 129–30, 137–8, 140, 143, 149,
151, 154–60, 162, 164, 175, 185,
190–2